"Elizabeth Lyon knows book proposals the way a surgeon knows anatomy."

—GARY PROVOST, author of twenty-two books
including *100 Ways to Improve Your Writing*

"This book is pure gold! I received an offer from a large publisher who stated that my proposal was professional and well written; even my agent said it would be the standard in the industry. I owe a debt of gratitude to Ms. Lyon."

—MARY JEANNE MENNA, author of *Mom to New Mom:
Practical Tips and Advice for the New Mom*

"Don't try to sell your next nonfiction book without consulting it."

—GERALD GROSS, author of *Editors on Editing:
What Writers Need to Know About What Editors Do*

"*Nonfiction Book Proposals Anybody Can Write* gave me the structure I needed to produce a coherent, organized proposal. Everything my agent wanted to see in my proposal was there because of Elizabeth's book. I was able to send my proposal within a week, and three months later, my agent was responding to bids from four large publishing houses. One of them paid me an unusually high advance for a first-time author. I will always be grateful to Elizabeth."

—SALLIRAE HENDERSON, M. DIV., author of *A Life Complete:
Emotional and Spiritual Growth for Midlife and Beyond*

NONFICTION BOOK PROPOSALS ANYBODY CAN WRITE

(REVISED AND UPDATED)

How to get a contract and advance <u>before</u> writing your book

Elizabeth Lyon

A Perigee Book

A PERIGEE BOOK
Published by the Penguin Group
Penguin Group (USA) Inc.
375 Hudson Street, New York, New York 10014, USA
Penguin Group (Canada), 90 Eglinton Avenue East, Suite 700, Toronto, Ontario M4P 2Y3, Canada
(a division of Pearson Penguin Canada Inc.)
Penguin Books Ltd., 80 Strand, London WC2R 0RL, England
Penguin Group Ireland, 25 St. Stephen's Green, Dublin 2, Ireland (a division of Penguin Books Ltd.)
Penguin Group (Australia), 250 Camberwell Road, Camberwell, Victoria 3124, Australia
(a division of Pearson Australia Group Pty. Ltd.)
Penguin Books India Pvt. Ltd., 11 Community Centre, Panchsheel Park, New Delhi—110 017, India
Penguin Group (NZ), 67 Apollo Drive, Rosedale, North Shore 0632, New Zealand
(a division of Pearson New Zealand Ltd.)
Penguin Books (South Africa) (Pty.) Ltd., 24 Sturdee Avenue, Rosebank, Johannesburg 2196,
South Africa

Penguin Books Ltd., Registered Offices: 80 Strand, London WC2R 0RL, England

While the author has made every effort to provide accurate telephone numbers and Internet addresses
at the time of publication, neither the publisher nor the author assumes any responsibility for errors,
or for changes that occur after publication. Further, the publisher does not have any control over and
does not assume any responsibility for author or third-party websites or their content.

PRINTING HISTORY
Second Blue Heron trade paperback edition / October 2000
Perigee trade paperback edition / December 2002

Perigee trade paperback ISBN: 978-0-399-52827-9

Library of Congress has cataloged the Blue Heron edition as follows:

Lyon, Elizabeth.
    Nonfiction Book Proposals Anybody Can Write / by Elizabeth Lyon.—1st ed.
        p. cm.
    Includes bibliographical references and index.
    ISBN: 0-936085-45-2
    1. How-to. 2. Nonfiction book proposals. 3. Marketing. I. Title.

PRINTED IN THE UNITED STATES OF AMERICA

20   19   18   17   16   15   14   13

Most Perigee Books are available at special quantity discounts for bulk purchases for sales promotions,
premiums, fund-raising, or educational use. Special books, or book excerpts, can also be created to fit
specific needs. For details, write: Special Markets, Penguin Group (USA) Inc., 375 Hudson Street,
New York, New York 10014.

This book is dedicated to
the memory of R. Gaines Smith,
writing teacher, mentor, and best friend.

Contents

Acknowledgments

Writing any book is a monumental task, and I have been especially blessed to have the help, encouragement, and love of many. My deepest thanks go to:

Dennis and Linny Stovall, my first publishers (Blue Heron Publishing); literary agent Natasha Kern, who over many years shared her knowledge and experience about proposals and publishing; literary agent Denise Marcil, who was the synapse that sparked my connection to the Stovalls; the writers whose proposals are an integral part of this book; the National Writers Association; and everyone who offered an endorsement.

Every writer needs a good editor. If editors are a measure of wealth, I'm the richest person in the world. My deepest thanks to Patty Hyatt, Stew Meyers, and Carolyn Rose. Without their incisive editing, continual support, and polite poetic prodding, this book would have been a shadow of its current clarity and content.

A special thanks to Aline Prince and Bill McConochie for reading and offering their critiques. For endless constructive criticism, I am grateful beyond words to my Colonyhouse friends, to Victor Rozek, and to my writing friends, past and present, in the Monday, Tuesday, Wednesday, and Thursday critique groups.

For the second edition, many authors have generously shared their successful proposals. Several Tuesday critique-group members offered invaluable advice. I am deeply appreciative of the friendship and support offered by: Carolyn Scott Kortge, David Congalton, Doris Colmes, Chanrithy Him, Bob Blonchek, Marty O'Neil, and Mary Jeanne Menna. I am also indebted to my friends, Michael

Vidor and Anne Sheldon, for supplying the clearest, most writer-friendly author-agent agreement ever written.

I owe special thanks to my literary agent and friend, Meredith Bernstein; to Linny and Dennis Stovall for going the final mile; to Ratina Wollner and Daniel Urban, editors extraordinaire; to the Good Luck Marketing Club; to Martha Holmes; and to my Perigee editors, Jennifer Repo, Christel Winkler, and Michelle Howry.

My family endured a particular strain during the pressured time period during which this book was produced, rewritten, and revised. As always my parents, Don and Ella Redditt, remain my anchor and inspiration. My great kids, Kris and Elaine Lyon, and my ex-husband, Charley Snellings, all gave selflessly of their time and help. Like it or not, they now know more about nonfiction book proposals than just about anyone else.

Foreword

When Elizabeth Lyon first told me she was planning to write a book about how to write and submit nonfiction book proposals, I was delighted. I had long felt I needed specific guidelines for my clients and prospective clients and found existing books to be inadequate. I knew Elizabeth was exactly the right person because I had sold several of the proposals she had worked on and mentored. They were far superior to the usual submissions we receive. In addition, I knew that Elizabeth's teaching expertise would lead her to organize the needed information in an accessible and understandable way.

There are many reasons why you would undertake the major work involved in writing a book. You may believe it will assist you with career advancement in another field; you may want to establish a new career as a writer; you may feel passionately and often altruistically that a certain subject must be presented to the public, and, you may believe publication will be a road to fame, fortune, self-understanding, or a legacy of your life's work.

Most writers are usually not prepared for the challenge of researching and writing a proposal. You may think this is a task that agents will do for you. Some writers resist the necessity of treating this literary child of the heart and mind as part of a business plan. Often, some parts of the proposal process are troublesome. In some cases, they discover they are really experts and not writers at all. Perhaps they need to work with a coauthor or ghost writer. The services of an editor of Elizabeth's stature are invaluable in helping writers to achieve their goals and grapple with the problems they encounter in moving from expert to author.

One of the things that is most important in going through this daunting process is to continually refocus on why you are doing this and clarify your goals. Eventually, if you get an agent, you will need to communicate these goals to her so that she can help you to get what you want from publishing. This focus will keep your sense of commitment to and passion for your subject alive.

It is important to keep in mind that the process of selling something to someone else is not a matter of convincing someone to buy something that they *don't* need or want. It is rather a process of sharing your vision so clearly that the other person is swept up in it, experiences a contagion of your passion and excitement, and wants to share it with others. You want the agent or editor to wish your book was already written, so they could share it with a friend or loved one or benefit from it themselves. When you begin to feel overwhelmed by the information you are accumulating about the market, publicity, chapter organization, and so on, when your book begins to seem like a term paper, always come back to what prompted you to start this process in the first place and tell us about that.

I have never worked with a writer on a proposal without the writer feeling, at some point, that the effort was too hard or not worth it. There is always a point where it seems easier to give up. Yet, without exception, writers have said at the end of the process of developing a proposal that they understood their books far better than they had before and were far more prepared to write them. Even authors of self-published books that have done well and are being presented to the industry gain new insights and often decide on revisions when they are thinking about how to tell editors why their books are new, better, different, more timely, or more insightful than other books available.

This book is an invaluable tool for achieving success as a nonfiction writer. There is no substitute for paying attention to what those in this arcane industry tell you. I am invariably appalled when I receive query letters from writers who have had their work read and rejected by agents and editors for sound reasons and yet have ignored the advice they have been offered. Pay attention to professionals in the industry rather than to relatives and friends.

In this book, Elizabeth has produced a compendium of methods and insights about getting published successfully that will spare you many problems on the road to publication. Read it through. Then proceed in exactly the order she has presented. Even if you determine that your project is not suitable for publication, you will have been spared much fruitless time and effort.

When you finish the steps she has outlined, you will at the very least have a preliminary proposal that will be understood and taken seriously. Chances are, you will join the ranks of the many writers she has helped to achieve publication. She is providing you with a set of keys to the fulfillment of your dream. Follow her advice so your dream can become a reality.

Natasha Kern, Literary Agent
Portland, Oregon
www.natashakern.com

Preface to the New Edition

Since the publication of this book in 1995, my greatest satisfaction has come from readers who report, "I followed your instructions and my book was published!" I have also been gratified by the many literary agents who recommend my book to their clients and consider it as the "standard" on successful book-proposal writing.

When I considered what needed revision for a new edition, a logical question popped up. If it isn't broken, why fix it? Certainly the basic information in the first edition remains as reliable today as it was in 1995. However, our changing world, as well as the changing publishing industry, call for several additions.

In this second edition:

- I've reported on the cutting-edge of electronic publishing. On-demand and e-publishing is rapidly expanding. Many experts predict that consumers will soon be able to buy formerly out-of-print books as well as new ones from production units in bookstores. These print-on-demand (POD) units will print and bind books in about fifteen minutes, from electronic files.
- I've expanded the instructions about writing memoir and autobiography. Formerly a category dominated by celebrity autobiographies, in the last five years, books written by everyday people about their personal experiences have even made bestseller lists. Frank McCourt's *Angela's Ashes* and Sebastian Junger's *The Perfect Storm* come to mind.

- I've added a writer-friendly, superb model of an author-agent agreement.
- I've introduced new competitive strategies for marketing yourself and your proposal, both prior to sale and after your book is published.
- The Internet has become an invaluable writer's resource, facilitating a writer's research on nearly every section of the proposal. While I have retained instructions for doing things the paper way, I've added Web addresses and resources.

In publishing and communications, we are just beginning to see how the apparent impersonality of the dot-com world can cross-pollinate with the flesh-and-blood world. Despite our culture's full entry into the electronic era, human beings, not Intel chips, continue to power the commerce of book publishing. After all, the impact of one author's book is a highly personal experience for its reader. Word of mouth, not one-stop-shopping, sells books.

However, Intel chips may indeed be facilitating relationships between writers and editors, writers and agents, and writers and readers. Thanks to our Internet genies, a few clicks of the magic mouse can put readers in direct contact with any person's Web site and e-mail address.

I trust that this second edition will help you transform your writing into a published reality. I also wish you the reward of wonderful relationships with your readers. To report on your successes or to say hello, just send an e-mail, or write in care of my publisher.

Elizabeth Lyon
Eugene, Oregon
www.elizabethlyon.com
www.4-edit.com

A Note to My Readers

As an editor and instructor, I've watched students and clients struggle to decipher the basic steps of writing proposals. As a writer and author, I've had to do the same—picking my way along with little help from inadequate sources.

For years, how to write a nonfiction book proposal—or even the necessity of one—has been insider's knowledge. This book demystifies a process that has remained largely unexplained by the pundits of the publishing industry.

> Nonfiction subjects include self-help, history, travel science, biography, naturopathy, psychology, personal experience, education, fitness, parenting, new age, writing, medicine, real estate, business, language, and more.

I've assumed that you know *nothing* about proposals and little, if anything, about the publishing world. As a result, I have organized this book in the order of reader need.

At each step in the process, I've interwoven examples from about nearly two dozen proposals that span a variety of nonfiction subjects. There is no need to flip to the back of a book and match instruction with examples. My primary criterion for selecting a proposal excerpt was that it serves as a good example of what I sought to explain.

I've designed the chapters to help you conserve your time and energy while enjoying the greatest productivity and quality. Each chapter begins with a statement of goals and a definition of terms.

Each section of the proposal is covered in its own chapter. I've also included a troubleshooting section in most chapters. The final chapters of this book show you how to assemble, polish, and market your proposal.

I use a writing style that features headings, boxes, and bulleted lists in order to make the presented information easier to absorb. This style also allows you to come back later to find answers without having to cull through lengthy unbroken text. Sidebars provide accessible summaries and reviews for experienced proposal writers.

While this book supplies the recipe for a proposal, you are the one who must combine the ingredients, and create one. Like bread dough, proposals take kneading, putting aside to rise, and kneading again.

Over the years of helping writers as an editor and "book doctor," I've identified those qualities you must possess to write a successful proposal and book. You need a willingness to follow directions, accept criticism, and rewrite. Finally, you must persist until you succeed, believing in yourself and your idea.

NONFICTION BOOK PROPOSALS ANYBODY CAN WRITE

CHAPTER ONE

Book Proposals: What Are They? Why Use Them?

Chapter Goal: To introduce and define proposals, explain who uses them, and present an overview of the publishing industry.

It's a great time to be a writer. It's an even better time to give birth to a nonfiction book. Never before have so many channels existed for publishing. Since the sixties, publishing has grown into a mega-industry with annual sales of over $23 billion, up $7 billion from 1995. Practically speaking, about 25,000 publishers now supply the reading public. From large conglomerates like Random House to regional publishers like Calyx, a publisher exists to match every reader's—and writer's—preferences.

Amazingly, the number of books published annually in North America has doubled in the last thirty years to an average of nearly 50,000 titles. In most years, about 85 percent of those titles are nonfiction. About 75 percent of those are by first-time authors. In other words, nearly 32,000 nonfiction books are written annually by first-time authors.

It's a great time to break in. A solid idea, the ability to communicate, and a well-written book proposal supply the practical means to manifest that dream. Not that you won't face competition. At a

Sidebar 1-1
Fascinating Facts About the Publishing Industry

- In 1963, the book industry reported sales were $1.68 billion for 25,784 titles. In 1993, total book sales reached $16.1 billion with an average of 50,000 titles. In 1998, sales soared to just over $23 billion.
- In 1997, on-demand book printing (done one at a time as a title is ordered) revenues were up 50 percent to $10.5 billion. Projections for 2002 are $32 billion.
- Launched in 1998, on-demand publisher iUniverse (formerly toExcel) expects to publish 50,000 titles in 2002.
- In 1998, children's book sales accounted for about 6 percent of the market, professional book sales captured 19 percent of the market, and university presses finished the year with 2 percent of all book sales.
- Women purchase the majority of all books sold, while men purchase about half of all paperbacks.
- The average production cost of a hardback book ranges from $20,000 with mid-sized publishers to $50,000 with giant publishers.
- About 80 percent of all books published fail to earn back the advance given to their authors.
- The average hardback book cost about $6.50 in 1963 compared to just under $25 in 2000.
- In 2000, customers in Houston were able to enter Majors, a 10,000 sq. ft. retail bookstore, order a title from the in-house print-on-demand (POD) system, wait fifteen minutes, and walk out with their purchase.

recent writer's conference, literary agent Mary Alice Kier of Cine/Lit Representation described a sales trip she made with her associate, Anna Cottle, to a dozen New York publishers. "With just about every editor we visited, there was a ritual held during the first five minutes before we could sit down: clearing boxes of manuscripts off chairs or moving them to give us room for our feet. In some instances, our meeting was not held in the office." Not, she explained, due to the widely held myth about power lunches to cut deals while dining at exclusive New York restaurants. "There was no room!" Mary Alice Kier told the audience. "Manuscripts were stacked on every desk, table, and chair."

Northwest literary agent Natasha Kern estimates that she receives about 15,000 query letters and manuscripts each year. (A query letter describes a book idea and asks agents or editors if they would like to see more.) East-coast literary agent Donald Maass averages 6,000 queries each year. By volume of correspondence alone, agents and editors must read shorter forms—queries or proposals—and be selective about reading entire manuscripts.

The sheer quantity of manuscripts presents a logistical problem for both agents and editors. They have no choice but to reject 99 percent of what they receive. This creates a competitive environment where agents and editors must choose the most well-written proposals. Despite this, don't assume that you've got about as much chance of gaining an agent or editor as winning the lottery. Only a small percentage of writers who submit manuscripts understand the importance of using a proposal or know how to write one. This book will give you a critical important edge on the competition. Chapters one through thirteen explain how to write a saleable proposal, and chapters fourteen and fifteen discuss agents, editors, and marketing.

Definition and Purpose of a Book Proposal

A book proposal is a marketing tool used to describe your book idea and sell it to a publisher. Virtually all nonfiction books are sold by proposal. It serves as the conventional means of communication between writer and agent/editor. In addition, it serves as a powerful aid to you, the writer, by helping you refine ideas, clarify organization, and speed the eventual writing of your book. Through the book proposal, you also address serious marketing questions for your publisher and present sample chapters from the actual book. In summary, a proposal accomplishes the following tasks:

- Presents the subject of your book
- Introduces your qualifications for wri
- Analyzes the market, i.e. the audience
- Compares your book to similar books
- Offers ideas about how you'll help pro
- Explains details about length, delivery,
- Contains a detailed outline of your boo
- Includes sample chapters, and
- Inserts supportive documents that furt
  yourself as its author

Parts of a Proposal

To fill its many purposes, the proposal has evolved into a document with many sections. Although no industry standard has yet been set for the titles of these sections or for their order, most agents and editors prefer using headings and an arrangement that correspond to the following:

Title Page
Concept Statement
Proposal Table of Contents
About the Book
About the Author
About the Market
About the Competition
Production Details
About Promotion
Table of Contents
Chapter Summaries
Sample Chapters
The Appendix

Without counting the pages in the sample chapters, a proposal might be as short as ten pages or as long as forty, depending upon the complexity of the book and the thoroughness of the writer. The chapters in this book are presented according to how you, the writer, will be most easily able to construct your proposal. Later, you'll assemble the proposal in the order shown above for agent/editor reading.

Why Not Send a Finished Manuscript?

Many times each year, I receive calls from writers who have completed their manuscripts and now feel ready for marketing and publication. You can imagine their surprise and disappointment when I inform them that nonfiction agents and editors do not prefer completed manuscripts. When agents or editors do receive completed books in lieu of proposals, they cannot forward them to the editorial review committee, because they have no answers to questions of marketing, competition, and production. Usually, they'll send you a form rejection letter and your book—assuming you enclosed return postage. If you're lucky, an agent/editor will read some of your book and send back a letter encouraging you to write a proposal.

Literary agents sell books to publishers on behalf of writers and are generally the first readers of a proposal. The proposal acts as the only vehicle of sale for your nonfiction book. Eventually, it will be scrutinized by editors, a production person, sales representative, publicity and promotions person, and possibly a publisher/owner. These people comprise the editorial review committee. If all parties agree on your book's merit, then you'll be offered a contract.

Before you throw up your arms and declare, "This looks too complex," let me assure you that writing a proposal is no more difficult than putting together a term paper, and it's a lot easier, by the way, than writing an entire manuscript. The detailed information offered by a proposal serves the many people who use it to make important marketing and publishing decisions. After all, you're asking someone to invest tens of thousands of their dollars in your idea. Believe me, they'll want to be fully briefed before they make a decision.

Who Reads Your Proposal?

Connecting books with publishers takes place through the efforts of:

- Literary agents
- Acquisitions editors
- Editorial committees
- Book producers

The pros and cons of marketing your proposal to an agent or editor are detailed in chapter fourteen. However, the descriptions that follow should give you some basic information about these different channels.

LITERARY AGENTS

A literary agent's relationship to writers and editors resembles a real-estate agent's to home sellers and buyers. Like most real-estate agents, literary agents work for the seller; that is, the writer. They get paid only when they sell your book to a publishing house; they work on commission. Literary agents typically receive 15 percent of your book's income—from any advance and royalties and from the sale of subsidiary rights.

An advance is money you receive on future royalties. Royalties are based on a percentage of the retail (or wholesale) price of your book. An advance is like borrowing money until pay day; it's money against revenues when your book sells. It's based in part on a formula: the number of books in the print run multiplied by the retail price of the book multiplied by the author's royalty rate (anywhere from about 5 percent for a mass-market paperback to about 12 percent for hardback). Fortunately, if your book takes a loss, you do not normally have to repay the advance. Publishers consider an advance as an investment in you and in future works.

Literary agents sell about 90 percent of all books. As the middle person in the chain from writer to publisher, literary agents select the most promising book ideas, offer editorial advice for polishing a manuscript, and take over the task of marketing your proposal to editors. An agent also acts as your cheerleader to editors and as your buffer from harsh words of rejection. Agents haggle with offers and know which parts of the publishing contract are negotiable. They iron out communications between authors and publishing personnel, recommend publicists, give advice on your career, and sell your book to other countries and to Hollywood.

In other words, literary agents have skills that make them indispensable to most authors. And to editors. During the last decade, the publishing industry suffered downsizing due to conglomerate mergers, changes in management, and changes in book distribution. As a result, publishers began to rely more and more upon literary agents to *find* books for them. Given the many manuscripts received by publishing offices, this made good business sense: less need for editorial assistants, less expense, and more efficiency by trusting reliable agents to recommend manuscripts.

Even though so many books are sold through literary agents, they are not the best choice for sale of specialized or regional books. With any book, in fact, you may choose to directly query editors at publishing houses.

ACQUISITIONS EDITORS

Acquisitions editors, whether full-time or freelance, work on behalf of publishers. They are the ones who communicate with agents and writers and make the initial decision about whether to accept or reject your query or proposal. Although some of the largest publishers now consider proposals submitted only by agents, many—if not most—of this continent's publishers still review query letters sent directly by writers. If the query piques their interest, these editors will request and seriously consider your proposal. At small, or even mid-sized publishers, the acquisitions editor may also be part or full owner of the company. In some cases, this editor has 100 percent control over which books get published. At larger houses, the decision usually falls to the editorial committee.

EDITORIAL COMMITTEES

In the early nineties, I began marketing my proposal for this book to larger publishers. An acquisitions editor at St. Martin's Press liked my proposal well enough to present it to his company's editorial committee—twice. In both attempts, his desire to take on the book was overruled. The sales department prevailed.

At larger houses, capturing the interest of the editor assigned to your kind of book is *only* the first step, although an important one. In fact, a larger publisher may have many editors, each vying for his or her favorite proposals to fill the slots in an upcoming list or season. Typically, a proposal must find acceptance from editorial committee members representing sales, promotion, production, and editing. Even the publisher/owner may express a view. This team must believe your book is worthy and would sell well before an editor calls you or your agent with an offer. This may seem as difficult as finding the proverbial needle in the haystack—to them and you—but books of all kinds and quality pass through this process every day.

In contrast, when this book was first acquired, Dennis and Linny Stovall, former owners of Blue Heron publishing, reviewed my proposal. They decided this book would be a good addition to their list. Some smaller publishers will check with their printer, graphic artist, and publicity manager to help determine if a book is profitable, but the entire decision about whether to publish a particular book rests with the publisher/owner.

BOOK PRODUCERS

Book producers, also referred to as book developers or packagers, are a hybrid of book publishers and agents. Only becoming a presence since the seventies, book producers provide publishers with services ranging from artists, photographers, and writers to completely edited and finished books. As subcontractors, they take some of the load off publishers, although they often approach publishers with book proposals.

The main advantage of a book producer to nonfiction book

writers is the opportunity producers offer for entry into publishing if other avenues close. Producers have editors who take time to work with and train writers. They employ writers-for-hire who may never receive direct credit for the books they write; yet they gain invaluable experience and pay. Book producers may purchase your book outright, providing no royalties, or they may offer you an advance plus royalties.

Some book producers produce only a handful of books each year; others churn out as many as several hundred. Among the approximate 100 book producers, only a dozen or so invite queries from writers about book projects. If interested, they will request a proposal. You may, however, write a letter describing your expertise and writing qualifications to go on file. Most of the time, producers contact writers they know or have referred to them. Since their use of writers varies so widely, you can learn more about this avenue to publishing by reading about book producers in *Writer's Market* and *Literary Market Place*.

Overview of the Publishing Industry

With approximately 25,000 publishers to select from, you or your literary agent must figure out which publishers are right for your project. About one quarter of the publishers do most of the publishing. That many still creates a quandary over where your book best belongs.

To narrow this field, you must match your subject and approach with your targeted audience and with the right size and type of publisher. By size, you can categorize your options into large—and everybody else. A conglomerate, like Simon & Schuster or Random House resembles an octopus. Each arm represents publishing houses or divisions, each of which has many, even dozens, of imprints. About six of these giants dominate nearly three-quarters of all publishing. In alphabetical order, these six conglomerates are: HarperCollins, Farrar, Straus & Giroux, Penguin Putnam, Random House, Simon & Schuster, and Time Warner. For a complete listing

Sidebar 1-2
Overview of Book Sales By Category & Outlet

Estimated book sales in 1998.
Book sales by percentage of total.
Based on $23,033.3 million in sales.
TRADE

Adult hardcover	27
Adult paperback	12
Juvenile hardcover	4
Juvenile paperback	2
Professional	19
Book clubs	5
Mail order	2
Mass market paperback	7
University press	2
Elementary/High School texts	14
Higher education	13
Standardized tests	1
Subscription reference	3
Bibles	5
Other religious	4
Other	2
Total	*122%

*Total greater than 100% reflects author's rounding off to nearest whole point (adapted from Publishers Weekly 3-1-99).

of their imprints, see *Writers Market* or *Literary Market Place* (www.literarymarketplace.com).

The remaining quarter includes mid- to small-sized publishers: regional publishers, university publishers, independent small presses, nonprofit publishers, and electronic (Web-based) publishers.

One of your tasks will be to figure out whether your book fits

Outlet Share of Adult Book Purchasing in 1998 by percentage of share:

Large Chain Bookstores	25.3
Book Clubs	18.0
Independent/Small Chains	16.6
Warehouse Clubs	6.4
Mass Merchandisers	5.9
Mail Order	4.9
Food/Drug Stores	3.6
Discount Stores	3.3
Used Books	3.0
Internet	1.9
Multi-Media	1.0

(*Based on Consumer Research Study of Book Purchasing, Publishers Weekly, 5-10-99*).

the demands of a conglomerate, or if it better meets the criteria of a smaller or specialty publisher. The proposal process is designed to lead you to this answer.

Writing for the Twenty-first Century

The use of the personal computer started a revolution in publishing that has spread to the Internet with no end in sight. The "electronic highway" has brought good news and bad news. Arguably, a writer's literacy now means facility with the Web as well as skill in writing. For authors, the good news is that more channels of publishing have opened and are still being defined. Electronic publishing is the new frontier. It includes e-books, books in electronic files available for downloading into computers or into small readers, and print-on-demand (POD) books. This form of publishing uses special equipment that stores books in electronic files. The equipment prints and binds a title only when a customer wants it. This was unheard of twenty years ago. The only agreement among publishing professionals is that we're only seeing the start of electronic publishing.

As we begin the twenty-first century, nearly every publisher maintains a web site with links to online purchasing. The last few years of the nineties saw a mad scramble to make new partnerships that have turned publishers into distributors and distributors into publishers. No one wants to miss a piece of the electronic publishing pie, although only 5000 titles had been converted to the right software language by the end of 1999. However, many companies predict an exponential growth in titles available for print-on-demand. As Sidebar 1-1 reports, iUniverse expects to have 50,000 titles available by 2002. In 2000, Majors Scientific Books, in partnership with POD wholesaler, Sprout, Inc., installed a POD production system in a Houston retail bookstore. Barnes & Noble is doing the same in a handful of its stores. Perhaps following the McDonalds' business plan—first install the outlets, and then they, the customer, will come. We have only seen the beginning of what is destined to be as revolutionary as the invention of the Gutenberg press!

As a global culture, we want to know more about our world, including its new inventions and its old ways. And, we want our information instantly. Demand is higher than ever for the printed word, and, now the electronic word.

The bad news is that everyone is a writer. Agents and editors complain about the logjam of manuscripts and hours lost spent sorting e-mail. Word processing made it possible to create multiple copies of a manuscript with no more than a few taps on the keyboard. One publishing expert estimates that half a million manuscripts are circulating at any given time in search of publication.

Regardless of whether, to paraphrase Dickens, now is the best of times or the worst of times, this book will lead you toward your goal of a book contract. If you follow the steps in this book, you'll have a superbly organized, professionally written, and marketable nonfiction book proposal.

The first step toward that goal is evaluating and refining your idea.

Evaluating and Refining Your Ideas: Preparing to Write Your Book

Chapter Goal: To refine your book idea—testing its worthiness and slanting it for greater salability.

Recognizing your expertise or enthusiasm for a particular subject, well-meaning people may have told you, "You should write a book." It's great to have their support, but don't take their encouragement as a signal to quit your day job, dash off a quick book, and bank on royalty checks rolling in.

The biggest mistake writers make is to start writing too soon, before they've done any planning or organizing or additional research. That process begins with deeper examination of your idea, of its merits

> Books require planning. This is always true of good books, books that endure and sell year after year.

and marketability, and of your writing skill.

Ideas Agents and Editors Seek

If you had a crystal ball, you would know exactly what agents, editors, and the unpredictable public are looking for. Without such aids you'll need to study industry forecast guides. *Publishers Weekly* is *the* trade journal of the industry. You'll become familiar with the major players, publishers, and their policies. By the time you read six months' to a year's worth of this magazine, including the fat fall and spring issues, you'll know what's selling now and what will be on the shelves in the immediate future. You'll identify trends, spot fads, and figure out which literary waves have already crested. You'll even begin to see who sells what to whom.

Literary agents and editors watch the market. They know what's hitting the bookstores now, as well as what is scheduled to come out. It usually takes a year or two to complete a proposal, find an agent, and sell your book to a publisher. For books on anniversaries of historical events, such as twenty-five years after the eruption of Mt. St. Helens or the 200-year celebration of Lewis & Clark's trek across the Oregon Trail to the Pacific Ocean, you must plan further ahead than publishers, who make acquisitions years in advance. Agents and editors are "idea people" and book lovers. They yearn to find outstanding books that will make the bestseller list.

> **WWW ADDRESSES FOR CURRENT TRENDS**
>
> Authorlink:
> *www.authorlink.com*
>
> Publisher's Weekly:
> *www.publishersweekly.com*
>
> American Booksellers Association
> *www.bookweb.com*
>
> Bookwire:
> *www.bookwire.com*
>
> Children's Writing Resource Center:
> *www.Write4kids.com*
>
> Editor & Publisher:
> *www.mediainfo.com*

Read *Publishers Weekly*, *The New York Times Book Review*, and the book section of your local newspaper. Keep current with books written in your field. Stay abreast of current trends, cultural shifts, and new discoveries. The presentation of your idea in the form of a proposal *must* excite an agent, who in turn *must* excite an editor, who in turn *must* excite everyone else on the editorial committee. After publication, the sales representative *must* like your book better than most of the other titles he represents, becoming so excited that he makes his retailers decide to carry it and talk it up to their customers. At each step, everyone should be excited about the market potential of your book, even if they themselves have no interest in its specific content, whether you're writing about Victorian gardens, parenting teens, or discovering Oregon on foot. Literary agent Denise Marcil said it well: "The best writing is from the heart. When a writer is truly excited about a topic, I get excited and say, 'Wow!' "

Evaluating Your Idea

Evaluating and refining your book idea are two of the most important steps in the success of your book project. The more you examine and dissect your idea before beginning your proposal, the more time you will save. You will also suffer fewer headaches.

> Consider your book idea as carefully as you would buying a house or a car.

PASSING THE PERSONAL TEST

Before you analyze the marketplace, I believe your book idea must pass a personal test—intellectually, emotionally, and spiritually. In particular, ask yourself the following questions. Be honest and make sure you are satisfied with your answers.

- Are you enthusiastic enough about this idea to stick with it for, say, five years, from conception through publication to promotion?
- Are you qualified (or could you become qualified) to write this book?
- Does writing this book match your long-term career goals? Can you describe how publication of this book will make a difference in how you view yourself and how you are viewed by others whose opinions you respect?
- Are you willing to learn how to write for publication?

Can You Stick With It?

I have met people who believe they *should* write a book on a particular subject, whether or not they want to. Often, they believe it would be a good career move, even though their hearts aren't in it. Some let themselves become strong-armed by a well-meaning spouse or friend. Don't get caught in that trap. Your time and life energy are too precious not to write about what you enjoy and about subjects that excite you. After all, if you're not excited yourself, how can you hope to interest an agent?

Are You Qualified?

Ask yourself if you would be qualified to write a book on your subject. If not, could you—would you—take the time to develop the necessary credentials? In our society, only doctors are permitted by law to diagnose and prescribe. Only attorneys can practice law. Outside of licensure and diplomas, our culture still demands substantial credentials before conferring the mantle of "authority." If your car needs repair, you would no more take it to your licensed hair stylist than you would let your dealer-certified mechanic style your hair.

You can be the writer half of a writer/expert team. To pursue this route, you must demonstrate professional writing and interview skills and be willing to immerse yourself in the knowledge and language of your expert's field. In essence, you would have to become a professional in two fields—writing and that of the expert's. It goes without saying that both writer and expert should sign an agreement about division of labor and money for the creation of the proposal and book, as well as for its promotion.

As an alternative to teaming up with an expert, you can also research, write, and publish articles in academic, technical, or professional areas. Many freelance writers make a living by studying the journals and conference papers, in science, for instance, and translating them into articles and books for the general public. Over time, you can build a reputation as a lay expert, and then write a proposal and book.

We've been discussing "the professions and the trades," but developing credentials (or teaming up with an expert) applies to nonprofessional areas as well. For instance, one would think that preparing three meals a day for all your adult life would qualify you to publish cookbooks. Before you sit down to whip up a cookbook proposal, I'd want to know if you've published articles on cooking. No? Taught cooking classes? No? Starred in a local TV cooking show? I didn't think so. Before you can share your secret sauce with the world, you've got to convince agents and editors that you know what you're talking about. Testimonials from sated family members are not enough.

Does Your Book Idea Match Your Long-term Career Goals?

Last of all, consider the career implications of publishing the book you have in mind. You may develop a following, become known or better known, after you publish a book. Some writers publish books in order to create new careers. For instance, a book may be used to launch a speaking tour, which then allows a person to become a consultant. In general, a trade-books editor will assume you want to write a book similar to your first one in order to capitalize on name recognition. I'm sure that helped me sell *The Sell Your Novel Tool Kit*, first to Blue Heron Publishing and later to Perigee.

Think about what shape you'd like your life and career as a writer to take in five years, ten years, and beyond. Make sure you would be proud to have a particular book as your legacy to the world. Publishing a book grants you instant authority—like Dr. Spock or Rachel Carson. Do you want to be remembered by your present book idea?

You must have clear and positive answers to these questions of personal impact. If you're still on solid ground with your book idea, ask yourself whether you're ready to refine, or even develop, the writing skills you'll need to go the distance.

Are You Willing to Learn How to Write for Publication?

Proposals showcase your writing, and your writing must show well. Writing for publication is vastly different from writing essays about "My Summer Vacation" or term papers about "Analysis of the Symbolism in Hemingway's *The Old Man and the Sea*." Most writers require specialized training to write successful proposals and books. The examples drawn from proposals in this book reveal the kind of professional writing and marketing style common to proposals.

Roger Devine, former assistant trade books' editor, stated, "Ninety-eight percent of the things that come to me are written by people who can't write." Echoing this sentiment, New York literary agent Denise Marcil cites poor grammar, punctuation, and prose as the most annoying weaknesses in proposals submitted to her.

Read several books on freelance writing; learn the techniques of writing for publication. In this book's Resource Directory, I've listed books, correspondence courses, and Web sites related to improving your writing techniques.

As used in this book, "writing for publication" does not mean writing for textbooks or academic journal articles. Writers with advanced degrees or years spent in professional or highly technical fields—people such as professors, doctors, therapists, computer buffs, scientists—often speak and write in three- to five-syllable words or in technical jargon. If you are one of the "higher-educationally impaired," you may have to unlearn high diction and techno-speak in order to communicate to a non-academic reader. Psychologist Marilyn Barrett, author of *Creating Eden: The Garden as a Healing Space*, faced this problem. Because her book was based on her Ph.D. thesis, she had to work through several revisions of her proposal with a professional editor until she recovered her "natural voice."

PASSING A PUBLISHER'S TEST

It's important to sensitize yourself to the publishing perspective shared by agents and editors. They are constantly on the lookout for great ideas and new trends. With any nonfiction book, you must fulfill four basic criteria:

- Fill a void
- Make a contribution
- Offer something different and/or better, and
- Meet the demands of the times

Fill a Void

When the public has an interest or need for which no book has yet been published, an opportunity exists for a writer to "fill a void." While doing research for his book the "savant syndrome," Dr. Darald A. Treffert failed to find a book written for the lay public. He filled the void with his book, *Extraordinary People*. What helps make a publisher willing to risk publication of a never-been-done book is the combination of heightened public interest and a qualified author to write it.

Make a Contribution

When other authors have already written in your subject area, but you have something substantive to add to the field, you have an opportunity to make a contribution. Often, making a contribution goes hand in hand with supplying a book that is different, and timely—the next two criteria. Some agents and editors assume personal responsibility to help into print those books that make a contribution in a social or moral way. Often, these works make little money. Even so, some agents or publishers go the distance to see that these books get published.

Offer Something Different or Better

While your book may not speak for a previously disenfranchised group or tap into a social problem, it should offer something different or better. When I first conceived the idea for this book, for instance, only one other book on proposals served the public. Unhappy with its limitations, I set out to produce a book that was both different and better, in content and accessibility.

Sidebar 2-1
Editorial Review Committee's Most Common Reasons for Rejection of a Proposal

1. It sounds like a magazine article.

   You may have narrowed the subject too much, researched inadequately, or chosen too superficial a topic.

2. It's already been done.

   Angels, for instance. Other topics that have run their course and would be hard to get published include the giant recovery market including the treatment of alcohol and drug addiction, and co-dependent relationships, etc. To avoid a rehashing of topics already covered, research what's been written in your area, and check *Books in Print*, *Forthcoming Books in Print* and Amazon.com.

3. It's never been done.

   This reason for rejection means that the editors don't see a market for your book. They believe the public either wouldn't be interested in your new topic or would have to be educated to create a desire to buy your book. If you tend to ride the leading edge in your field, then write and publish articles first, in order to prepare the world for your new ideas.

4. Topics like that don't sell.

   Publishing has ingrained prejudices. Cat books sell; dog books don't. (Never mind the bestseller, *The Secret Life of Dogs*.) Baseball books sell; football books don't. World War II books sell; unknown authors' life stories don't. If you intend to overcome these biases based on bottom-line profits, you have extra work to do. You must have a well-developed slant and prove why your book will sell.

(Continued)

5. There's too much competition.

Perhaps another publisher has a similar book coming out—an insider fact you and your agent may not know. Perhaps they've just received six proposals on opossums and other marsupials. Agents and editors alike share their amazement in the synchronous phenomenon of receiving proposals for books on the same subject in a relatively brief time period. We do all seem to be swimming in the same sea of shared thought. Publishing goes in waves. Again, the remedy to entering an overly competitive field is to keep an eye on *Books in Print, Publishers Weekly,* and publications in your field.

6. It's too expensive to produce.

So what if you've spent the last ten years writing the definitive tome on forest slugs. Nine hundred pages is too long and the color plates for fifty photographs will break all budgets. You'll either have to find a publisher with deeper pockets or adjust your ideas.

7. The author's qualifications, name recognition, or promotional outreach is insufficient for the publisher's sales goals.

A conglomerate or imprint may decide that less than 10,000 copies in sales of a first print run is not worth its while. A small publisher might consider the same number to be a bestseller. If you want to break in with the big guys, you've got to carry big guns.

Our global culture has been oriented around a virtually insatiable thirst for information-supplying books and how-to's. Picador editor George Witte, speaking at a writer's conference, said, "There are lots of books that are not works of genius but provide solid information." As you read through the proposal examples in this book, you'll see that nearly every author fulfills the criteria of offering a book that is different or better.

Meet the Demands of the Times

The million-dollar questions in publishing are "Why this book? Why now?" In a real sense, timing is everything. Although books must be different and/or better and fill a void or make a contribution, if the timing isn't right, none of these reasons particularly matters. Your book must fulfill the demands of the times and meet the ever-changing interests and needs of the public. Scientist Linda Jean Shepherd might not have been able to sell her book, *Lifting the Veil: The Feminine Face of Science* in, say, the fifties. But it was precisely the right book for the zeitgeist of the nineties.

In contrast, space engineer Ralph Nansen had a hard time selling his revolutionary book, *Sun Power: The Global Solution for the Coming Energy Crisis*. He may be the most qualified person in the country to know whether our technology could reasonably and economically shift to his solar-energy plan, yet the editorial feedback he received indicated that he may be ahead of the demands of the times.

In an entirely different sense of "the demands of the times," some authors intentionally capitalize on the short-lived fads of popular culture and big events. Have you ever noticed how quickly books hit the stands following a major disaster, such as a hurricane, flood, or earthquake? Not to mention books on high-profile criminal proceedings and celebrities. Some writers make a comfortable living just by seizing the element of timing.

Agents and publishers, too, must keep apprised of long-range anniversaries of historical events and begin planning books for them years in advance. If you wanted to sell a book on the impact and vision of the movie, *2001: A Space Odyssey*, you would have had to written your proposal and sold the book in 1998 or 1999 for publication in 2001.

Many other books are perennials, not heavily affected by time, except when their information becomes dated. When I asked several publishing professionals what kinds of books they considered as perennials, they said: childcare/parenting, personal finance/planning, pet care, home how-to, personal health/fitness, entrepreneurial, pop culture, how-to's and cooking, to name a few. Your best barometer for what's selling now and in the near future is reading *Publisher's Weekly*.

Like a lab tech testing a product for *Consumer Reports*, Sidebar 2-1 will help you measure how well your idea will stand up to the demands from an editorial review committee before you commit to a proposal and book.

Refining Your Idea

You can't adequately refine an idea for a book without taking into consideration a market. Make sure you can answer these four marketplace questions:

- Who is my reader?
- How many readers could my book capture?
- What is the best slant for my idea?
- What is my selling handle?

WHO IS MY READER?

Although you'll be asked to go into greater detail about your potential readers when you write the proposal section, "About the Market," for now create a cameo of your intended readers. Who are they? What gender and age group would be most interested in your idea? What interests or professions do your targeted readers hold?

If you fail to ask and answer these questions early on, you may make a big mistake. A psychologist I'll call Howard decided he wanted to write a self-help book for the mass market. In one sense, Howard had defined his audience, because *mass* means everybody. However, within a few paragraphs, his sentences grew top-heavy with polysyllabic words, and his technical jargon overrode his message as he made lengthy detours into abstraction. In short, he ceased to communicate with his audience. Readers of self-help books want immediately useful ideas to apply to their lives, and the ideas must be reasonably simple. Howard also had another problem in his early draft: his examples inadvertently featured women in a poor light.

Keep in mind that women purchase the majority of all books; some experts say as much as three-quarters of all books and about half of all paperbacks.

> Discuss your book idea with booksellers, librarians, and potential readers to ensure that the scope of your idea is appropriate.

Another one of my students described a book idea based on her homespun solutions to raising children from birth to age eighteen. Since, at the time, I had two children, one teen and one preteen, I fit the profile of one of her potential readers. So far, so good. But, after a brief review, I knew I'd never buy her book; nor would an agent, editor, or, I believe, any parent. Why? Her idea covered too great a scope for her targeted readers' needs or interests. I no longer need to learn how to handle the trying twos, toilet training, or bedtimes. Not anymore. Instead, I needed advice on piloting my teenager through high-school homework and on keeping both of my children away from negative peer influences.

In contrast, school counselor Dean Walker thought deeply about his book's audience. By the time he brought his proposal to my critique group, he had already narrowed his idea. This was evident by his working title: *Organic Parenting: Raising Real People Through the Art of Human Relating, Birth to Six.* Although his title seemed cumbersome, it did reflect careful thinking about his audience—parents of younger children. His distinction of "organic parenting" also targeted a particular readership, parents whose values probably lean toward organic foods and "Mother Earth" lifestyles.

How Many Readers Could My Book Have?

Estimate the size of your market. Talk with bookstore owners or managers and listen to their advice. Ask if they'd expect your book to be published by a small, regional, or specialty publisher, by a mid-sized publisher, or by an imprint of a conglomerate. If a bookseller's answers are clear, focused, and immediate, then your idea is clear and communicates well, and you're probably on track. If the person you talk with hesitates, puzzles over your idea, and gives you vague answers, take that response as a signal to spend more time thinking about what you want to write and who will want to read it. Also pay attention to these retailers' nonverbal responses; gauge how much excitement your idea generates.

Ask a bookseller where your book might be shelved—to profile your intended readers, to estimate the size of your market, and to see which publishers are already interested in your subject. Knowing the size of your market will allow you to make reasonable claims in your proposal, and it will save you time in marketing it to the right publishers or agents. For example, this book on proposals is a specialized book. I'm unlikely to see this book on the *New York Times* bestseller's list. Only readers interested in writing nonfiction book proposals will pick up a how-to book on this subject. That market, though narrow, is large enough to have earned the label "bestseller" by my first, small, publisher. As you can see, it's all relative.

HOW CAN I SLANT MY IDEA TO ATTRACT MY READERS?

One afternoon I received a call from a woman who had completed a program to qualify as a Master Gardener. She had recently moved from the Northeast to my part of the world, the Northwest. After telling me about her credentials, which were substantial enough to write a book, she said, "I want to write a book on gardening." We talked further and I expected her to become more specific in her description of her book idea. Instead, she repeated, "Just on gardening."

She needed to prune her idea, to narrow its scope. Even though she could define her readers—gardeners, and could guess at the size of her potential market— she would never be able to write a proposal on "gardening" and sell it. Bookstore shelves sag under the

Sidebar 2-2

The Most Common Slants to Capture Reader Attention

Below, you'll find two examples in each category. The first is a published book. The last is an imaginary title as if I was brainstorming for a slant on a book about "cats."

NEW—what's never been done before, the cutting edge. Example: *New French Thought: Political Philosophy* (Mark Lilla); or *New Cat Breeds*.

MONEY—any allusion to the buck attracts attention. Example: *Big Profits from Small Stocks* (Samuel Case); or *Million-Dollar Cats*.

SEX—either direct reference or sexual innuendo. Example: *Nuts! The Battle of the Bulge* (Goldstein, Dillon, & Wenger); or *Furry Bedwarmers: The Cat in Your Life*.

SECRETS—inside accounts, behind the scenes. Example: *Secrets of Fat-Free Baking* (Sandra Woodruff); *or Behind Bars: The Untold Story of Impounded Cats*.

PROMISES—this slant offers the moon and better deliver. Example: *Eat More, Weigh Less* (Dean Ornish, M.D.); or *Cats That Can Change Your Life*.

FIGHT OR FLIGHT—meant to arouse brain-stem feelings of survival, this slant gets adrenaline rushing. Example: *Jungle Rules: How to be a Tiger in Business* (Imlay and Hamilton); or *Catting Around: Stalking Big Cat Home Videos*.

FEAR—when you want to make your reader afraid, this slant is the one to use. Example: *Outrageous Practices: The Alarming Truth About How Medicine Mistreats Women* (Laurence and Weinhouse); *or An Endangered Species: Big Cats Fall to Small-Armed Men*.

(Continued)

NUMBERS—whether the number refers to time, pounds, age, or anything else, it is a classic slant. Example: *The 7 Habits of Highly Effective People* (Stephen R. Covey); or *Ten Ideal Vacations for Kittys*.

LOCATION—any idea that implies place. Example: *In the Kitchen with Rosie* (Rosie Daley); or *Bedroom Designs for Catting Around*.

AMAZEMENT—a slant that gives you a believe-it-or-not feeling or elicits amazement. Example: *Remarkable Discoveries!* (Frank Ashall); or *The Cat Who Dog-Paddled the Channel*.

SUPERLATIVES—any title that involves extremes, such as worst, best, longest, shortest, richest, poorest, etc. Example: *The Greatest Team of All Time* (Acocella and Dewey); or *The Sleepiest Cats in the World*.

REVERSALS—minority viewpoints or an opposite stance from the prevailing views on a subject. Example: *Roughing It Easy* (on camping by Dian Thomas); or, *Seeing-Eye Cats*.

TRAVEL—Unlike location, or in addition to it, the travel slant makes clear the out-and-about orientation of the book. Example: *A Cat Abroad: The Further Adventures of Norton, The Cat Who Went to Paris, and His Human* (Peter Gethers), or *Cruises Cats Love*.

HUMOR—a humorous slant on an idea is enough to provide the sharp focus that every subject demands. Example: *I Purr, Therefore I Am: Never Before Collected Observations on All Things Cat* (compiled by Merrit Malloy), or *Paw-Print Picassos: Your Cat as Artist*.

weight of gardening books. Entire books have been written on roses, composting, or organic control of pests. Even so, room exists for one more book; in fact, there's room for bushels more. However, because so much has already been written on gardening, new books require well-focused slants. They should be narrowed to a smaller scope and to niches not already filled, such as "Postage stamp gardening for college dorm rooms," or "Dashboard gardening for the full-time RVer."

Sometimes students and clients don't understand what I mean by narrowing an idea. It does evoke the idea of ending up with less. Yet, in the book world, less usually means more. The best way to narrow your idea is to understand *slant*.

Slant means the focus of your subject or the angle you take in presenting it. A slant helps make your book unique and gives it a sales angle. Slant establishes bias and "colors" an idea throughout, from title to chapter content. Imagine a beautiful sunset described for meteorologists compared to a description of the same sunset written for tourists. Different audience. Different slant.

> You have to end up with so strong an idea that it can stand up to intense editorial scrutiny.

Take an afternoon and visit your local bookstores or use the online bookstores. Browse through titles in your subject area and descriptions of similar books. Which titles grip you? Can you identify the slant? The intended audience? Use Sidebar 2-2 to identify slants of the books that most attracted you and slants that might best fit your idea.

Clarity of subject is by far the most important feature of your book's concept. If you have ever started a business or searched for a service by name, you will understand the need for a descriptive name rather than a cute one. Until name recognition, i.e. McDonalds or Levis, can sell your product or service, it's generally best to choose a business name like Magic Carpet Cleaning rather than Sam's Service Specialties. What specialty? What service? Who's Sam?

The same holds true for marketing your book. It's better to err on the side of plain description than to miss the mark with a fancy title or approach that reveals nothing of your book's contents. Consider some of these actual book titles: *The Prostate Book*, or *Beachcomber's Guide to Florida Marine Life*. Descriptive and clear. In Carolyn Cotter's first draft of a proposal on a model for countering manipulation, she and coauthor George H. Green titled their book, *Don't Even Try!* What does that mean? Give up? By the time she sent it out for agent consideration, it bore the title, *Earn Your Verbal Black Belt* with a descriptive subtitle. Personally, I preferred this title to the one eventually used, because it reflected the metaphor of the martial arts, a part of the book's actual content. Needless to say, I couldn't argue with the clear title selected by Elizabeth Beier, Green and Cotter's editor at Berkley Publishing Group: *Stop Being Manipulated*.

Titles offer an important reflection of the slant. It may take you many tries and many months to find a title you are happy with, but start your thinking processes with a working title that reflects a slant. It's crucial to your idea's success to present your subject matter in a special way.

In her book, *How to Write Irresistible Query Letters*, Lisa Collier Cool identifies over a dozen slants. I've listed the most common slants and given examples from published books in Sidebar 2-2. For instructional purposes, I've followed each example of an actual book with one based on the idea of writing a book about "cats." Take your narrowed book concept and check it against the list of slants. Refine your idea by rewriting it with a slant. To explore the possibilities of a slant for your idea, write a title for your book using each slant.

As you can see from the examples of slants, just taking the simple (and broad) category of "cats" allowed me to create a narrowed subject with diverse avenues of sales appeal. Select the title that you think reflects your strongest and best slant. You may eventually change your title, but use this as your first working title.

Your publisher may later change your working title into

WWW ADDRESSES FOR BOOK TITLES AND DESCRIPTION

www.abe.com

www.publink.net (a portal to 170 online retailers of books)

www.booksense.com (site for independent booksellers)

www.amazon.com

www.bn.com

www.borders.com

www.bookzone.com

www.powells.com

WWW ADDRESSES FOR
WRITING INSTRUCTION

Freelance Success Institute:
www.freelancesuccess.com

Gotham Writers Workshop:
www.writer.org

UCLA:
www.onlinelearning.net/

Word Museum:
www.wordmuseum.com

Writer's Village University:
www.4-writers.com, or,
wvu.com

Writers Write University:
www.writerswrite.com

a more descriptive one. Never forget, however, that you'll make your first sale to sophisticated buyers—an agent and editor. Because I was directly involved in presenting Green and Cotter's book to several agents, I watched them perk up when they heard the working title, *Earn Your Verbal Black Belt*. I'm not sure they would have been equally interested in *Stop Being Manipulated*, yet this title may better reach the book's mass-market readership.

WHAT IS MY SELLING HANDLE?

Once you have selected the slant that defines your book as different from all others like it, you're ready to write a first selling handle. According to literary agent, Thomas Grady, former executive editor at HarperCollins, a selling handle is "a memorable, succinct, crystal clear, and possibly clever way of describing the purpose and promise of a book." How long is a selling handle? Two sentences. Not three. Two.

To craft your book's selling handle, Tom recommends that you step outside your book and think about it in the third person. It might help you to fill in the following blank. "Next on Oprah, _____."

Who uses a selling handle? First, it gives you a center of gravity for thinking about, talking about, and writing your proposal and book. Second, in this era of speedy everything, it gives your agent the gold nugget he or she needs to offer prospective publishers.

When your book is finally in the chute, awaiting delivery from

---

Sidebar 2-3

Ten Questions to Answer Before Committing to a Book Project

1. Can you write well enough—with correct grammar, punctuation, and coherence? If the answer is *no*, are you willing to learn how to bring your writing up to standard?

2. Do you have sufficient enthusiasm for a project that may span years?

3. Are you qualified to write your book? Can you develop qualifications?

4. Will publication of your book satisfy your long-term career goals? Will you be proud of this book in years to come?

5. Is your book idea better than or different from other books already published on your subject?

6. What is the size of your market? Will your book appeal to a small, middle-sized, or large audience?

7. Do you have enough material for an entire book?

8. Does your subject have staying power? Will it reach beyond a current trend and sell copies in three, five, or ten years?

9. Does your idea spark enthusiasm? As you share your idea, do your friends, booksellers, and prospective readers become excited?

---

printer to warehouse to stores across the continent, the sales rep will instinctively, perhaps intentionally, choose books with powerful, clear, and catchy selling handles. It makes sense. According to Tom Grady, sales reps hate content; they want handles to save them time. Who better to write your book's selling handle than you? Consider the following examples of selling handles.

Mom to New Mom: Practical Tips and Advice for the New Mom is a parenting-tips book for new moms with babies from birth to age one. (by Mary Jeanne Menna, Times Books).

Act Like an Owner: The Power of an Ownership Culture is the first book to demonstrate that an ownership culture can create an environment where ordinary people accomplish extraordinary things. (by Robert Blonchek & Martin O'Neill, John Wiley & Sons).

Three Cats, Two Dogs, One Journey Through Multiple Pet Loss is the unflinching story of confronting and surviving every pet lover's worst nightmare—sudden multiple pet loss. (by David Congalton, NewSage Press).

Now it's your turn. Oprah's people have just phoned you; what will you tell them?

It takes time to arrive at a solid book idea. Preliminary research will help you continue to evaluate and refine your idea. Research will also form the foundation for drafting "About the Competition," the first section you'll write for your proposal.

CHAPTER THREE

Research Made Easy: What Data Will You Need?

Chapter Goal: To create a foundation for writing your proposal by recognizing and planning what research you will need.

Research is necessary and invaluable, but it need not be protracted and painful. When graduate students begin doctoral theses, they sometimes spend a year or more researching their subjects. Such research is the foundation for a successful proposal too, but some shortcuts can get you in and out of the library before you have to put another quarter in the parking meter.

To many people, research is an eight-letter bad word. Their negative experiences may have been based upon the laborious ways we formerly did research—with stacks of index cards, piles of books, and mounds of photocopied paper. It is my intent to relieve your suffering by streamlining your task, first, by letting you know what kinds of research you'll need, and second, by introducing you to the most effective research tools available. Then, you can maximize results and minimize labor.

Overview of Research Requirements for Your Proposal

Although it's likely that you'll do most research little by little as you develop your proposal, a comprehensive overview may help give you the "big picture" of your research needs. Sidebar 3-1 provides this overview.

Research Tools—Libraries and the Internet

I'm one of those individuals who enjoys research. Often, I become so fascinated with tidbits, I find that I easily go off on tangents, nearly forgetting my original goal. If you're already familiar with doing research, you may not need this section. To some extent, the school system taught all of us how to do research "the old way," that is, by physically searching through mountains of paper—card catalogs, journals, magazines, and books. If you have begun to use and explore the Internet, chances are that you primarily use it for your research needs. Doing research on your home computer using the Web is still new enough in the history of the written word to be called "the new way" of researching. In the following sections, I'll outline both ways of doing research. The following six research tools should help you find the information you seek.

- Libraries and librarians
- Directories, databases, and clearinghouses
- Periodicals and newspapers
- Books in print and out of print
- Book reviews
- Authorities in your field

LIBRARIES AND LIBRARIANS

Long live librarians! They are a writer's invaluable resource. Librarians at college or university libraries will assist you with computerized searches for information and use of more traditional reference

Sidebar 3-1

Overview of Research Needed for Your Proposal

Proposal Section	Research Needed
Concept Statement	ranges from no special research to some research to development of slant, statistics, or startling facts
About the Book	statistics, interesting facts, quotes from published sources, quotes from experts and people-in-the-street, a solid background understanding of your book's idea, knowledge of most competitive books like yours, identification of your targeted reader
About the Author	a good memory
About the Market	statistics to document the demographics of your audience and the size of your market; checking *Literary Market Place* for possible book clubs
About the Competition	*Books in Print, Cumulative Index,* and *Forthcoming Books in Print*, as well as books most similar to yours; trips to well-stocked bookstores and interviewing owners or managers; online research of book titles and descriptions
Production Details	permissions forms, individuals to endorse book and write a foreword, costs to complete the book
About Promotion	books on marketing books; Web sites on book promotion; books and Web sites on design and utilization of author Web pages
Table of Contents	books like yours to compare organization and style
Chapter Summaries	information that goes into each chapter
Sample Chapters	details—facts, statistics, information to write these chapters
The Appendix	magazines, journals, and newspapers for material related to your subject; personal archives for clips, flyers, public-relations materials on you and your subject

texts. Sometimes a writer will feel stymied, overwhelmed by the need to drum up statistics for the proposal sections that require them. Befriend a reference librarian. You'll get the most help if you fully inform them of your project and the information you need. To save hours and days, call a reference librarian and set up an appointment. Let these professionals lead your search. They get specialized and on-going training in the latest research tools.

If you don't live near a university library, librarians at many local public libraries remain "at your service," even for phone inquiries. The last time I called, I was working on a proposal and called to find out how many times in a lifetime the average American changed residences, careers, and spouses. The librarian called back within a few hours with these statistics and their source.

Most libraries have replaced traditional card catalogs, which show the books in inventory, with computerized catalogs. Using these, from your home computer or at the library, you or a librarian can track down books available at your library or branch libraries—searching by title, subject, author, or other key words. These references can give you descriptions of individual books and help you find synonyms of your topic. Use these words to cross-index your topic with related subjects.

Online resources abound. In preparation for writing "About the Competition," you'll be required to review other books similar to yours. But it won't be necessary to read every one of them. Online references provide summaries of each book that help you eliminate those you don't need, decipher slants and audience, and alert you to comparable books that you should spend time reading from cover to cover. In the Resource Directory, you'll find Internet addresses for finding book titles and their descriptions.

For your competition section, you'll need to describe other books like yours and offer a comparison of the similarities to and differences from your own. Take notes on the library descriptions of these competitive books, including their library call numbers, such as the Dewey decimal numbers or Library of Congress numbers. File these for later reference so you don't need to repeat your initial search. When you find a book online that you want to refer to, print out its description and perhaps also its table of contents.

For any book that might end up in your "About the Competition" section, whether you do your research the new or old way, get the following bibliographic information:

- Author's name
- Book title
- Publisher
- City and state of publication
- Publication date of most recent edition
- Number of pages
- Retail cost of hardback or paperback—if available

DIRECTORIES, DATABASES, AND CLEARINGHOUSES

Moira Andersen Allen, author of the book *writing.com*, defines the differences between three research tools: directories, databases, and clearinghouses.

Directories are compilations (made by someone—a person not a computer) of information on a specific, often narrow, subject. They exist in book and electronic forms. For instance, *Guide to Literary Agents* is a compilation of approximately 600 listings of literary agents. This is a directory.

The reference section of most libraries has shelf after shelf of directories. Online, one of the most well-known search engines is *Yahoo!* When you enter a keyword into this online directory, it will spit out a list of 25 or more Web sites and a place to keep clicking to get the next grouping and the next.

Databases are the motherships of directories. Containing enormous amounts of information, they may hold the archives of magazines and newspapers, many directories, statistics, encyclopedias, etc. Databases bring an entire planet of research to your fingertips. Think of a database as a library that specializes in a particular subject area. Reference librarians need only type the correct Web addresses to discover the specific information you require in virtually every field of interest.

Clearinghouses, as Allen defines them, describe "subject-specific sites that offer extensive resource links." For a clearinghouse related to writing information, for instance, you can't beat ZuZu (*www.zuzu.com*).

Doing in-depth research has never been so quick or so comprehensive. Get to know directories, databases, and clearinghouses—and/or your neighborhood Internet-savvy librarian. Also know that at least once a year, *Writer's Digest* features the best Web sites for writers. See the Resource Directory for more Web sites and books on the subject of research.

PERIODICALS AND NEWSPAPERS

You can find information about periodicals and newspapers, as well as articles from these sources, through directories, databases, and clearinghouses. Because they are such an important part of research for a proposal, they deserve special mention.

Periodicals and newspapers can reflect the ever-changing fads of our culture more quickly than books do. One of the critical questions you must answer for an agent/editor in "About the Book" is: "Why this idea; why now?" Magazine and newspaper articles will tell you whether your idea is passé, in vogue, or just about to be "discovered." Through these serial publications, you'll also find current statistics, facts, and quotable passages that add pizzazz to the Concept Statement, About the Book, and Marketing Sections. Periodical and newspaper directories and databases go back years, or even decades.

The traditional *Reader's Guide to Periodical Literature* and other directories give extensive indexes of trade, technical, religious, and college publications. They fill in gaps by providing indexed and abstracted descriptions of magazine and journal articles published on this continent and around the world.

Once again, on the Web, you can go to sites that put nearly every magazine, journal, newspaper, and newsletter—in English and every other foreign language—at your fingertips. Besides the Web addresses listed in the prior section, you can also use Librarians' Index to the Internet (*www.sunsite.berkeley.edu/*), or, for newsgroups:

CaraList, the Official Catalog of LISTSERV Lists (*www.lsoft.com/lists/ listref.html*). Last of all, consider checking the site: Using the Internet for Research (*www.purefiction.com/pages/res1.htm*).

From serial publications, you should:

- Confirm that your book supplies a current need or fills a publishing void.
- Make sure that your subject offers enough substance for a book, enough slant to attract your readers.
- Begin to define how your book will be different and better than existing books.

When you find articles related to your book's subject, photo-copy them and record the bibliographic information, or bookmark them online. At a later date, you may wish to review articles for quotes to use within your chapters or for verification of facts and statistics. You may also decide to include copies of some articles in your proposal's appendix and in your query package to demon-strate the popularity of your topic.

BOOKS IN AND OUT OF PRINT

For your About the Competition section, you need to know what books on your subject are in print, and perhaps, what books have gone out of print. I'm convinced that a high percentage of writers conduct a search of the literature by going to their local bookstore and finding "nothing much." If you rely on memory, on your per-sonal collection of books, or on only those books in stock at a favorite bookstore, you risk writing a proposal that has shallow development and makes an inadequate comparison of your book with others. This means searching beyond your local library and bookstore. You *must* check Bowker's *Books in Print*, *Forthcoming Books in Print*, and an Internet bookstore such as

> Find out what's been pub-lished, and review those books most similar to yours for eventual use in your pro-posal's competition section.

Amazon.com. If you want to write a nonfiction book for children, check *Children's Books in Print*. These are major reference books, frequently updated and carried by every library.

These directories are divided by subject, author, and title. The subject index allows you to directly check your topic. If necessary, ask your reference librarian to help you create a list of synonyms for cross-referencing. Remember to jot down bibliographic information and notes about each book's slant and content, if you intend to profile it in About the Competition.

BOOK REVIEWS

One of the most difficult references to come by using the old way of research are book reviews. For one thing, hardbacks get reviewed much more often than trade or mass-market paperbacks, yet your competition may be published only in paperback. In my pre-web experience, spending hours at the University of Oregon library—renowned as a research library—finding the reviews I needed was purely a matter of luck.

Once again, the Web solves the problem of finding book reviews, if you can go through a university site or use a university computer and avoid prohibitive subscriber fees. If so, the site *booksinprint.com* has 300,000 full text reviews from *Library Journal, Publisher's Weekly,* and other sources. Baker & Taylor's site, *btol.com* features 77,000 reviews.

AUTHORITIES IN YOUR FIELD

Plan to interview authorities on your book's subject for purposes of acquiring original, unpublished contributions to your book or proposal (with credit), and for recommendations of other books on your subject. Interviews with experts in your field can add information you simply won't find in publications.

You'd be surprised at how willing authors and experts are to offer information and interviews. These days, you may get a quicker response if you e-mail someone rather than send a letter. However, it may also be to your advantage to send a professional letter on attractive stationery, offering your own e-mail and phone number, and possibly indicating that you will contact the authority by e-mail or phone in a few days.

If you don't know experts in your subject by name, I recommend finding them by going to one of the two following Web sites (or ask a librarian to do it for you): ProfNet (*www.profnet.com*) or Experts (*www.google*).

If your research does not indicate you have a viable book idea, your investment of time will have spared you rejection down the road. Preliminary research can reveal some of those editorial reasons for rejection, such as "it's already been done," or "it sounds like a magazine article," or "it's never been done." If this turns out to be the case, you've saved yourself time, effort, and disappointment.

Despite thorough research into the competition, what if your results are inconclusive, or you're simply unsure whether your idea is worth developing into a book? Perhaps you found dozens of books like yours, but still believe yours is significantly different. Or perhaps you couldn't find any truly comparable books in print, yet believe you have a book the world needs or would enjoy. I'll address these uncertainties in the next chapter.

CHAPTER FOUR

About the Competition: What's Already in Print?

Chapter Goal: To compare and contrast your book to others like it, and to write a powerful analysis of books comparable to yours.

Concept Statement
About the Book
About the Author
About the Market
* About the Competition
Production Details
About Promotion
Table of Contents
Chapter Summaries
Sample Chapters
The Appendix

Seeking publication is similar to selling a new product. You wouldn't think of ignoring competing models. Your buyer (in this case your publisher) would be foolish to offer you a contract without knowing the competition. It may surprise you, but competition for your book may actually be a good thing. In fact, finding other books in your field demonstrates public interest and prior publisher confidence.

Definition and Purpose

The profiles of competitive titles for your proposal are in the section called "About the Competition." Here, authors typically profile half a dozen to a dozen books most like their own. In each profile, list the bibliographic information mentioned in chapter three, summarize the contents and slant of each competitor's book in a short paragraph, and compare and contrast it with yours.

Although the competition section is usually the fifth section in a finished proposal, I recommend addressing it now, as part of the process of determining if your idea fills a publishing void and whether your book will make a contribution to the field. If you can't substantiate that, there's little point in making a heavy investment of time and energy in the proposal process.

You don't want to reinvent the wheel. Your research of competitive titles should validate your unique spin on your subject. Learning what the competition has already written will help you refine your idea, allowing you to further slant it for greater salability.

Like many of my clients, you may be surprised that it is the job of the writer, not the publisher, to profile the competition. However, realize that the entire proposal represents a market-research report, and that the burden of proof of your book's need rests with you. You're the party seeking financial backing.

Similar to selling any product, the sale of your book depends upon briefing the publisher about your competition and providing a convincing argument why your book is better or different or both— why your book represents the *zeitgeist*, the spirit of the times.

Your list of books in "About the Competition" also tells the publisher where you see your book being shelved. The shelving locations for some books are easy to determine. *Mothering Twins: From Hearing the News to Beyond the Terrible Twos* clearly belongs with books on family, parenting, or birthing (depending upon the volume and diversity in a bookstore). But where would a bookseller put *Creating Eden: The Garden as a Healing Space*? Gardening? Nature and ecology? Self-help? Where you position your book—by comparison to others—helps crystallize your vision of it and how it will be marketed.

Sample "About the Competition"

In the lead of the competition section of *Act Like an Owner*, authors Blonchek and O'Neill reiterate the size of their market, i.e. "exploding," then state which categories of business books are most comparable to their own, namely, corporate culture and leadership. They also describe the uniqueness of their book within these broad categories and differentiate their book from ones that are academic. Sidebar 4-1 shows how they handle the transition into the body of "About the Competition" and features one of their seven summaries of competitive titles.

Performing Background Research

Begin your search for books for your "About the Competition" section by checking several online bookstores or directories, or by using the index to *Books in Print*. It gives short descriptions of books, including bibliographic data. Because most writers discover more books than the six to twelve needed for their competition sections, you should:

- Eliminate dissimilar books
- Check recent out-of-print titles
- Use shortcuts to reduce reading
- Write your section "About the Competition."

ELIMINATE DISSIMILAR BOOKS

From the title of many books that you may first find in one of the big directories, you may think there are more books like your own than there really are. Your first job is to eliminate from consideration any and all that really are dissimilar. Even from the brief line or two in the traditional *Books in Print* directory, you can tell if the scope, audience, or slant is far from your own. Sometimes you can take note of a book that is really booklet in length, or, on the other

Sidebar 4-1
Sample: About the Competition

Act Like an Owner by Robert Blonchek and Martin O'Neil (Wiley)

Proposal	Comments
...Our research on other books of this nature indicates the concept of corporate culture is an important topic; however, there are no books that specifically address the concept of an ownership culture as *the key to creating an empowering workforce.* [their emphasis]	Reiterates what makes their book special.
Recent books that are similar in nature include:	
Beyond Engineering by Michael Hammer, Harper Business, 1996.	Lists bibliographic data, although incompletely.
In this book, Hammer puts into perspective that the reengineering revolution is more about people and business change than about processes. He also mentions that he hears almost daily the refrain that everyone must think and behave like an owner. We couldn't agree more. Hammer also calls *Beyond Engineering* a prospectus for a series of books. He believes that the ideas surrounding process-centered work, including the culture of a process-centered organization, deserve volumes on their own. We take him up on this challenge. *Act Like an Owner* is about corporate culture. It is about an Ownership Culture. And, it is about building businesses around people. This is where we depart from Mr. Hammer's views .	Summarizes the slant of the competitive book and how it is the same as their own.
	Strategically, it's better to repeat your book's title and not the competition's.
	Politely states the contribution that their book adds to the field.
	States clearly how their book differs from this title.
Hammer says it's all about processes, but don't forget the impact on people. *We say it's all about people—from the start.*	Clear, powerful statement of their book's slant. In the original proposal, italics were presented in bold.

(continued)

Sidebar 4-1 (Continued)

Proposal	Comments
Value Migration by Adrian J. Slywotzky, Harvard Business School Press, 1996	Incomplete bibliographic information. Recent title for their proposal written in 1998.
Slywotzky introduces the concept of a business design as a business chess game. He shows conclusively how business design is a key differentiating factor of successful businesses today. He illustrates how the value of company migrates to new companies with better business designs, and he presents several general modes of how business value typically migrates.	Excellent summary of the competitor's subject and contribution.
Act Like an Owner builds on Slywotzky's case for the value of a solid business design. It presents a process that the reader can go through to identify his or her current business design or formula and shows how the reader can use this process to stay on top of changes in customer needs and market trends. *Act Like an Owner* takes *Value Migration* to the next logical step. Unlike Slywotzky, we show the reader how to take a solid business design and implement it. Slywotzky simply defines business design and shows how many companies have failed because of their out-of-date designs.	Explains how their book builds on the competitor's ideas. Emphasizes the practical application of the theoretical in the competitor's contents. Good repetition of authors' title. Emphasizes how their book contributes to the field. States how their book differs from the competitor's book.
Five more titles reviewed....	

end of things, several times longer than your own. This may prove enough to simply strike it from the list.

In general, eliminate books that are over five years old. By the time your book is published by a large publisher, another two years may pass, so the titles of competitors' books will be seven years old—if they are still in print.

Who is the publisher for your list of books that might need to be included in your competition section? If you intend to sell to a mid-sized or large publisher, you would not want to include books that seem self-published, corporately published, or possibly done by a regional press. Too many of these books might send the signal that your book, too, is most appropriate for a narrow, regional, or specialized market.

CHECK RECENT OUT-OF-PRINT TITLES

About 90,000 books go out of print each year, although the development of electronic publishing may change all that. Backlist sales are presently the foundation of most publishers' revenues. Yet, large publishers today tend to let books slide into extinction at a faster rate than in the past. In contrast, small to mid-sized publishers make every effort to keep a book active in their backlists, because every penny, so to speak, counts. But it may not be financially viable for larger publishers to keep your first printing in stock or to maintain reprints, even with apparently acceptable sales. Why? All publishers must pay taxes on books they warehouse from one tax year to the next, so they have little incentive to keep slower-moving inventory.

The revolution in electronic publishing is quickly changing the legal definition and practical considerations involved in the designation, "out of print." Any book can exist in a digital form forever. New publishing-technology companies in partnership with publishers, distributors, or booksellers can print a hard copy of selected titles, or download the equivalent books, per consumer demand.

In 1998 and 1999, the Association of Author's Representatives, the Author's Guild, and the National Writers Union demanded an industry-wide revision of the book-publishing contract clause regarding "out of print." Most new publishing contracts generally include a clause describing the "duration" of the book's publication in paper form and include a separate clause that encompasses electronic publishing rights.

In 1999, a new online publisher, iUniverse (formerly toExcel), offered to bring any out-of-print books authored by members of the

Author's Guild back into print as on-demand electronic books (See Author's Guild site: *backinprint.com*).

If you are relying upon the old way of finding information, *Cumulative Books in Print* may help you catch other titles that meet the five-year-or-less criteria.

Use Shortcuts to Reduce Reading

Through your research, you've collected the list of titles and some descriptions of similar books for use in the "About the Competition" section. You may have one or one hundred. Since you will have to provide a paragraph or two of description and analysis about each truly comparable book, you would not want to spend months or years reading through *every* title you've researched. There are ways to trim this task to a manageable size.

Assuming you have already eliminated dissimilar titles, ask a reference librarian to help you locate book reviews of the other books remaining on your list. Reviewers usually provide enough description and analysis for you to fairly compare your idea with the published book. If your book is similar, then determine if the review provides enough material to draft the one or two paragraphs you'll need.

Since the print media limits most of its reviews to hardcover books and bestsellers, your best recourse to get good information on most books is to check the online bookstores such as Amazon.com, BN.com, and Borders.com. For most books they list, you'll find a description, a table of contents, and often reviews from several sources.

If you cannot find reviews or descriptions for some books, you must find copies in your library, or through interlibrary loan, or in bookstores. If you still have dozens of books that qualify, gathering a stack may sound like a year's work, but don't panic; you're not going to "read" them all. Your job is to extract the details you need by reading the book jackets, scanning the indices, studying the tables of contents, and spot-reading enough to confirm or deny your conclusions.

The book jacket summarizes a book's essence. From the contents and index, you can determine how a book differs from yours.

In a well-written book, you can read the introduction, chapter one, and the last few pages of the book to glean a succinct summary of an author's purpose or a book's theme as well as its slant—exactly what you need for your description and analysis.

By the time you apply this scanning method to the books you intend to describe, you'll only have a few books left—those books most like your own. *Read them.* Take notes about the similarities and differences between those books and yours. Finally, read them to learn how other authors handle the job of writing a book on your subject.

Writing Your "About the Competition"

With your research notes and bibliographic information on each title you plan to include in your competition section, you're ready to write. This section of the proposal should contain the following parts:

- Lead
- Analysis of each book, including:
    - —a listing of bibliographic data about each competitive title
    - —a description of each book
    - —several lines to one paragraph of text comparing and contrasting your book to each one described
    - —transition paragraphs, and
- Conclusion

Lead

In the lead or introductory paragraph, you should restate the subject—and possibly the background—of your book to indicate why it should be published now. Identify your targeted reader and use the lead to

> Remember, as in all sections of your proposal, plan to sell what is different and special about your book, emphasizing your authority to write it.

generate excitement. You may want to add a reminder of your credentials. In other words, constantly sell your book and yourself.

Here is the lead for Blonchek and O'Neil's competition section that was omitted in Sidebar 4-1.

> The market for business books is exploding. It is one of the fastest growing segments of the publishing industry. Business books encompass leadership, management, finance, marketing, and strategy. Within each of these categories, books written by academicians and appropriate for business schools, and those written by practitioners dominate the market. Since Blonchek and O'Neill rely heavily on their own business experiences, *Act Like an Owner* is a practical, easy-to-follow leadership book for creating a highly productive ownership culture....

Compare their style and sales approach to instructor Val Dumond's lead paragraph from the competition section for her book *Grammar for Grownups*:

> I am always looking for useful books about grammar to recommend to students, business clients, writers of all kinds. Whenever a new class is scheduled, I dash hopefully to the bookstore to pick up the latest and best grammar guidelines only to discover that while there are many grammar books out there, none wants to help grownups apply the rules they already know in an organized easy-to-understand approach.

In this one short lead, the author has reminded us of her audience—students, business clients, and writers. She's reminded us of her qualifications—she teaches grammar; and she's put us on notice that none of the existing books satisfy the needs of her students. She's done something else: she's given us a sample of her warm personal style, which we must believe will be the style of her book as well. The businessmen who wrote the prior lead may have done essentially the same thing but in a style entirely their own and perhaps more appropriate for a business book.

Biochemist Linda Jean Shepherd, Ph.D., uses her lead for

"About the Competition" section to reiterate the benefits her book offers to readers and to generate excitement.

> *Lifting the Veil: The Feminine Face of Science* is a book that integrates the exciting trends of the new sciences and the related, holistic world view that is a gift of the feminine. It uses the actual experiences of scientists to help readers reconnect with their enlivening qualities and to counteract the arid, one-sided masculine approach to the world.

ANALYSIS OF EACH BOOK

Limit your analysis of each competitive book to no more than three short paragraphs. If you have several categories of books—perhaps to identify different readers—you should provide headings for these markets.

List Bibliographic Data

Introduce each title by listing bibliographic data, including author, title, publisher, publication date, and, if possible, retail prices, edition, and hardback or paperback. There are two basic styles to do this. If you lean toward a well-ordered universe, you might prefer a more organized presentation, first listing the bibliographic data and then describing and analyzing each book. If you're the type who leans toward the artistic side, you might prefer to present the same data but in a more casual style that works the information into the paragraphs.

I prefer a more organized style for graphic clarity and, therefore, clarity of content. The five coauthors of *Mothering Twins* demonstrate this more formal style:

> *Twins From Conception to Five Years* by Averil Clegg and Ann Woolett (from Great Britain), Van Nostrand Reinhold Co., revised edition, 1988. (127 pp), $11.50.
>
> A short, practical guide written in an outline format with suggestions often listed for the reader. It supports women in making individual choices concerning preg-

nancy, birth, and early care of twins.... It does not address the emotional side of having twins.

In a proposal for her memoir, *The Iron Butterfly*, author Doris Colmes uses a more open, narrative style. Here is one of her descriptions of the competition with the bibliographic data worked into the paragraph:

> Like *The Seventh Child* (Freddie Mae Baxter, Alfred Knopf-Random House, 1999), the author's story encompasses over seventy years of living and learning. Ms. Baxter, however, tells her story through the eyes of only the African-American culture, while *In a Garden of Eden, Honey* addresses multicultural and cross-generational phenomena.
>
> In *Angela's Ashes* (Frank McCourt, Scribner, 1996), Mr. McCourt presents a dismal, poverty-stricken childhood, while in *1185 Park Avenue* (Anne Roiphe, The Free Press, 1999), Ms. Roiphe illustrates how being born into wealth can be just as miserable. While both Mr. McCourt and Ms. Roiphe stop their narrative at young adulthood, *The Iron Butterfly*, not only discloses how a child manages to grow up unhappily within both of these economic extremes, but follows this person all the way through adulthood and explains how early trauma affected an entire life.

As you can see, the description and analysis of a competitor can take up only one or two paragraphs, and it is far from a complete summary of the book's contents.

A Description of Each Book

Don't aim to be neutral; your job is to show your book in a more favorable light than those you list. Select the most important highlights that demonstrate the similarities and differences you wish to emphasize.

Notice how the coauthors of *Act Like an Owner* (Sidebar 4-1) left no doubt about the contrasting (as well as different and better) feature or benefit of their book by italicizing (in the original, they used bold) that feature or benefit.

Let's consider one more example. The following presents one of two books listed in Dr. Derek S. Lipman's book on how to stop snoring:

> *Snoring*, by Marcus H. Boulware (American Faculty Press, 1972), was written by a speech therapist. Because its publication preceded the establishment of sleep-disorder laboratories and the development of the surgical procedure known as UPPP, this book no longer provides current medical information on the subject.

Dr. Lipman made short order of a competitive title in a field where he found only two books on his subject.

Compare and Contrast Each Book With Yours

Notice, too, that in all of the quoted examples, the authors showed respect for the books written by other authors, yet emphasized the shortcomings. Criticize your competitors but don't insult them. Realize that your proposal might end up in the hands of an editor who acquired and loved one of the books you feel inclined to trash.

When your book is similar in content, style, or theme, use phrases such as: "similar to," "in a like manner," "also," "the same as." When highlighting your book's superiority and differences, use transitional phrases, such as: "in contrast to," "unlike," "different from," and use superlatives, such as: "much wider," "less daunting," "stronger sense," "more defined," "broader," "more inclusive."

Transition Paragraphs

Paragraphs before or after particular profiles help interpret your conclusions and orient an editor to view the competition the way you would like. Use of "sandwich" paragraphs also works most effectively to transition from the competition profiles in one market, such as "self help," to another, such as "women's psychology."

Transition paragraphs are also a necessity to explain why you would profile books not directly related to your subject. Perhaps you don't find any directly similar books. But, you do find others that are similar in style, format, or theme (although not in subject). Perhaps a book mentions your subject, but only in one chapter. Or, you may decide to describe novels in order to show the popularity of your nonfiction subject. Use transition paragraphs for explanations prior to offering your profiles and analyses.

CONCLUSION

Conclude your "About the Competition" section by summarizing the superiority of your book. Continue to sell excitement. For example, notice the strong conclusion written by linguistics educator Rosemarie Ostler:

> In short, the three books described above fail to provide the reader with the same scope of information as *The Hidden Life of Language*. Either they fail to mention modern theories of language or they focus heavily on cognitive neurolinguistic aspects. In contrast, this book presents detailed yet non-technical analysis of casual and regional speech, a summary of the latest findings on language origins, and substantive but easily grasped details of language change, as well as current information on the neurological and psychological aspects of language. This breadth of outlook cannot be found among the books now available.

Troubleshooting

Use the following list to diagnose problems in writing "About the Competition." Then apply a remedy from the suggestions that follow.

- The where-to-shelve dilemma
- Too few comparable books
- Too many comparable books

The Where-to-shelve Dilemma

Perhaps your dream is to walk into your local bookstore and see 100 copies of your book on a publisher's stand next to the cash register, not in the bowels of the store. Dream on, but in your proposal, get real.

What's the big deal? The big deal has to do with distribution, delivering the goods to your customers. If a book doesn't fit a clear shelving category, then it risks being put somewhere your reader may not think to look. If your book's success doesn't depend heavily on bookstore sales, then the impact of shelving is, of course, lessened.

The successful sale of a book may depend on whether a bookstore owner can place it on the right shelf to reach the customer who habitually browses in only one area of the store.

What can you do? To some degree, sharpening your title may be the answer. In chapter two, we discussed the advantage of a descriptive, but perhaps boring, title over a cute but obscure one. Everyone in publishing—including booksellers—complain of overload. Even John Baker, Editorial Director of *Publishers Weekly,* once complained that too many books and too many different books were being published. Add into the equation all of the new titles from online publishers and the out-of-print titles being raised from the dead, and you'll begin to understand the necessity of a clear title and strong slant to make your book stand out.

If the shelving location (and therefore, possibly, the market) for your book is not clear from your title, make doubly sure it is self-evident from your subtitle. Otherwise, an overloaded bookseller may misshelve it, and an underpaid clerk in an online bookstore may list it in the wrong category. End result: A customer can't find your book to purchase it.

Consider psychotherapist John Gray's bestseller, *Men Are From Mars, Women Are From Venus.* Science fiction? Astronomy? Religion? Okay, probably everyone gets the implied joke and guesses this is a book about relationships and the struggle between men and women. But Dr. Gray has made sure we do. Check out his subtitle:

"A Practical Guide for Improving Communication and Getting What You Want in Your Relationships." He leaves no room for doubt. The where-to-shelve dilemma is resolved.

Certainty about shelving means a clear, definable market. If you decide that your book fits more than one shelf in a bookstore, then your headings in "About the Competition" should reflect these different markets. Diagnostically, if you come up with more than one subject category for your book, you could be writing for too broad a market. Ask yourself, "Can I narrow my book to one readership?" If you can't, if your book reaches more than one category of readers because it is cross-disciplinary, then you may have a cross-over problem.

Books with multiple readerships are called "cross-over" books, because they ask readers to cross over from their favorite subject areas and peruse unfamiliar shelves and subjects. Some books have no clear, single category, because they include many disciplines of study. They may confuse the retailer, and your book may fall through the cracks. Beyond the where-to-shelve dilemma, you may have too many audiences with no single audience strong enough to carry your book.

Recall from the start of this chapter my question about psychologist Marilyn Barrett's proposed book. She divided her competition section into three categories: nature and ecology, gardening, and self-help. She introduces her section with a lead that explains why she made these choices:

> *Creating Eden: The Garden as a Healing Space* is a book that integrates exciting trends in gardening, holistic environmentalism, and self-help psychology. It uses the actual *and* metaphoric garden to help readers reconnect with the restorative processes of nature, feel more balanced and aware of themselves, and counteract the treadmill effect of urban living.

Dr. Barrett's decisions about where her book would be shelved seem well-thought-out and accurate, but let's look into this further. Do you sense a compatibility between her three categories—

nature/ecology, gardening, and self-help? On the surface, my answer is yes. On closer examination, I'm not sure. Many ardent gardeners haven't expanded their interests or philosophies to nature and the environment. Certainly neither environmentalists nor gardeners are necessarily self-help readers. I believe Dr. Barrett's most dominant market is self-help, but a particularly specialized nature-loving, garden-loving, self-help reader. Fortunately, they number plenty.

If you, too, have defined more than one market in your competition, make sure that the divergent categories are few, perhaps two or three, and that each category has a solid reading market. For instance, I recently purchased *The Long Quiet Highway* by Natalie Goldberg. In fact, I was surprised to find it where I was browsing—autobiographies—because I associate her with a book for writers called *Writing Down the Bones*. In a moderately sized bookstore, you'd find copies in both locations, even though *The Long Quiet Highway* is an autobiography more than it's a book on writing. Booksellers want to capitalize on name recognition and capture her prior readers. Yet, the fact that I found her book in autobiography tells me that the retailer read the jacket and also hoped to pick up readers whose allegiance runs toward autobiography. In any case, she has a solid market for both categories—books on writing and autobiography.

Consider *Mysteries of the Dark Moon*, a book about recognizing and using the difficult, i.e. "dark," experiences of life. Demetra George, self-described mythologist and counselor, lists her comparable or competitive books under two categories: 1) women's psychology and 2) new age, recovery, and personal growth/healing. Separating the catchall of the latter category could produce a total of four possible shelving choices, not two.

With this expanded number of categories, George hoped to demonstrate a wide market and draw the interest of a larger publisher. *Mysteries of the Dark Moon: The Healing Power of the Dark Goddess* was published by Harper San Francisco (a division of HarperCollins). Obviously, the editorial committee saw the potential for the book and must have believed the many markets were compatible, rather than producing a cross-over problem. It's also possible that George had demonstrated a following, name recognition, and loyalty from readers of her two prior books, which had been about astrology. While the combination of book idea, description in "About the Market," and author credentials worked for Demetra George, you should know that multiple markets always mean some risk of being perceived as a cross-over problem.

If your book seems to cross subject lines, go back to the drawing board and ask yourself if you should alter your idea. Perhaps it needs further simplifying and narrowing. Reread chapter two on refining ideas. You may have had a well-defined slant, but perhaps you need to change your slant to produce a single, definable audience. At the very least, visit a well-stocked bookstore and ask the manager to help you determine your primary market and define the categories that you can use in "About the Competition."

Too Few Comparable Books

When Dr. Darold A. Treffert proposed his book on savants (gifted but mentally impaired individuals), he had no comparable books to put in his competition section. He could have risked editorial rejection based on, "It's never been done," except for one fact. Several other sections of his proposal made mention of his own recent appearances on *CBS Evening News*, *60 Minutes*, and other shows. His credentials as a specialist on the savant syndrome inspire awe, and he'd

> Remember that less is more, especially in writing. Rethinking your book at this point might be the best thing you ever did.

already taken steps to put the fascinating subject before the public. His book was published under the title *Extraordinary People*.

If you find few or no other popular books on your subject, it could mean your idea is too obscure for mainstream publishing. If you have academic or professional qualifications, you may need to pitch your book to a university or technical publisher. Or, ask yourself whether you've included too much for one book or only enough for a long magazine article. If you decide that your idea is worthy of pursuit *as is*, then be willing to go to extra lengths to win over a publisher. You may need to postpone marketing until you expand your qualifications. On the other hand, the problem may be remedied by nailing down more statistics that prove your book will have a large market. Expand the section promising your willingness to promote the book.

Another strategy for putting "something" in this section is to mention and describe recent articles in popular magazines, or even novels, to build a case for the public's growing interest. To write "About the Competition," lay historian and travel writer Susan Lloyd had to overcome the paucity of books to compare with her proposed book, *The Last Zapatista*. Beginning with her introductory paragraph, she builds the case for why a book on a Mexican folk hero is worthy of publication.

> Because of his popularity and timeliness of subject, *The Last Zapatista* represents the kind of book, touching on history, myth, politics and travel, which is of interest to the general reading audience. Never has the subject of Mexico, in particular, been of such interest to the U.S. public because of a recently passed trade agreement, rebellion brewing in Mexico's south, and an ever growing Mexican population north of the border. Attesting to its popularity, it is interesting to note the number of books on Mexican or Latin American subjects that have been made into feature-length Hollywood films—including many books in this competition listing. It is also exciting and especially timely that a feature Hollywood film is being made about Zapata, scheduled for release in 1995. (*Note: Proposal was written in 1994.*)

Having positioned her book as timely based on political events in Mexico and from novels and movies, Lloyd goes on to describe her book relative to Latino classics and bestselling Mexico-based novels, including: *One Hundred Years of Solitude* (Marquez), *The House of the Spirits* (Allende), *Like Water for Chocolate* (Esquivel), and *The Mambo Kings Play Songs of Love* (Hijuelos).

> If you find few or no books like yours, stop all work on your proposal until you determine why.

In the subsequent paragraphs of her competition section, she introduces novels where Zapata is mentioned or featured. She cites a planned Hollywood movie for one novel and their settings in others to the *Zapatista* uprising in Chiapas. This information supplies "evidence" to the case about her book's timeliness.

Writers of memoirs often bemoan the difficulty of finding comparable books to their own. It's true, for instance, that you don't have the advantage of entering a subject at amazon.com's site, like writers of parenting, business, or gardening books. What can you do?

First, your memoir's slant should reveal some unifying theme. You may in fact be able to identify a subject that corresponds to your theme, such as shattering the glass ceiling, beating a terminal illness, or reconstructing a successful life as an immigrant. If you can find a subject within your memoir, this may aid and narrow your search for comparable books.

You may also find books for your competition section by looking for authors with gender, age, race, or situations similar to your own. Independent booksellers can be enormously helpful, because they often possess a depth of knowledge about books found less often among clerks at the big chain bookstores.

Last of all, you can compare your style of writing with other well-known memoirs, whether or not the subject matter or author's profile matches your own.

Occasionally, a book is rejected, not because it wouldn't be great, but because it is literally ahead of its time, the first in a new field. Before you decide you might just be the next Rachel Carson (ecology), Paul Erlich (environmental philosophy), Marilyn Ferguson (new age), Stephen Hawking (science), or Paul Senge (business), do some deep soul-searching. Most of the time, writers of "firsts" find no comparable books because their subject is:

- too specialized or obscure
- too limited to produce a large enough readership to warrant book-length treatment
- too broad.

Nevertheless, if you genuinely believe you have something new to share with the world, you should establish credibility by writing and publishing magazine articles on your subject, giving workshops, and by gathering endorsements from recognized authorities in the field—before you seek book publication. Doing so is a great test of your ideas and should make even clearer whether yours is a pearl of great price or a good-looking but less valuable imitation.

If your book is at the cutting edge, your best bet may be to market directly to a small or specialty publisher of books in your field, rather than to seek an agent for sale to a larger publisher. Success with a small publisher could lead to word-of-mouth sales and ultimately to a reprint by a larger publisher.

TOO MANY COMPARABLE BOOKS

I'll never forget the elation of my son when in second grade he "discovered" knock-knock jokes. He couldn't wait to try them out on me and was stunned when I knew the punch lines. "You've heard it before?" he asked, eyes wide with surprise.

> Read deeply enough on your subject to assure yourself, agents, and editors that you have something to add to the field.

When your search in *Books in Print* or with Amazon.com exhumes dozens, or perhaps hundreds, of books apparently like yours, you may experience a shock similar to my son's. Your book may have already been done. Your contribution must be a substantial enough addition to warrant book-length treatment.

Business consultant Lucia Hedrick faced and overcame this problem for her book, *Five Days to an Organized Life*. Literally hundreds have been published on the subject. Can you imagine her task, first convincing her agent, Denise Marcil, and then editors, that the public really does need another book on getting organized? In fact, knowing that any sane agent or editor would think of this immediately, the second sentence in her proposal reads, "There are more than 300 organizers, or personal planning aids, on the market...[with sales] expected to exceed $300 million."

With the flooded field acknowledged up front, she goes on to convince the proposal reader why her book is different *and* better. In "About the Competition," Hedrick escapes the task of itemizing hundreds of these competitors with a first sweeping contrast:

> There are many books available on personal organization, including a few "classics," but they are too long. Like so many self-help books today, they are 90 percent filler and 10 percent substance, the kind that cause my students to throw up their hands and cry, "But I don't have time to read it!" After reading *Five Days*, no one will ask, "Where's the beef?"

Later she practices the organization she preaches by stating:

> In a sea of many titles, organization books fall into four categories, based on target audiences: those written for executives, for homemakers, for women, and the general organization guides.

Having established this distinction, she then introduces representative books for each category, only two or three, as if these few competitors represent the same strengths and failings of all of the rest of the books in that category.

This author cleverly elevates her book above all others in this crowded field by this summary paragraph:

> In short, *Five Days* is a nuts and bolts—knit-one, purl two—kind of book. Its approach is different from previous works in three ways: 1) *brevity:* it makes its points in fewer pages, 2) *philosophy:* I emphasize rewards and having fun, and 3) *mechanics*: I keep it simple…

Her argument in favor of her system convinced me of its worth. Feeling an urgency to read her book, I quickly found that it had sold out in all the bookstores in my city. She transferred her conviction and enthusiasm so effectively that I waited impatiently for the book to come in. I wouldn't even look at a competitor's system. That's a successful "About the Competition!" With over 80,000 books sold, the author successfully transferred the enthusiasm expressed in her proposal into her book.

CHAPTER FIVE

About the Author: Selling Yourself

Chapter Goal: To present yourself and your qualifications in the best possible light.

Concept Statement
About the Book
* About the Author
About the Market
About the Competition
Production Details
About Promotion
Chapter Summaries
Table of Contents
Sample Chapters
The Appendix

Years ago, I hammered out résumés for people as part of a business. I suggested that my clients write down their job histories and make notes about other accomplishments such as awards, memberships, and volunteer activity. Most of the time, independent of education or job status, my clients arrived at my office with a meager and incomplete record. Some brought old résumés, but most people "forgot" relevant accomplishments. Don't make that mistake in your proposal. Trumpet your accomplishments, your experience, and your virtues. Sell yourself to help sell your book idea.

Definition and Purpose

In "About the Author" you must detail your qualifications to write the book you propose. While this section may seem like a résumé, it varies in format and style. Its purpose is to impress agents and editors and make a publisher trust you with a five-figure capital investment in your idea.

Vocation, personal experience, research, or hobby/recreation encompass the most common ways to show your qualifications. Less common ways include: celebrity status—Nancy Reagan's astrologer or the late Princess Di's bodyguard—or access as a coauthor or writer-for-hire to a celebrity or expert. Nowadays, larger publishers give considerable weight to an author's connections— how many people you know in your field or in the media who can aid in your book's promotion. As literary agents Mary Alice Kier and Anna Cottle put it, "More and more New York houses actually look for a national franchise on the aspect of [author] credentials." Or, as another agent expressed it, "I'm sick and tired of editors only wanting to hear about a book if the author has a national platform."

Because "About the Author" requires no research, you should craft a rough draft after you've written "About the Competition." If you write this author section early, it will give you an objective reflection of your authority to write the book, which is as essential as the merits of your idea itself. A rough draft of this section should make you feel certain you possess the qualifications to write the book or signal you to suspend work on your proposal until you've developed the necessary qualifications. If you remain in a quandary, see the later section of this chapter called "Troubleshooting."

Last of all, this section of the proposal should give an agent/ editor a sense of who you are as a person, not just as an authority. Without going into excessive personal detail, you might state where you live, where you were born, and whether you are married with kids.

Style of Writing

Because this is an easier section of the proposal, its guidelines are simple. Write in first- or third-person, though most writers use third-person. Speaking about yourself from this narrator's position lets you tout your qualifications without sounding like an egomaniac. First-person, however, may be perfect for a book of a highly personal nature. The advantage is that you can express your qualifications in a personal way.

This section resembles a résumé, but your qualifications should be expressed in complete sentences and paragraphs, not in lists or fragments. If the number of credentials calls for it, include a résumé in your proposal appendix.

Present your author qualifications with active, exciting verbs, rather than dull to-be verbs. Aspire to use only one to-be verb per hundred words. Emphasize specifics over generalities, i.e., "past president of the New Jersey Business Association" rather than "active in trade groups." Finally, present your credentials in descending order of importance.

Before reading what you should include in "About the Author," study the example in Sidebar 5-1. This author section was written by journalist and walking expert, Carolyn Scott Kortge, author of *The Spirited Walker: Fitness Walking for Clarity, Balance, and Spiritual Connection* (HarperCollins).

The Six Parts of "About the Author"

While this section may seem like a standard curricula vitae, it offers a different way of presenting yourself to the world. Here's a list of information you should address:

- Subject credentials
- Career credentials
- Educational background
- Credits (awards, publications, and memberships)
- Promotional skills
- Personal data

Sidebar 5-1
Sample: About the Author

Carolyn Scott Kortge

The American Association of Sunday and Feature Editors called Carolyn Scott Kortge one of "The Best" when they announced winners of a 1990 journalism competition. The endorsement echoes the opinions of newspaper readers, editors, and journalism judges. A skilled reporter, interviewer, and feature writer, Kortge has won national respect and attention for writing excellence throughout a twenty-year journalism career.

The American Academy of Family Physicians acknowledged her contributions to medical education with its top media award. The International Delta Society praised her for coverage of human-animal bonds. The International Reading Association cited her for contributions to illiteracy awareness. Twice she was selected by Women in Communications, Inc., to receive the organization's highest newspaper award. She was runner-up for the Catherine L. O'Brien Journalism award and the Penney-Missouri Journalism Award. The Biomedical Synergistics Institute, Inc. honored her coverage of innovative health care.

Kortge's journalism career began at the *Oshkosh* (Wis.) *Daily Northwestern* and carried her to *The Wichita Eagle-Beacon* in Kansas where she produced an award-winning series of articles on the impact of the women's movement on nuns in religious orders. In 1979, she returned to Oregon as features editor at *The Register-Guard* in Eugene. She remained at the newspaper until 1992. Now a freelance writer, Kortge continues to produce a newspaper column for *The Register-Guard* and was recently published in the "My Turn" column of *Newsweek* (October 23, 1995). She has also written for *Modern Maturity*, *GEO*, and *Special Reports*. A biographical profile of legendary Oregon runner Steve Prefontaine that she created for Oregon Production Group inspired a 1995 television documentary and brought the athlete, who died tragically at age twenty-three, to the attention of Hollywood film makers.

In 1989, Kortge expanded her achievements into the area of athletics as a competitive race walker. After an intimate, first-person article about her training appeared in the local newspaper, readers turned

(Continued)

out to support her first 10K competition, an international meet for athletes thirty-five and over. For two years after the event, she taught walking classes at a community recreation center and introduced hundreds of walkers to the exhilaration of vigorous, fitness walking. As a competition walker, she added medals for track and field achievements to her journalistic awards. She holds bronze and silver medals from the National Masters Championships of the USA Track & Field Association and has been ranked in the top five women walkers nationally in her age group. Two years ago, she stepped back from the rigors of athletic training and competition and settled into a fitness walking program that has evolved into an aerobic, walking meditation.

Journalism nourished Kortge's spiritual appetite with opportunities to interview authors and teachers from diverse faiths and backgrounds. Travel broadened her range. In mountain monasteries of Nepal, she sat beside Tibetan Buddhist monks and learned to chant "Om Mani Padme Hum." In gilded Catholic cathedrals of Ecuador, she discovered a tradition of gratitude. At a Mayan Indian ceremony in Guatemala, she bathed in fragrant clouds of incense in a ritual of protection and prayer. At England's majestic Canterbury Cathedral, she stood at the tomb of martyred Thomas à Beckett and lit candles for peace. Some of her journeys have been internal. She's traveled the crags inside herself. She knows the bumps and bliss of a long, committed marriage and has written of personal explorations in columns that touch the common core of human connection.

Kortge's impassioned approach to life and her accomplishments as an adventurer, interviewer, writer, editor, and traveler have made her a popular speaker. She has been a featured presenter at the annual "Women on the Move" conference in Eugene and at "Women Emerging," a seminar presented by the Eugene-Springfield Chapter of National Association of Accountants. She has spoken to the Oregon Association of Hospital Auxiliaries, the Southern Willamette Private Industry Council, and Oregon Homebuilders Association. She has been a frequent guest lecturer in journalism at the University of Oregon and at Lane Community College and a featured presenter at the University's High School Press Conference.

A two-term past president of the Professional Women's Network of Oregon, she remains active in the organization. She is also a member of Oregon Track Club Masters and USA Track & Field. A

(Continued)

past board member of Oregon Track Club Masters, she has served as an organizer of the Hayward Classic Masters Track & Field Championships and volunteers as public-address announcer for the annual two-day meet. As a certified track-and-field official, she assists at area track meets including Special Olympics and the Prefontaine Classic at the University of Oregon's Hayward Field.

Kortge lives in Eugene, Oregon, with her husband Dean. She considers their thirty-two-year marriage her most amazing accomplishment and credits at least part of it to a shared interest in travel, exploration, and long walks. They have walked the 100-mile Cotswold Trail in England and traveled 120 miles on trails in the rugged English Lake District. In Costa Rica, they climbed volcanoes and slogged through rain forests. In Ecuador, they hiked the high heaths of Andean peaks. At home, they roam the Cascade range. Next on the list of dream treks: the Incan trail to Machu Pichu and the Santiago de Compostela trail in northern Spain.

SUBJECT CREDENTIALS

By the time agents or editors read your author section, they will presumably have already read other sections of your proposal. Some agents and editors, however, will flip from "The Concept Statement" to "About the Author." They want to quickly evaluate the author's qualifications before reading further. For this reason, you must continue to sell yourself in this section.

Although subject qualifications and career credentials often overlap, some writers seek to publish books unrelated to their careers. Then, subject credentials must come from other sources, such as research, hobbies, co-writing with an expert, or personal experience.

Susan Lloyd's book, *No Pictures in My Grave: A Spiritual Journey in Sicily*, was based on personal experience. She had received artist's fellowships and other funding related to her book's theme and setting, and she had produced and directed an award-winning documentary related to the book's theme. Even so, she opened her "About the Author" in a highly personal way that matched her book's introspective tone.

My experience growing up in Oregon in an Italian-American Catholic family provided the initial nucleus of remembered experience for *No Pictures in My Grave*.

The lead paragraph provides details about the author's grandmother and how she taught the author to pray to the Madonna. A second, long paragraph develops the author's personal relationship to her education and her discovery of the Black Madonna, a key metaphor in her book.

Another writer made a lifelong study of his passion, economics, but his advanced degree and life work had led him into business administration. He pursued two strategies to overcome the deficiency in his qualifications to write a book on economics. First, he collected "Advance Scholarly Review and Endorsements" on his book from recognized professors, authors, and scholars in the field of economics. After his persuasive presentation got him an agent, his agent placed these reviews and endorsements directly after "The Concept Statement," *before anything else* in the proposal. Not only did these endorsements supply missing credentials, he had also captured several awards for papers in economics "way back when" in his undergraduate work. While he was not, on the surface, qualified to make a scholarly contribution to the study of economics, his subject credentials supplied everything he needed to gain an agent and then a publisher.

CAREER CREDENTIALS

Your work may offer the inspiration for your book idea. If so, put your professional qualifications first in the lead paragraph of the author section (Sidebar 5-1). Carolyn Kortge's qualifications

> List and develop your career credentials in descending importance—from most important to least.

to write on this subject depend on her journalism skills and on her experiences with walking and meditation. Indeed, a feature she wrote on race-walking supplied the initial inspiration for all of her walking experiences thereafter.

Dr. Lipman gains his authority to write a book on how to stop snoring not just because he is a medical doctor, but because he specialized in otolaryngology. (I had to look that up; it means he's an ear, nose, and throat doctor.) Dr. Lipman's second sentence in his "About the Author" states: "He has studied at leading sleep disorder centers in Europe and the United States." Thus, he has put his most relevant career credentials first.

Another doctor, a naturopathic physician proposing her book, *Body Salts: The Way to Health, Naturally*, opens her author section with this short and sweet statement: "Dr. Skye Weintraub is a graduate of the National College of Naturopathic Medicine in Portland, Oregon. She specialized in homeopathy and botanical medicine." Her status as a naturopathic physician gives her the qualifications to write any book on natural health, but her specialty in homeopathy and botanical medicine supports why she could write a book on the limited, if not esoteric, subject of body salts.

Writing instructor Val Dumond, author of *Grammar for Grownups*, offers a unique variation in how to open with subject/career qualifications:

> Val Dumond has taught courses in business writing and grammar over the past ten years to government clerks and managers, college students, business executives, secretaries, lawyers, nurses, sales representatives, loggers, utility workers, shipbuilders, law officers, and data processing staffs. (A list of clients is found on the following page.) After a day-long intensive session of Grammar For Grownups, their evaluations of her techniques include comments like *fun, time went fast, forgot I knew that much, enjoyable, useful, wow! I already knew that stuff.* [her italics]

This opening to "About the Author" does a lot of work for her. How clever to list the walks of life of her clients after she presented her career credentials—ten years teaching. This delivers the message: My experience is vast, the book's contents are based on different people's needs, and my market has a potentially large audience. Last in the paragraph, she closes with client endorsements of the most powerful kind—students who have been exposed to her method. Sales!

She continues detailing career credentials by mentioning prior publications of grammar books. You'd think she would have opened with this publishing credit. Because *Grammar for Grownups* is aimed at a general readership, and her other books were published by Prentice-Hall, she might have chosen to avoid planting the idea of an academic audience in her agent or editor's mind.

EDUCATIONAL BACKGROUND

Generally speaking, any degree from the masters level up carries weight, independent of the subject of your book, but agents are wary of book ideas written by academicians. You

> Decide whether your level of education helps or hinders your success, and feature it accordingly.

may be qualified, but you'll have to demonstrate an ability to translate your knowledge into the style of writing enjoyed by your particular audience. In some cases, I instruct erudite clients to bury the mention of their doctoral theses, or sometimes their doctoral degrees, *until* they've interested the reader in their subjects.

In each of the proposals I have written, I only mention my master's degree in counseling in the final paragraphs of "About the Author." Neither Val Dumond (*Grammar for Grownups*) nor Lucy Hedrick (*Five Days to an Organized Life*) lists her educational background at all. Their degrees may be irrelevant, possibly because they are in areas different from their book's subjects, or unimportant against the weight of their other credentials.

Susan Lloyd made a similar choice by listing her Bachelor of Science degree in Art Education and Master of Fine Arts degree in Photography/English in the last paragraph of her author section for her inner-journey memoir, *No Pictures in My Grave*.

If your educational degrees or nonacademic training seem relevant to your project, make sure they appear early in the author section. Also indicate the specific college or university where you earned them. If your education is not particularly relevant, you have no pressing need to mention it. However, if you have graduated from a prestigious institution, mention your degree and the institution, whether or not it is directly relevant. In other words, you're allowed the sin of omission, or the sin of inclu-

> Never mislead anyone about your qualifications. Highlight or underplay, yes; embellish, no!

sion, in presenting your credentials. Just know that when you leave information out, you may be subject to wild speculation, which may or may not be to your advantage.

In addition, never include a comprehensive accounting for every school you attended or every job you've held. List only items that relate to your proposed book.

CREDITS (AWARDS, PUBLICATIONS, AND MEMBERSHIPS)

Awards indicate that you rose above others to receive recognition. Publications show your success as a writer. And, memberships suggest current interest and involvement. All three count.

Awards

Awards might include grants and fellowships to pursue work, such as Susan Caperna Lloyd's Oregon Arts Commission Individual Artist Fellowship Award, her Flying Springbook Writing Competition Award, and her Helen Wurlitzer Foundation Writers in Residence Grant, all included in her author section, and, as you can see, specifically mentioned. In a similar fashion, Carolyn Kortge's author section (Sidebar 5-1) proudly and appropriately lists her awards in specific detail.

Perhaps you've received some award in your work; by all means include it. The same holds true for any placement award in writing contests. Whether or not you have published your writing, a contest placement demonstrates recognition of your ability.

Publications

It seems self-evident that you would include your publishing credits; after all, you're pitching a book! However, you wouldn't necessarily want to include mention of *all* of your credits. For instance, none of my proposals mention my published articles in *The Ascendant*, a magazine for astrologers.

Be specific about your credits. Author Mary Jeanne Menna didn't just say that her parenting article was published. In her author section, she wrote:

> Menna was especially proud to have received the Silver GAMMA Award in the Best Feature Writing and Reporting category at the Magazine Association of Georgia conference last year for an article she wrote: "New Opportunities for Children with Disabilities," *Atlanta Parent,* October 1997.

Whether or not a book publication bears directly on your present subject, cite it by title, publisher, and date. General descriptions make a *generally* good impression. Specifics make a powerful impression. Take grammarian Val Dumond's author section, for example. She informs the reader that her *Elements of Nonsexist Usage* was released

> Omit mention of any award, publication, or membership that would diminish you or your proposed work.

by Prentice-Hall with a first printing of 30,000 copies. Because the topic is relevant to her proposed *Grammar for Grownups*, she spends a full paragraph describing its contents. She continues with specific mention of an earlier self-published project, also on nonsexist language, and describes by title her three books about history. Last of all, regarding her publication history, Dumond tells of publishing a newsletter for the past three years called *Words and Music* (being specific again) and describes its language/grammar-related contents.

If you have a substantial publishing history in newspapers and magazines, plan to add a list of your credits in the proposal appendix, but only if you feel that doing so is important to convincing editors of your qualifications to write your book. On the other hand, the details you include in "About the Author" might make the addition of such a list unnecessary.

Your credits may range from published articles or essays in high-circulation magazines to projects that you have self-published for your own enjoyment and distribution. You increase your authority to the degree that your writings reflect the subject of your proposed book and were published by nationally circulated magazines.

Memberships

Use the same criteria for your memberships or affiliations: If they are relevant to your proposed book, include them.

For instance, coauthors Emily Kay and Anita Seville sought publication of a biography titled, *We'll Remember in November: Molly Yard's Gift to Women's Rights*. Since the woman they featured was a past president for the National Organization for Women (NOW), it would be a strange omission were they not to mention and enlarge upon their own activities as NOW members. Consider the first of two paragraphs:

> Both Ms. Saville and Ms. Kay are longtime activists in the women's movement. Inspired by Molly Yard's call to arms, they founded a local chapter of the National Organization for Women in 1989. Through their work with NOW, they have played key roles in organizing a number of successful projects—including a fund-raiser for survivors of battering and rape, which has raised more than $100,000, and a legal advocacy network for women in Massachusetts.

Memberships listed in "About the Author" can alert an agent/editor to your connections. They contribute to the all-important picture of your ability to promote your book.

PROMOTIONAL SKILLS

In chapter twelve, I'll show you how to develop a complete promotional plan. In the author section, however, you have a chance to present *past* experiences that display your promotional skills. If you don't believe you have these past experiences, don't panic; not everyone includes something related to promotion in "About the Author." Before you quickly dismiss this "hole" in your background, consider past teaching, seminars you have led, television or radio interviews, speaking clubs, all of which demonstrate promotion skills. Business consultant Lucy Hedrick devotes two paragraphs to her past experiences, as follows:

> I am a sought-after speaker for agencies, professional associations, and business organizations, including the United Way, the PTA Council, the Junior League, the National Organization for Women, the Entrepreneurial Women's Network, the National YWCA ENCORE program, the Women's Council of Realtors, and many others.
>
> As an expert on personal organization, I appear regularly on cable television, am interviewed extensively, and am quoted in the national press.

Notice the confidence with which this author projects her promotional skills. Is she successfully selling herself? I believe so, and her specific list in the first paragraph substantiates her claim of being "a sought-after speaker" as a matter of fact, not of egotism.

Likewise, mythologist Demetra George, author of two prior books, shows no hesitation in presenting her promotional skills in her "About the Author," as follows:

> Ms. George is a captivating and dynamic speaker and has presented workshops in Boston, New York, Minneapolis, San Francisco, Phoenix, Seattle, Portland, and all across Canada.

This list of major cities spanning the continent certainly telegraphs her capability of promoting a book nationally and internationally. These authors offer great models for the unhesitating way you should present your qualifications.

SEQUELS OR FUTURE BOOKS

Some books lend themselves to sequels, or you may have another related book idea that you are working on. By all means, add a sentence or two describing the work, perhaps offering a working title. After Lucy H. Hedrick sold *Five Days to an Organized Life*, she sold in rapid succession, *365 Ways to Save Time, 365 Ways to Save Time With Kids,* and *365 Ways to Save Money,* seizing upon the success of her first work and the wave of number-slant and list books, popular in the early nineties.

Agents and publishers are looking for experts who want to write more than one book. Because only about 25 percent of all books earn out the advance paid the author, it makes good business sense to recoup publisher investment through an author's subsequent books. Typically, first advances are lower than subsequent ones (perhaps because of the poor track record of most first books), so agents, too, stand to profit by long-term relationships with authors over the span of many books. Knowing this, Mary Jeanne Menna adds the following paragraph in her author section:

> Also, immediately following the completion of this book, the author will begin work on a series of related tips books to be written in rapid succession...*[and then she offers working titles of two more books].*

PERSONAL DATA

One purpose of the author section is to convey to the editor a sense of who you are as a person. Some writers elect to omit any personal data. Still, just a sentence or two can add warmth and provide both a personal dimension and a satisfying conclusion to this section. Consider Demetra George's final paragraph, which wraps personal data together with her book's concept:

Demetra George lives on the Oregon coast with her two teenage children whom she co-parents with their father. Her daily contact with the Pacific Ocean attunes her to the rhythms of the tides, which are regulated by the phases of the moon. She was born during the dark phase of the moon.

A small bit of personal data transforms you from a mass of qualifications and credentials into a person an agent or editor might even like to meet some day.

Troubleshooting

Fortunately, "About the Author" is one section in the proposal where very little can go wrong. If you've made an effort to include all six parts, to give specific detail, and to write a lively narrative with lots of active verbs, then you've met the most important criteria. Only four difficulties give some writers a problem:

- Inadequate qualifications
- An excess of qualifications
- Qualifications of more than one author
- The special case of memoir/autobiography

MINIMAL QUALIFICATIONS

If you decide that you are inadequately qualified to write your book, you must consider the appropriateness of undertaking it. Perhaps you should find an expert in your chosen subject and team up as a coauthor. Perhaps you should choose another idea that better matches your existing qualifications.

Consider what a senior editor at a large New York house had to say about minimal qualifications:

Minimal credentials can be difficult, because book reviewers, booksellers, and everyone else will want to know why the publisher has chosen this book to publish and why this author is qualified (other than enthusiasm) to write a book. An exciting book idea does not necessarily translate into an exciting, or even a good, book.

I remember the sinking feeling I got when one of my students approached me with a well-written continuation of the thinking of philosopher and mystic, Teilhard de Chardin. Now, that's a big undertaking. My student had spent decades in deep contemplation straightening out the bugs. She worked as some kind of computer technician with no educational credentials beyond the bachelor's level. To convince any editor that she had the authority to write such a book, she would have had to show subject qualifications, such as the publication of articles, or membership in organizations of philosophical inquiry, or serving as a famous philosopher's apprentice.

Lacking any career or subject credentials, this woman wanted an editor to consider her manuscript—her life's passion—on its own merit. I wish it could be so. I have heard this plea often from writers long on passion and short on credentials. Unfortunately, it's like asking Stanford to admit you because you're smart, even though you're missing a high-school diploma. The last time I inquired, my student had amassed a stack of rejections but had not yet decided to fortify her qualifications to write about Teilhard de Chardin.

If you are committed to writing in your chosen subject area, then plan to take all the time necessary to develop missing qualifications. This may involve returning to school, writing and publishing articles, and teaching workshops or classes. It may involve travel, so that you can increase your name recognition beyond your immediate locale. However you have built your qualifications, save all evidence of doing so—clips of published articles, flyers about seminars, class descriptions about teaching posts, or anything else that is visual. These items should become part of the appendix of your proposal.

Sometimes an author is not so much lacking in qualifications as in the willingness or skill to fully present them. Other writers may feel more comfortable promoting themselves. Consider how you feel about this; then, show more or less detail, more or fewer of your selling points, to present yourself in the best light.

AN EXCESS OF QUALIFICATIONS

If you've been President of the United States, what do you think you'd put on your next job application? While presidents probably don't have job applications, you can be sure they don't fill in the details of everything they've done. All they need to do is list, "Former President of the United States."

When you have stacks of qualifications for a book you are writing, eliminate lesser positions and experience related to the subject. Inexperienced writers give themselves away by mentioning every publication and award dating back to Boy Scouts or Girl Scouts and eighth-grade penmanship. Just provide your strongest, most recent, and most impressive qualifications.

A retired physicist once consulted me about a book he wanted to write on prostate cancer. He erroneously believed he was supposed to include a list of every article in every journal in his decades-long career as a scientist. Not one of these articles covered prostate cancer. I suggested that he exclude the itemization of credits, instead summarizing them with a statement like: "John Doe has written and published over 100 articles in scientific and technical journals."

Another way to handle long lists of accomplishments is to give the specifics of one to three of the most impressive ones and then summarize the rest. If an agent/editor sees a long paragraph block with long listings of credits, he or she may go from impressed to fogging out. Direct attention to what's important and immediately relevant to your book.

QUALIFICATIONS OF MORE THAN ONE AUTHOR

When five mothers of twins decided to publish a book on raising twins, they agreed to be equal coauthors of the book. They held business meetings and writing meetings. They worked out a collaborative contract that specified how they would distribute the labor of writing and promoting the book, and how they would divide the monies from the book's sale. In their author section, each coauthor used three to five paragraphs to describe her qualifications. Each one highlighted subject, work, education, credits, and promotional accomplishments. Taken together, Albi, Deurloo, Johnson, Catlin, and Greatwood have the authority to write *anything* related to child development, rearing, or parenting. In a sense, because they are five coauthors, their author section could have raised the problem of over-featuring their qualifications. I bet they were aware of this, because four of the five coauthors pared their biographies down to three tight paragraphs. Still, presenting themselves took up three single-spaced pages.

You must provide agents and editors with biographical details of anyone whom you consider as a more or less equal participant in your book's creation. This might include experts and their coauthors or artists and illustrators.

Coauthors Carolyn Cotter and George Green had no collaborative agreement for their publishing partnership until they were accepted by literary agent Denise Marcil, who requires one for all her coauthoring clients. Because George Green is the expert—a psychophysiologist—and conceived the five-step model their book features, his author biography was presented first. In fact, three of the four paragraphs detail his qualifications for the book.

Cotter, who did all of the writing, penned one short paragraph about her qualifications as follows:

> Carolyn Cotter (M.B.A., with a B.A. degree in Social Psychology) is a former business manager. She also is editor for books by her husband, Richard (Prentice Hall: *The Business Policy Game, Modern Business Decisions, Commercial Banking*).

Cotter had no publishing credits of her own prior to writing the book for George Green. Yet, this short paragraph summarized her strongest credentials while reserving primary billing for her coauthor.

If your book has substantial art work or photography, you should ask the artist for biographical information. This data should follow your author qualifications. It doesn't matter whether you have hired the artist or agreed to share the advance and royalties. In some books, illustrations or photography become as invaluable to the "statement" of the work's identity as the idea and actual writing. The professional accomplishments of your artist are not only important but may compensate for perceived weaknesses in your own qualifications.

THE SPECIAL CASE OF MEMOIR/AUTOBIOGRAPHY

Writers of memoir and autobiography would appear to have the easiest time writing "About the Author." In answer to the question, "Why are you qualified to write this book?", the answer is, of course, "It's about me!" The author is the subject.

For purposes of clarity, Philip Gerard, author of *Creative Nonfiction: Researching and Crafting Stories of Real Life,* defines autobiography and memoir as follows:

> Autobiography…refers to a long account of one's own life, encompassing a fairly complete lifetime, or focused within formative years or some other limiting time frame…. A memoir…strikes the same emotional note as autobiography—written memory—but is usually focused on some triggering person or event in the narrator's experience,…memoir is always a memoir *of* something outside the narrator's interior life.

Memoir writers, hoping to sell a book, face special demands. The portion of their lives developed in the memoir must be "bigger than life." It must transcend the realm of private experience and strike a universal chord based upon its theme.

The author section for memoir or autobiography must convey the richness of your life experiences and convince the agent/editor of its relevance to a large readership. It must also accomplish one more task that is echoed in nearly every other section of the proposal: *Your writing—its style, voice, and expression—must be professional and compelling.*

It's not enough to have a story to tell or a message of urgency. You must demonstrate that you have the writing skill to professionally tell your life story. For this reason, published writers of memoir or autobiography have paid their dues by taking writing courses and by reading books on how to write memoir, creative nonfiction, and autobiography (See Resource Directory for recommended reading). They should have written short personal essays and sought publication of these to further demonstrate their writing skill and interest by editors in their life experiences.

If you're sure you want to seek publication of your life experiences, then dedicate yourself to strengthening your writing and publishing credits before you seek an agent or editor.

Consider this lead paragraph in an author section of an autobiography proposal written by Doris Colmes for her book, *The Iron Butterfly*.

> My life has been a series of adventures, some planned, some inadvertently foisted upon me by fate. In the process, I have embraced such a variety of lifestyles that I am able to comment authentically on a great many vagaries of the twentieth century. I have lived on two continents, as refugee, as housewife/mother, as hippie, as student, as criminal, as bona-fide member of an other generation than the one into which I was born.
>
> I received my Master's Degree (summa cum laude) at age sixty-eight while working full time as administrator of a residential facility for teenage boys....

From this point on in her author section, Colmes describes a wide diversity of careers that reinforce the impression that this writer has lived a fascinating life and possesses no small amount of wisdom that readers can look forward to receiving. Near the end of the two pages of author qualifications, Colmes adds a paragraph that reiterates what unique benefit her readers can expect to get from her book:

> As detailed in the enclosed "About the Book" section, not only did I experience at first hand most of the pivotal experiences that shaped this century, this very culture, but, in the process, found my true identity as a woman and as a spiritual being. My escapades were at times dangerous,

more often hilarious, and always instructive. This almost century-long journey towards spiritual salvation, fulfillment and—most of all—forgiveness makes my story universal for all of us at this time of millennium.

After you write your "About the Author," ask a few trusted friends to read it and make suggestions. Include some readers who know you well and who understand that the purpose of this section is to sing your praises. Or, ask a writer or editor familiar with nonfiction book proposals. If my experience writing résumés for others is any measure, you're more likely to be too modest than to overstate your abilities.

After you've thoroughly defined your qualifications, you're ready to move on to define your audience.

CHAPTER SIX

The Concept Statement: Tell Me Why I Should Buy Your Book

Chapter Goal: To explain the purpose, advantage, and goals of a concept statement, and to show how to "hook" an agent and publisher.

* Concept Statement
About the Book
About the Author
About the Market
About the Competition.
Production Details
About Promotion
Table of Contents
Chapter Summaries
Sample Chapters
The Appendix

It's a busy day at Borders Bookstore. The manager of the Springfield, U.S.A., branch sees a sales representative enter the store. Like other publishing-firm reps who visit large and small bookstores throughout the country, he has one goal: to sell the books carried by his publishing house, matching titles with each retailer's special needs.

The larger the house, the more titles from which the rep must choose; he cannot present every title to the bookseller.

Although booksellers rely upon reps—either in person or over the phone—to help select books appropriate for their stores, they can't carry everything. Space is limited. A sales pitch must be quick; the product must match the store's identity.

Imagine that today the sales rep has your title among the fifty he wants to sell. In the five to ten, or perhaps fifteen, seconds he has to describe and sell the book you sweated over for two years, what will he say?

What would you say? Let's be generous. You have 250 words or less, preferably 50–100 words, to describe your book and get your agent, editor, review committee, sales rep, clerk, and purchaser to salivate with anticipation. Those 50–250 words are called the "Concept Statement."

Definition and Purpose

A concept statement is a first, short summary of your book, written in a marketing style that I describe in the section on generating excitement. After the title page, the "Concept Statement" provides the first words—and therefore, the first impression—to an agent/editor. It must generate enough excitement to stimulate agents and editors to read the rest of your proposal. It must clearly and convincingly describe your book's subject and why it's different or better (or both) than other books on the market. A concept statement may also serve as written copy for the publisher's catalog, as a description offered to an online bookstore, or as a script for a sales rep's rap.

Not every proposal has a concept statement set apart from the section describing the book. However, those writers who go to the trouble to create one will be rewarded, because these first words can accomplish so much. Write it well enough and it becomes the fuse that ignites editorial enthusiasm for the rest of your proposal.

Take a second look at your selling handle. It will serve as a jumping-off point for drafting a concept statement. After editorial acceptance, the "Concept Statement" may be used for pre-publication catalogs and copy for reviews. Who knows your book better, you, or some overworked editorial assistant who may or may not take the time to thoroughly read your proposal or book?

The Six Goals of an Ideal Concept Statement

Before you can write an effective concept statement for your book, you need an even more specific understanding of what it intends to accomplish. An ideal concept statement will reflect all parts of the proposal that an agent or editor is about to read. It's like a movie theater's trailer of coming attractions. It must accomplish the following:

- Generate excitement
- Clearly describe the subject and scope of the book
- Convey uniqueness and timeliness
- Make clear your book's greatest benefit and features that deliver this benefit
- Mention the book's audience
- Reveal author credentials

As you'll see through the examples in this chapter, not all parts of these will be present in every concept statement. This is a more recently delineated part of proposal writing, and many writers and authors have yet to discover its advantages and use it.

GENERATE EXCITEMENT

What, in the writing of my concept statement (Sidebar 6-1), generates excitement? Granted, excitement is a subjective experience. If an editor has been searching, for instance, for a book on proposals, or knows that a niche for one exists, the subject matter alone may be sufficient to create excitement. If an editor has been looking for the particular kind of book you happen to offer, average writing in a proposal may suffice to yield a contract offer.

Sidebar 6-1
Sample: the Concept Statement
Elizabeth Lyon

Because my concept statement for this book includes all of the six goals, I've used it as the sample and provided analysis of it.

Concept Statement	Analysis
Too many qualified writers are rejected out of hand, simply because they lack insiders' knowledge of how to write book proposals. *Nonfiction Book Proposals Anybody Can Write* answers the plight of these writers by leading them in the construction of a report-style proposal. By integrating successful proposals into the text, this how-to guide shows, in detail, exactly how to write each section. As the most instructional book on the subject, it features simplicity, step-by-step directions, and offers a template for standardization of the proposal format.	Problem/audience Slant: promise Subject of book generates excitement. Why now? Subject of book Features Excitement through features/scope
Written by freelance editor and instructor Elizabeth Lyon, *Nonfiction Book Proposals Anybody Can Write: How to Get a Contract and an Advance Before Writing Your Book* makes liberal use of examples, exercises, and checklists to guide the inexperienced proposal writer from inspiration through finished saleable proposal.	Author's qualifications Full book title repeated Features Audience Excitement through benefit

However, in most proposals, you must back up an exciting subject with writing that enhances your book idea. When drafting your concept statement, generate excitement by using:

- Active exciting verbs;
- An upbeat tone;
- Teasing or tantalizing offers;
- Statements of promise; and
- Emotionally powerful descriptions.

CLEARLY DESCRIBE THE SUBJECT AND SCOPE OF THE BOOK

Your book's title and subtitle should help describe the subject of your book. They certainly create the first impression about the subject and scope. In most cases, descriptive, accurate titles and subtitles that match the content and uniqueness of your book are better than dramatic titles. Remember the example of the proposal submitted to me for editing that bore the title *Don't...Even...Try!* Try what? You'd have to consult a psychic to know what the authors had in mind. By the time the book hit the stands, it bore the title *Stop Being Manipulated: How to Neutralize the Bullies, Bosses, and Brutes in Your Life*. Title and subtitle now revealed the book's intended content.

Select descriptions of your book that deliver a clear picture of its scope. Some books involve diverse, interwoven subjects that appeal to more than one audience. Others feature particularly complex ideas. Still others break new ground. Teacher, psychologist, and hypnotist Dr. Michael Rousell faced all three of these challenges for his innovative book, *Breaking the Spell: Spontaneous Events That Shape a Child's Life*. Springing from his doctoral thesis, his concept statement nevertheless needed to simplify complex and original research while still conveying his book's depth and breadth. Here's how Dr. Rousell handled this sticky wicket in the first paragraph of his concept statement:

> Clinical hypnotists generally agree that hypnosis may take place at any time or place, without a formal induction, if conditions are conducive to its presence. My research reveals that the elementary classroom is teeming with hyp-

notic conditions. *Breaking the Spell: Spontaneous Events That Shape a Child's Life* describes how the common elementary classroom abounds with hypnotic conditions that inadvertently affect students. This book reveals how the teacher-student relationship, student characteristics, and classroom conditions virtually parallel what professionals currently know about hypnosis and spontaneous trance states.

In contrast, other book ideas may be deceptively simple. This presents the author with the job of showing unseen depth, breadth, or importance enough to warrant a book-length treatment.

Author David Congalton offers a good example of such a concept statement from his book proposal for *Three Cats, Two Dogs, One Journey Through Multiple Pet Loss*.

> Returning home from a holiday party on December 14, 1997, a California couple turns the corner on their street and, tragically, a new corner in their lives. Their house is on fire, engulfed in smoke and flames. Inside, their five beloved pets—three cats, two dogs—lay dead of carbon monoxide poisoning.
>
> *Three Cats, Two Dogs, One Journey Through Multiple Pet Loss* is the unflinching story of confronting, and surviving, every pet lover's worst nightmare—sudden, multiple pet loss. Radio talk show host and columnist David Congalton mixes personal anecdotes with his previously published essays on pets to take readers beyond the traditional clinical and spiritual books on pet loss. This straight-from-the-heart account profiles the harsh lessons in Grief 101 learned by both Congalton and his wife during that critical first year after the fire. Their struggles, and eventual triumph, resonate with anyone who has ever loved and lost—or will lose—a companion animal.

CONVEYS UNIQUENESS AND TIMELINESS

An important aspect of the "Concept Statement" is to assert the way in which your book is unique. That's why it's best to develop a slant and to review the competition before setting out to write a proposal. Ask yourself how your reader will benefit, in a unique way, by purchasing yet another book on gardening, business, love relations, or history. Biochemist Linda Jean Shepherd made clear what's unique about her book in both her title and in her concept statement:

> *Lifting the Veil: The Feminine Face of Science* is a journey of discovery of the soul of science. Using stories from practicing scientists, this book explores how the long neglected feminine viewpoint can enliven science. It creates a bridge between the masculine and feminine, and invites science to welcome the contributions of the feminine principle into this masculine realm.

At this point, you may see from these examples how some phrases accomplish more than one of the six goals. A book's subject may be what makes it unique and generates excitement. Features can create excitement; so may author credentials. A description such as Linda Jean Shepherd's of enlivening science by creating "a bridge between the masculine and feminine" can function as a reader benefit

> Multiple revisions can "boil down" your concept statement and increase its potency.

(inform, offer understanding) and as a reflection of being the right book for the times.

Be patient. Expect to polish your concept statement from the time you write the first draft until you send it to an agent or editor. I revised mine throughout the creation of my proposal and, once again, on the same day I mailed out my proposal.

MAKE CLEAR YOUR BOOK'S GREATEST BENEFIT AND FEATURES THAT DELIVER THIS BENEFIT

Benefits are the positives your reader hopes to receive from your book. Features are the vehicles for delivering benefits. As book purchasers, we might not articulate what benefit we anticipate from a given book, yet we probably register it, or we wouldn't make the purchase.

For instance, recently I bought:

A new dictionary
- Benefits: new words, latest hyphenation decisions
- Features: more examples, derivations, synonyms, pre-ferred usages

The Carbohydrate Addict's Healthy Heart Program by Heller, Heller, and Vagnini
- Benefits: scientific understanding, greater health, weight loss (over 40 pounds so far!)
- Features: personal stories, instruction, lists, charts, menus

Simply put, features help deliver benefits. My proclaimed benefit to you, the reader, is that my book "guides the inexperienced proposal writer from inspiration to finished salable proposal." My features include step-by-step instruction, examples, and lists.

Benefits may be concrete, such as saving money, losing weight, or writing a professional proposal; or they may be abstract, such as gaining understanding, becoming inspired, or being entertained. Whether benefits are concrete or abstract, features can always be described in specifics.

Because you'll also need to have a firm grip on the difference between benefits and features to write "About the Book," you should examine the concept statement in Sidebar 6-2 by real-estate investor Mabel Armstrong and study the column identifying benefits and features until you are sure you understand the differences.

MENTION THE BOOK'S AUDIENCE

Before you write your concept statement, review your book's audience and how broad—or narrow—your market will be. Sometimes, the audience defines your book's uniqueness, such as Mabel Armstrong's "women who've never invested in anything before." The audience for the book you're reading now is specific and narrowly defined: "inexperienced proposal writers."

Sidebar 6-2
Sample: The Concept Statement
Mabel Armstrong

Concept Statement	Benefit or Feature
The Practical Woman's Guide to Real Estate Investment is an introductory real-estate investments book aimed at the entry -level investor. It presents the logic and process of real-estate investing in lively, easy-to-understand language with examples, anecdotes, self quizzes, forms, and work-sheets to help the beginning woman investor develop skill and confidence to get started.	Benefit within title
	Feature
	Features
	Benefit
[It] brings financial independence within the reach of most women. Using clear and understandable terms, author Mabel Armstrong shows that investments in real estate are not easy or mysterious. But they are straight-forward, and can be understood and managed successfully by women who've never invested in anything before.	Greatest benefit
	Feature
	Benefit

Authors of proposals for books aimed at general-interest readers have a tougher time defining their audiences than authors of books aimed at a specific, and usually smaller, readership. For instance, Green and Cotter's book, *Stop Being Manipulated*, seems potentially usable by everyone. Yet, because "a book written for everyone is a book written for no one," Cotter spent extra brain-power defining who *wouldn't* be interested in her book, and why.

REVEAL AUTHOR CREDENTIALS

One of the many questions in the minds of agents or editors when they read your concept statement is "Does the writer have sufficient qualifications to write about this subject?" A writer can, of course, become an expert or team-up with an expert to write a book on *any* subject. Without too many words, and without creating more questions than answers, work your credentials into the "Concept Statement."

Notice how I briefly took care of author credentials in my concept statement with the phrase, "freelance editor and instructor." Demetra George captured her author qualifications about her women's psychology/astrology book, *Mysteries of the Dark Moon*, in three words: "mythologist and counselor." Dr. Michael Rousell writes: "teacher, psychologist, and hypnotist." In Sidebar 6-2, Mabel Armstrong should have used something more than "author," even a phrase such as "successful real-estate investor" or a related author qualification would have been more helpful. Make your tag brief, knowing that "About the Author" permits elaboration on your qualifications.

If accomplishing these six goals in 50–100 words strikes you as a task of enormous proportion, you're right—but don't fret. Take as long as you must to create a rough draft. Rewrite and refine; then lay your effort aside. Get critiques from astute friends and writers, then revise again. If you end up with 250 words that you can't live without, that's fine. However, shorter is usually better. Eventually, a long concept statement will be cut for promotional ease.

Another benefit of all this hard work may be the difference between a puny advance and a respectable one. Remember, the number-one goal of your concept statement—and your proposal—is to generate enthusiasm in agents and editors, igniting their passion for championing another worthy book. It feels great to believe in a book and to want to see it published.

Critique of Two Concept Statements

Use the list of the six goals of an ideal concept statement listed in the beginning of this chapter to analyze each of the two concept statements that follow. Because you may have different interests and tastes—like any agent or editor—your analysis of what works and doesn't work may differ from mine.

Title: *The Hidden Life of Language*
Author: Rosemarie Ostler, Ph.D.

Concept Statement: *The Hidden Life of Language* is for people who want to know what the Great Vowel Shift has to do with their spelling problems; why it's easy for English speakers to learn to count in Swedish, French, Spanish, and even Hindi; when the "bow-wow," "pooh-pooh," and "ding-dong" theories of language origin were popular; whether *hopefully* to mean 'I hope' is here to stay. This book, written by linguistics educator Rosemarie Ostler, answers these and many other questions that ordinary people ask about language. It offers straightforward yet substantial explanations for many intriguing or puzzling features of our speech.

Among other questions answered by the book are why all infants start out with the same grammar, no matter which language they are going to speak, what anthropology can tell us about language origins, why English contains so many words from French, and how someone's pronunciation of *roof* can tell you where he or she is from. This book offers a host of fascinating facts about language while revealing the details of its inner workings.

Analysis: Of the six goals, only one is not stated or implied: what makes this book unique. To add this information would take only minor revision. Ostler could use the simple phrase: "unlike any popular book on language," or, "unique by addressing the interests of the general public." The reader then receives a clearer understanding of the audience than what was provided by "ordinary people." Together these two phrases about audience would distinguish this book's general market from other books aimed at linguists or scholars.

You may have also wondered what the greatest benefit is of Rosemarie Ostler's book. I believe the benefit, which is implied but not stated, is entertainment, arousing and answering reader curiosity, delivered by the feature of "substantial explanations" and "fascinating facts." Her lead in the concept statement gives us plenty of specific examples and hooks my curiosity.

I chose this next concept statement by Susan Lloyd because it represents an entirely different kind of book. The success of this travel narrative depends on how well the author gives the reader the feeling of walking in the author's shoes. In Lloyd's book, she must also make her readers feel as renewed as she felt.

Title: *Return to the Mother*
Subtitle: A Holy Week Journey
Author: Susan Caperna Lloyd

Concept statement: Journey with award-winning photographer, Susan Caperna Lloyd, to Sicily, New Mexico, the Philippines, Guatemala, and Spain to witness Easter-week rites seldom photographed, in which this western reporter becomes a participant transformed. *Return to the Mother: A Holy Week Journey* documents the survival and potency of pre-Christian, but contemporary, goddess rituals. It evokes the passion and mystery of these "living myths" and powerfully draws us into a journey to reclaim our own roots and sense of *communitas*. As we join the author who is of Italian and Spanish ancestry in her "return to the Mother," we too receive the gift of renewed personal power.

Analysis: In 1989, when Lloyd and I first worked on her proposal, we believed our principal job was to convince agents and editors that the main benefit to readers would be a vicarious journey of personal growth and exploration through Susan's experiences. We hoped her readers would feel renewed as she did. We also knew that her book idea was complex and one of a kind.

As I look over the concept statement now, I am again struck by Susan's originality and the multiplicity of ideas. Because the book covers a lot of ground, this concept statement could have been simplified and extended by several more lines. The listing of the five locations could be simplified to read "Spain and her former colonies." In rewriting, I would also state: "...in which this western reporter participated," instead of "...in which this western reporter becomes a participant transformed."

Another problem with this book is revealed, in hindsight, through its concept statement. Who is this book's audience? Catholics? Feminist/goddess readers? Cultural anthropologists? Inner-journey readers? Women of Italian or Spanish ancestry? While each of these audiences might be enthusiastic about some aspect of her book, each might also be nervous about other aspects. *Return to the Mother: A Holy Week Journey* was the author's first proposal. Although an agent represented Lloyd, the book did not sell. A second proposal (based on the same personal experiences) became her first book to sell: *No Pictures in My Grave: A Spiritual Journey in Sicily*. The author decided to rework *Return to the Mother* for readers of cultural anthropology.

Draft a first concept statement for your book. Include a clear statement of your book's subject and scope. At the same time, convey your excitement to score high on the pizzazz meter. Next create a list of your book's major features and corresponding reader benefits. Rewrite your concept statement to include your book's features and benefits, as well as its uniqueness and timeliness. Make reference to your audience and add author qualifications. Think of writing the concept statement as though the words were modeling clay; keep molding them until you arrive at an acceptable creation. Last of all, rewrite for brevity, clarity, and smoothness.

With your book idea shaped into a word sculpture, turn your attention to defining your audience and market in greater depth in the next chapter, "About the Market."

CHAPTER SEVEN

About the Market: Defining Your Reader

Chapter Goal: To provide a detailed description of your targeted readers, your market size, and how to reach it.

Concept Statement
About the Book
About the Author
* About the Market
About the Competition
Production Details
About Promotion
Table of Contents
Chapter Summaries
Sample Chapters
The Appendix

Whether I walk into my city's independent bookstore or one of the chain superstores, I am in awe over the tremendous number of books on the shelves.

Who buys them all?

In 1992, Americans spent $16.5 billion on books. In 1998, they spent just over $23 billion. Canadian and Mexican readers spent billions more. A significant portion of books published on this continent supply foreign markets. When you send your proposal to an agent/editor, you must have a clear and specific answer to the question, "Who will read this book?"

Suppose you're an old car buff. Can you describe other old car lovers who would buy a book on restoring running boards? Or, let's say you want to write a book about the next evolutionary step of humankind—and are qualified to write it. Who is your reader? In other words, how can you direct a publisher to your book's market?

In chapter two, I asked you to define your reader in broad strokes: man or woman, lover of old cars, self-help reader, or college-educated. In terms of market, you estimated the size as small, medium, or large. Now, in "About the Market," you must further define these two concerns—audience and market.

Proposal writers often confuse the term "market," as it is used here, with "marketing." Market refers to your audience, your book's reader. Marketing describes what you and your publisher do to reach your market. In "About the Market," you must describe your targeted reader in narrower terms, such as by their income, educational level, marital status, or size of family. Specifically, your audience might be a middle-income, college-educated, divorced woman with children.

Contents

When I taught freelance writing, I liked to lead my students through a kind of Rorschach test for the magazine market. We studied the covers of magazines and their ads. From these, we made guesses about a magazine's reader demographics: male or female, age, occupation, income level, education, values and beliefs, and tastes. To get you in the spirit, grab a pen and paper and write thumbnail sketches of who you think would buy *Backpacking*, *Bride*, and *Country Gentleman* magazines.

Granted, you would probably need to look at the covers and ads before your guesses would be completely accurate. While the cover of a magazine, like a book, must produce a click of recognition with its viewer, advertisements offer the key to reader demographics. Advertisers pay big bucks to get their pictures and copy in print. They can't afford to target their products incorrectly. You can enlighten yourself about this side of publishing by contacting any magazine's advertising department and requesting a display-advertising packet. Besides rate sheets and a sample or two of the magazine, you'll get a market-research report based on surveys of the magazine's readers. This report will offer statistical answers to questions of age, gender, occupation, income, and much more.

In this section of your proposal, you should adopt the same attitude as a magazine's sales manager. Consider the publisher as your potential client and your book as the product they might buy. You want the publisher to be delighted with that product, and ask for more.

If you can, find a statistic showing the success (how many books sold) of your competition. If you get these statistics, highlight them to document the potential of your market. Often, how many books a particular title has sold is considered a "trade secret." But, if sales have been good, publishers (and authors, too) like to boast with numbers. Each year, usually in the first quarter, *Publishers Weekly* reports on the closing year's winners and losers for both fiction and nonfiction books. Another place to find sales statistics is in the "Category Closeup" features included in *PW*. You can sometimes get lucky by calling an author's publisher, specifically the sales or publicity departments, and asking how many copies of a particular title have sold.

Whether you approach a regional publisher like Seattle's Seal Press or a conglomerate like Simon & Schuster, the editors all look to "About the Market" to answer three questions:

- Who is the market?
- How large is the market?
- Through what special venues can the market be reached?

In the rest of this chapter, I'll answer these questions, and discuss troubleshooting and special cases. First, read the model "About the Market" by Mary Jeanne Menna for her book, *Mom to New Mom: Practical Tips and Advice for the New Mom.*

WHO IS THE AUDIENCE?

If you've been building your proposal as you work through each of these chapters, the time you've spent researching and refining your idea and writing "About the Competition" will serve you well in defining your audience. Now, however, contemplate your average reader and answer the following questions about your audience:

- Male or female? Keep in mind that about three-quarters of all books are purchased by women.
- Age? Estimate by categories, such as young adult, X-generation, yuppies, baby-boomers, seniors, or describe age by decades, such as 20–30s, 40s, 30–50, or over 55.
- Education? A reader's level of education has a great deal to do with reading tastes. A high-school graduate is interested in different subjects and appreciates a different style of writing than a reader with a master's degree.
- Income? A book on "getting by" will appeal to a different income reader than "playing the futures." Feel free to place your reader in broad income categories: low, middle, or upper, rather than by gross annual income.
- Social class? Generally tied closely to income, the three major social classes—lower, middle, and upper—often divide by attitudes, prejudices, buying habits, and tastes. A person thinks differently if her major concern is making the food stamps last until the first of the month rather than deciding whether to spend the holidays in the Bahamas or in Paris. Each group reads and buys different books.

While these basic sociological categories will get you started, you should go a little further. See if you can answer what media, entertainment, and publications your reader supports. Would you expect your reader to buy a book in hardback, trade paperback, or mass-market paperback? Go to the best-stocked bookstore in your area and study books like yours. Talk with bookstore personnel. You'll find answers to your questions and get a much better picture of your audience.

Read how real-estate investment advisor Mabel Armstrong profiled her audience in the "About the Market" section for *The Practical Woman's Guide to Real Estate Investment*:

> The most likely reader of *The Practical Woman's Guide to Real Estate Investment* is the twenty-five-to-fifty-five-year-old woman who has a couple of years of college and who is grappling with the financial issues of the day. She realizes that, even if she is married, her spouse will probably not provide her main financial support for the rest of her life.
>
> ...*The Practical Woman's Guide to Real Estate Investment* is written for the woman who recognizes her need to execute a long-range financial plan, but who is not ready to attend a foreclosure auction or build a shopping mall. She needs and wants to have the advantage of real-estate investing made clear and the intricacies of the process laid out in small, easy-to-follow steps. This profile fits the majority of my readers.

Because others can be more objective toward your idea, they may suggest a market different from the one you had assumed. They may or may not be 100 percent correct, but you'd do well to listen to their ideas.

> Ask informed friends, family, and booksellers to help you define your market to a tee.

How Large Is the Market?

A publisher exists for almost every well-written book idea, whether it be narrow or specialized. But, no matter how great your book idea, no publisher will be interested if your market is too small to make a decent profit. You, the author, may have to adjust your expectations to match your book's true market size.

Your next job for the "About the Market" section is to find statistical support for the most optimistic view of your market's size—unless you have a true mass-market idea. For my proposal of this book, written about a narrow subject and specialized market, I quoted several statistical references to document the size of my market: 25,000 books sold of another proposal book, 300,000 subscribing writers to magazines on writing, 600 agents. While I don't predict the exact size of the market, these figures help create a picture of the book's potential.

Proposal writers can supply statistical support for the size of their markets by listing:

- Magazine circulation figures from periodicals to which your reader might subscribe. *Writer's Market* or *Ulrich's International Directory* are the most common references for this information.
- Number of people who belong to certain trades, organizations, or associations. Ask a librarian, and/or consult *American Statistical Index, Encyclopedia of Associations, Statistical Source, U.S. Census*, and glean statistics from your preliminary research.
- Trends that are supported statistically, such as a 20 percent increase in whitewater rafters over two years. Ask a librarian and use the same references indicated above.
- Statistics about the numbers of books sold annually by subject, a fact that can be accessed from *The Bowker Annual Library* and *Book Trade Almanac*.

If you use the Web, you can find the sites of many of these references, or use some of the directories or databases mentioned in chapter three. Some proposal writers list their statistical results in a graphically appealing way. Here's an example of how psychotherapist Marilyn Barrett presented the data for her book, *Creating Eden: The Garden as a Healing Space*. The format is her own.

Recent trends substantiate the timeliness of a book which links healing and gardening. The following facts indicate this is an idea whose time has come:
- The Gallup Poll recently conducted for the National Gardening Association lists gardening, together with walking

and swimming, as one of the top three recreational activities of Americans.

- Since 1984, three articles on the therapeutic aspects of gardening have appeared in *Organic Gardening* (which now has a circulation of over a million) and two have appeared in *Prevention*.
- The *Time* magazine cover article of June 20, 1988, entitled "Paradise Found," mentions that:
  — 78 percent of American households garden;
  — nursery owners say business has doubled in the past few years;
  —"recent surveys suggest that the most fervent converts (to gardening) are between 30 and 49" and that "baby boomers get much of the attention, because they account for the record $17.5 billion that was spent last year on things horticultural."

Dr. Barrett's marketing section continues with five more pieces of evidence to support the size of her book's market.

THROUGH WHAT SPECIAL VENUES CAN THE MARKET BE REACHED?

In addition to knowing the size of your market, the publisher must know how to reach it. The five major venues for books are:

- Bookstores and book sections
- Specialty stores
- Institution sales
- Special sales
- Subsidiary sales

Bookstores and Book Sections

Bookstores include every size, from the nationwide chains—Borders Books, Chapters (in Canada), Barnes & Noble—to independent booksellers whose stores are typically smaller. As you know, you can also purchase books from book sections of grocery stores, pharmacies, airports, and one-stop shopping stores. If your book is aimed at the masses, then you and the publisher will recognize that your book will be sold through all of these outlets.

You should not state the obvious in "About the Market." Omit listing that your book should be sold in bookstores, book sections, and libraries, unless you think it's important to specifically identify subject specialties for these venues (as did Mary Jeanne Menna in Sidebar 7-1). Instead, use your market section to identify the next four venues for book sales.

If you believe your book targets the general public, document that belief and identify any of the following special venues.

Specialty Stores

A sporting-goods store stocks books on rafting. A music store sells books on music method and artists. A giant hardware store sells books on home repair and gardening. We refer to these as specialty stores because they are in business primarily to sell something other than books.

Naturopathic physician Skye Weintraub sold some of her first edition of *Body Salts* in health-food stores that also carry body salts. Literary writer Susan Caperna Lloyd suggested that her memoir "...be promoted at Italian cultural centers and museums...."

The five coauthors of the book on twins handled this category of the market by setting it off as follows:

> General reading or specialty stores, such as children's, women's, and birth and parenting. Booksellers' conventions, catalogs, and mail-order companies.

It is especially important for anyone whose proposal is not for a general-interest book to discover and list specialty stores where a particular book can be sold. If your market is narrow, you will need to find specialty markets or other outlets to give the publisher confidence that your book has a solid audience and easily reachable market.

Sidebar 7-1
About the Market
Mary Jeanne Menna

At one time, parenting bookshelves held only a few dozen favorite titles and authors, such as Dr. Spock and T. Berry Brazelton. However, in recent years, booksellers and publishers have witnessed an explosion of new titles and expanded categories. Baby boomers have been the primary drive behind this surge, as they are no longer living close to their childhood homes (and don't necessarily agree with their own mother's advice, anyway). Boomers are seeking fast solutions to their baby-care problems, and are clearly turning to books and magazines to get the answers.

The success of Frances Wells Burck's *Babysense* (over 100,000 copies sold); Vicki Lansky's *Practical Parenting tips: Over 1500 Helpful Hints for the First Five Years* (over 500,000 sold); and Vicki Iovine's *Girlfriends' Guide* books (series has over 300,000 copies in print) documents the demand for such books.

Despite the number of competing parenting titles on the shelves, booksellers report that this category is not over published, but in fact, expecting and new parents are purchasing "two or three" books at a time.

In addition to the popularity of parenting books, the market has witnessed a proliferation of parenting magazines in recent years (over fifty-five currently in distribution). Combined with double-digit surges in the number of subscriptions, this confirms once again that new parents are hungrily seeking advice on raising their children. Below are the titles, target markets, and circulation figures of the top six, national parenting magazines.

(Continued)

Title	Market	Circulation
American Baby	Birth–2	1,650,000
Baby Magazine	Pregnancy, Baby	850,000
Baby Talk	Birth–2	1,500,000
Child	Birth–12	930,000
Parenting Magazine	Birth–12	1,450,000
Parents Magazine	Birth–12	1,825,000
Total:		8,205,000

There are four major markets for my book in which sales potential is substantial. They are as follows:

- Bookstores: Parenting shelves; special promotional areas for holidays, such as Mother's Day.
- Specialty Retailers: Over 1700 maternity stores nationwide, such as Motherhood and Pea in the Pod; also various baby, children's, and women's retailers.
- Catalog Companies: Maternity and baby catalog sales, such as The Right Way and One Step Ahead.
- Internet: Author's own Web site, easily accessed through the major search engines and links from parenting sites, with a planned link to amazon.com; iBaby.com, childbirth.org, and the over fifty other baby and maternity products' Web sites.

Institution Sales

More than one small press has secured a toehold in the publishing world because of library sales. Public libraries, university libraries, and corporate libraries must stock and update books. Like bookstores and book sections of speciality stores, institutions are an obvious market and need not be individually mentioned. However, if you believe your book makes ideal supplementary reading for a course, then do mention that fact.

Rosemarie Ostler devotes a short paragraph to the course-adoption potential for her book, as follows:

> A secondary but possibly significant market exists among teachers of survey courses on language and related topics. Few introductory books are available that do not require some training in linguistics. *The Hidden Life of Language* fills that gap.

If you can get a professor or two to commit to using your book, give the name of the instructor, the class, and the institution. Even though Cotter and Green wrote a mass-market book with guaranteed bookstore sales, Cotter included a paragraph on the book's potential for course adoption:

> Some college courses will be market targets. These include courses in self-improvement, leadership, psychology, stress management, etc. Dr. Green's class at the community college in Reno, for example, will certainly be using this book as a text. In addition, at least one business faculty associate already has decided to assign it to her college classes in North Carolina as soon as it is published.

Special Sales

Sometimes, perhaps rarely, a book will make an ideal promotional gift for a business. Imagine every purchaser of a food processor finding a cookbook in the box. One came with my purchase of a Cuisinart. Giant corporations are the best bet for these bulk orders. If you can find one and guarantee their order, by all means include it in "About the Market."

Subsidiary Sales

Your agent may negotiate the right to retain sales of your book to book clubs. If not, your publisher will retain this subsidiary right. You can use the *Literary Market Place* (*literarymarketplace.com*) to find a list of book clubs. Select the ones that seem right for your book and include them in "About the Market."

Susan Lloyd defined two audiences for her memoir, *No Pictures in My Grave*: readers of "spiritual travel" and women's studies. She then listed potential book clubs under each category. For her "spiritual travel" readers, for instance, she listed these book clubs:

> Aquarian Agent Book Club, Greenwich, Connecticut
> Intercultural Book Club, Vershire, Vermont
> Preferred Choice Bookplan, New York
> Word Book Club, Des Moines, Iowa
> Reader's Subscription Book Club, New York
> (Note: One Spirit book club had not yet been created
> at the time of her proposal.)

In her "About the Market," Aline Renauld Prince added some compelling research to her book club listing for *Cheapskate Decorating*:

- Reflecting the upsurge in this category, Meredith's Popular Science Book Club changed its name as early as 1992 to Homeowners-Do-It-Yourself Book Club. "We offer virtually every home improvement book published," says Mary Freeman in *Publisher's Weekly*, page 34, June 22, 1992.
- McGraw Hill's How-To Book Club (over 40,000 members) manager stated, "Home improvement is the second largest single category for us after woodworking...."

After listing several more book clubs, Prince points out how the eighteen projects covered in her book lend themselves to separate videos. Then she continues her marketing section by listing the subsidiary sales potential of "Audio/Video/TV Trends," as follows:

- Taunton Press produces videotapes to supplement individual titles.
- Sunset Western Gardening Book is offering a CD-ROM, and updating six home-improvement packages into a "New Basics" series....
- Dean Johnson of Hometime Video publishes and distributes videotapes.

Sidebar 7-2
Fastest-growing Independent Publishers by Titles Produced in 1998

Independent Publishers	Titles in 1998
1. Seven Stories Press/NY sevenstories.com	20
2. Sourcebooks/IL	179
3. Sleeping Bear Press/MI *sleepingbearpress.com*	12
4. Overlook Press/NY *overlookpress.com*	74
5. Chelsea Green Publishing Co./VT *chelseagreen.com*	17
6. Turtle Publishing/MA	126
7. Hay House/CA *hayhouse.com*	72
8. The Lyons Press/NY lyonspress.com	121
9. Charlesbridge Publishing/MA *charlesbridge.com*	80
10. Adams Media Corporation/MA *adamsmedia.com*	80
11. Graphic Art Center Publishing Co./OR *gacpc.com*	30

- PBS television shows weekend programs geared to the do-it-yourselfer covering projects both large and small, from remodeling "This Old House," to "Sewing with Nancy."

If you foresee strong possibilities of other subsidiary sales, by all means mention them; if possible, back them up with specific facts and figures. Other subsidiary sales include: foreign-language translations, movies, software, audio and video, merchandise (T-shirts, dolls in your likeness, and so forth). You may want to take some time to talk to software experts to explore whether your book lends itself to electronic media.

Style of Writing

Make your data easy to read. Because you're likely to have listings, statistics, or other categories, make liberal use of lists, indentations, bullets, bolds, and underlines. Be upbeat and enthusiastic. The proposal is a technical report, but it is also a sales brochure designed to get your product into print.

Troubleshooting and Special Cases

Most of the difficulties that writers encounter in "About the Market" are symptomatic of problems with their concepts, rather than in presentation of market data. Let's examine four situations: two common problems, one special case, and one frequent error:

- Audience too diverse
- Market size extra small
- Market size extra large, i.e. mass market
- Putting promotional material in "About the Market"

AUDIENCE TOO DIVERSE

When you define more than one audience for your book, such as teachers and parents, or patients with a certain illness as well as health-care providers, or writers and agents, you must address each market under separate headings. Each readership needs statistical support describing its potential size as a market, and each readership requires suggestions about how to reach it.

Multiple markets only become a problem when they are too diverse. This creates what is referred to as a "crossover problem" (discussed in chapter four). This means that one set of readers won't "cross over" subject lines to read books shelved elsewhere. This is most problematic when the material in the book aimed at one reader antagonizes or alienates the other targeted reader.

I consulted with a writer who wished to write a book for both teachers and parents. Her book idea could have, in fact, served both audiences. However, teachers are "learning experts" who may read material for its instructional potential. Parents often require more explanation than needed by teachers and may feel too much pressure from extensive lists of exercises and the materials' requirements. Teachers and parents often form entirely different readerships and require material that is presented in a different way. Same idea; two books.

I'm a crossover reader, meaning, I'm one of those less-common readers who enjoys books that blend disciplines and divergent ideas. If you think many different types of readers will read your book, determine which of them will be your strongest market. Then, figure out whether your secondary audiences will be turned off for the very reasons your primary audience is attracted to your book.

For any book with a diverse readership, put on the hat of one group and look at your proposal from that point of view alone. Would you buy this book? Does it really speak to you? Can an editor count on all of your book readers?

If you emerge from these questions with doubts, consider recasting your proposal for *one* of the many markets, and/or relegating the others to a secondary status.

MARKET SIZE EXTRA SMALL

A small, dedicated readership is not in itself a problem. I remember a woman who consulted me for her proposal on a book about scuba-diving locations off the Pacific coast. She'd done impressive market research by finding out exactly how many (and where) retail stores existed in the western coastal states selling scuba-diving gear. She'd targeted these for special sales. She had researched the numbers of divers and the growth of interest in the sport. She was ready to approach a publisher and convince them that her book would fit a niche and sell well.

She'd also researched appropriate publishers. If she had possessed fantasies of trying to sell her book to Simon & Schuster or seeking an agent to sell it to the larger publishers, she would have faced disappointing rejections. Her market research defined her book as ideal for publication by a regional or specialty publisher. For this, she would not need an agent and would waste no time trying to interest agents or large publishers.

While you should seek and substantiate the most optimistic viewpoint of your book's potential sales, you must be realistic. This process of estimating the size of your market and choosing the appropriate publisher is difficult for some authors with niche-specific book ideas.

The research for your proposal's "About the Competition" should have alerted you to the publishers of books similar to yours. If your competitors' books weren't picked up by the New York publishing giants, why should yours? A small targeted audience may lead you to more realistic expectations and the pursuit of a small publisher. Sidebar 7-2 shows the fastest-growing independent publishers by titles published.

MARKET SIZE EXTRA LARGE

If you have written a book with a general audience in mind, you may be unnecessarily nervous about what to put in "About the Market." How many ways can you say, "Just about everyone could benefit from my book?" Earlier in this chapter, I gave examples of how other authors wrote a first paragraph defining their book as intended for a general reader or general audience. However, rarely does this paragraph suffice for "About the Market." More often, writers take the opportunity to continue selling their concept or their qualifications by embellishing on the book's qualities and its general appeal.

Consider the following description by space engineer Ralph Nansen in the market section of his proposal for *Sun Power: the Global Solution to the Coming Energy Crises,* a book he believes has a general readership. His first three paragraphs reiterate the problem his book addresses and introduce his ideas as the solution:

> …The message of *Sun Power* strikes a responsive chord
> in people. When the author talks about how solar power

from space can solve the problems that seem unsolvable, the excited response from every audience is, "Why don't we get on with it?" or "What can I do to help?" Nansen's book will be read by: policy setters in Washington; anyone and everyone connected with the oil, gas, electrical, and other energy-related businesses; environmentalists and members of the many organizations supporting them; leaders of industries dependent on affordable energy sources; technological experts; trend watchers; economists; and every sort of concerned citizen including students, professionals, executives, government employees, and anyone interested in the future of energy sources for this country and the world.

Much of this is sophisticated "schmoozing," and it is up to you whether you feel comfortable chatting. However, it's customary to add a few paragraphs after defining your proposed book as one that is written for the masses and, like Ralph Nansen, to take advantage of the opportunity to drive home information about who will read your book and why.

PUTTING PROMOTIONAL MATERIAL IN "ABOUT THE MARKET"

Some styles of proposals blend sections that in this report-style proposal are dealt with separately. Certain styles may blend the "Concept Statement" with "About the Book" into one "Overview." I've also seen a blending of the "Market" (meaning readership, including special venues and subsidiary sales) with "Marketing" (meaning author promotion).

For clarity, I think it is best to develop the market and promotion sections separately. Each of these two sections has a mass of data for you to convey. The author usually bears no obligation to distribute books to specialty bookstores, for instance. Moreover, agents or publishers sell book-club or foreign rights.

In contrast, the "About Promotion" section details what the author volunteers to do. It describes author, not agent or publisher, responsibilities. Keeping the two sections of the proposal separate maintains clarity of who is expected to do what.

At this point in crafting your proposal, you've answered the fundamental questions that determine whether you should continue or stop further development of your proposal and book. "About the Competition" proved that your book supplies a demand and offers a unique contribution. "About the Author" outlined your qualifications to write the book you envision. The "Concept Statement" translated your ideas into a "selling handle." "About the Market" defined your market, its size, and specialty venues.

In the next chapter, you'll learn how to integrate all of these into the all-important section "About the Book."

CHAPTER EIGHT

About the Book: Inform, Dazzle, Persuade

Chapter Goal: To learn how to hook and sustain agent/ editor interest while introducing the subject of your book and featuring its timeliness and originality.

Concept Statement
* About the Book
About the Author
About the Market
About the Competition
Production Details
About Promotion
Table of Contents
Chapter Summaries
Sample Chapters
The Appendix

Throughout school, I played the flute in bands and orchestras. One night, in eighth grade, I got to play the much-coveted piccolo part in *Stars and Stripes*. I pretended to have confidence I didn't feel and played my best ever. I knew why. I'd practiced the solo every day for weeks. I had learned that to play well, I needed consistent practice. Thirty years later, I can still play it, though not as well.

"About the Book" is your performance, your first solo. To ask you to write this section in chapter one would have been like asking you to play a solo without practice. Although agents and editors get a sample of your writing and your ideas from the "Concept State-ment," "About the Book" shows whether or not you can deliver the goods. If this section is poorly written, they are unlikely to read fur-ther. To write it well, however, you must have refined your idea, done research, and written the sections about the competition, author, concept statement, and market. That task probably required weeks and weeks of practice, practice necessary for a winning per-formance. When agents or editors read about your book, they should feel your confidence and enthusiasm, and should know that you are the best writer for the part.

Definition and Purpose

This section of the proposal expands on your concept statement. It reflects the same six goals and more. In "About the Book," you lay out your book's subject and answer an agent's or editor's questions, such as, "Why should we publish this book?" and "Why now?" You must document your book's unique-ness and explain how the reader will benefit by reading

> If done well, "About the Book" will gain agent or editor acceptance and a request for an encore. Done poorly, it may bring down the curtain pre-maturely.

it. You must list special features, such as checklists, quizzes, graphs, or interviews. In addition, you must persuade the agent/editor that your book will make a contribution to the field and fill a publishing void. "About the Book" must elicit excitement and allude to your audience, size of market, competition, and author credentials.

Because this section has multiple purposes and an organiza-tional structure more demanding than the other sections of the pro-posal, I'll break everything down into steps: First, read one sample of "About the Book" with my explanatory marginal comments. The sample was written by time-management and business consultant, Lucy H. Hedrick, for her book, *Five Days to an Organized Life*.

Sidebar 8-1
Sample: About the Book
Lucia H. Hedrick

Proposal	Comments

Everyone wants to get organized. There are more than 300 organizers, or personal planning aids, on the market, and sales of organizers in 1987 are expected to exceed $300 million. Desk and office supplies manufacturers, too, are enjoying record profits: a place for everything and everything in its place.

Overview of context for this book

Time-management seminars are prominent offerings on business training menus. Likewise, get-organized articles appear in every consumer magazine with predictable regularity.

In spite of these aids, *people are floundering.* They complain they have too much to do and not enough time. They purchase elaborate and expensive organizers, write in them judiciously for several days, but soon abandon their good intentions for more pressing deadlines... they're spinning their wheels—they're not moving forward, and *they're not having any fun.*

Author identifies problems: floundering, no fun

These planners are what most people think organization is all about. It's not. The real *benefit* of getting organized, and my personal philosophy, is *greater freedom—freedom to have fun*, to do the things we've always dreamed of doing.

Greatest benefit of book

In our frenetic, fast-paced lives, we all have 800 things to do. Someone who has the typical view of getting organized says, "I'm only doing 600 of these things. How do I get from 600 to 800; that is, get more done in less time?"

Anecdotal quote

I feel that's not the right approach. We have to choose the most important tasks and get rid of, or let go of, the rest. This gives us the *free time* to do what we enjoy.

Unique approach of this book
(Continued)

Also, getting organized is not about what most people think they need—a crack of the whip, a kick in the pants, or a mega-dose of self-discipline. Personal organization is learned, and achieved, more by the carrot than the whip; that is, by *rewarding ourselves for accomplishment.*

Benefit

As a time-management consultant who has taught hundreds of men and women how to get organized, once and for all, I have observed three reasons why people feel disorganized and out of control. First, they don't have a system, a *simple* system for getting on with their lives, in an organized way, one step at a time.

Author qualification

The problem

Secondly, they need someone to show them *how* to use the system. *We're not "born" organized or disorganized.* Some people learn as children to put similar items together—laundry in the laundry basket, pencils in the pencil box, books on the bookshelf. Some learn to plan ahead.... And some of us are taught certain values like being on time.

More context

Specific examples

However, *we can be taught*, at any time, to be more organized, just as we can learn to play an instrument, to operate a computer, or to make a tasty omelet. All too often those already trained dismiss the uneducated as untrainable.

Everyday examples

The third reason so many men and women today are overwhelmed and disorganized is because they don't *reward themselves for accomplishments*. When we give ourselves a reward—a coffee break, a walk in the park, a browse in a bookstore—after completing a job, we boost our morale as well as our energy and feel eager to tackle our next job. But . . . men and women have to be taught *how* to use rewards to increase their productivity, and self satisfaction. Furthermore, *my system emphasizes rewards*, which is unique in approaches to getting organized.

Uniqueness

Five Days to an Organized Life, marketed as an affordable trade paperback, will provide a simple, unclut-

(Continued)

tered method for getting organized, getting going, and getting things done. Just as I do in my classes and workshops, I will offer specific tools and techniques for accomplishing goals. How to break down a goal into bite-sized pieces and how to use lists and calendars will be shown in detail. *Five Days* will be organized into five chapters, one for each "day," or step, in the process, of getting organized.

Features

The five-day framework is a vehicle for presenting my system a little at a time, not a structure that the reader will continue to follow every five days.

…However, the overriding goal of *more freedom*— and thus a more satisfying life—will remain front and center. My purpose is not to show the reader how to get more done in less time, but rather how to get their work done so they can relax and have fun. And most important, *Five Days* will show *we earn the freedom to have* more fun by giving ourselves some fun along the *way*….

Greatest benefit

Structure

By having a lead, a body, and a conclusion, "About the Book" follows the deceptively simple structure of all nonfiction. Because "About the Book" must satisfy many purposes, its content within this simple structure, is quite complex.

Imagine "About the Book" as a closing argument made by an attorney. By the end of this section, you want an agent/editor— judge and jury—to:

- Recognize your book's subject and slant
- Appreciate its importance and place it in the realm of other books similar to it
- Feel an urgency to read and share it
- Be able to clearly articulate the greatest reader benefits and the primary features

THE LEAD

Every good painting has a point of visual attraction, a place where the viewer's eye is drawn. It may be a point of light, the convergence of lines, or a burst of contrasting color. Your lead should rivet the attention of the overworked agent or editor who's looking for any excuse to reject your proposal quickly and have one less on the desk to remind him how far behind he is.

Like a painter with dozens of colors, you can choose from many types of leads. The most common are:

- Anecdotes
- Impressive facts or statistics
- Quotes
- Startling statements
- Narratives
- Questions
- Metaphors or analogies

There are other leads as well, but these seven are the most common. The point is to find a lead that seems to match your book and creates the most powerful hook. The examples in Sidebar 8-2 feature actual leads to "About the Book" sections.

THE BODY

Artists draw viewers' eyes to a point on the canvas by using perspective. We've all seen a picture with a winding road. Where the road disappears into the distant mountains, it has narrowed to a single point. In the foreground of the picture, the road is wide. Details in the foreground—a flower, a rock—can draw the viewer's eye as much as the point in the distance. Proposal writers also make use of something similar to an artist's use of perspective. Years ago, agent Natasha Kern explained the structure of "About the Book" as a funnel, larger at one end than the other. After a lead, a writer could begin this section from either the wide end or the narrow end.

Sidebar 8-2
Leads to Begin "About the Book"

Example	Type of Lead
My wife and I liked to tell our friends, "We always spell love with a T." There were five very special reasons why: Topper, Triptych, Tripper, Trio, and Tess. Three cats. Two dogs. One big, happy family. Then we arrived home from a holiday party on December 14, 1997, to find the inside of our house engulfed in smoke and flames. All five pets were dead. (*Three Cats, Two Dogs, One Journey Through Multiple Pet Loss*)	Anecdote
Everyone wants to get organized. There are more than 300 organizers, or personal planning aids, on the market, and sales of organizers in 1987 are expected to exceed $300 million. (*Five Days to an Organized Life*)	Impressive facts or statistics
Sleep . . . Poets have praised it and enshrined it as the ultimate metaphor for quietude . . . Longfellow referred to it as "night's repose"; Shakespeare, as "nature's soft nurse." For Milton there was the "timely dew of sleep," and for Keats, the exultation: "O magic sleep! O comfortable bird / That broodest o'er the troubled sea of mind / Till it is hushed and smooth." (*Stop Your Husband From Snoring*)	Quotes
Last year, over 1,600 world scientists and Nobel laureates gathered to issue *A Warning to Humanity*. Their statement says, in part, that "...a great change in our stewardship of the earth and the life on it is required if vast human misery is to be avoided and our global home on this planet is not to be irretrievably mutilated." Among the actions called for is to reduce the use of fossil fuels and to increase the use of solar energy... (*Sun Power*)	Startling statements

(Continued)

Place has a voice: At dusk, in the early summer in the pea fields, we could sometimes see the chestnut-colored, white-tailed deer, like magical beings from a special world we were only temporarily visiting. (*Tales from Coon Creek Farm*)	Narratives
What has twenty toes, four arms, and two heads, and screams loud enough to spark even the most placid of mothers into action? No, it's not a wild love scene from an afternoon soap opera, it's TWINS! (*Mothering Twins*)	Questions
Grammar is not for kids. We were taught the rules of grammar in a way similar to the way we were taught sex, before we had a chance to experiment. The rules, therefore, became meaningless until we had some experience for reference. (*Grammar for Grownups*)	Metaphors or analogies

The wide end corresponds to a beginning with a wide view. You accomplish this wide view by describing the social, political, or cultural context for your book—the milieu or climate. Some writers spell out the problem for which their book offers a solution. After drawing this backdrop for their books, they narrow the perspective of the agent/editor by giving the title of their book, listing its unique features, and proclaiming its benefits as one solution to the problems of the times.

Other writers begin at the narrow end. After a lead, they introduce their books before giving any context. They list their books' unique features and promise reader benefits unlike any previous books. Then, later, in "About the Book," they delve into deeper reasons why their books should be published. Perhaps they offer a profile of our collective problems and sketch the need that their books will fill— from the specific book to the general climate; narrow to wide.

Each approach has advantages and disadvantages. More proposal writers start with a wide view rather than a narrow view for one powerful reason: "About the Book" must persuade an agent/editor to read on. Establishing the wider context for a book builds a case for its need. Remember the idea of persuading a judge or jury. The more pressing the social need, the greater the publisher's urgency to get this book published now!

For clarity of definition, starting with the wide perspective is called an inductive method of organization. Starting with the narrow perspective is called a deductive method of organization. Read the explanations and examples for each, and select the approach that best fits your book. See Sidebar 8-3.

The Inductive Method of Organization

Introduce the general social, political, and/or cultural climate as the context for your book. Make generalizations relevant to your book's concern and support them with facts and statistics. In addition, state any problems for which your book offers solutions. Later, narrow your discussion to your book alone, highlighting why it offers exactly the right solution at the right time.

In the examples of leads, the quote lead by Dr. Lipman on his book about snoring is one example of the inductive method of organization. He doesn't start by telling us about snoring; he starts by discussing sleep, which sets the general context for the book.

Susan Lloyd's *About the Book* demonstrates my point about establishing the "climate" for a book, as follows:

> As we enter the 1990s, the thirst for self-knowledge is epidemic. And with it, the knowledge of other cultures and ways of living. With more affluence, it seems everyone is traveling. Not content to take twenty-one-day package tours as amateur anthropologists and adventurers, we seek out exotic locales in the Amazon. We climb sacred Buddhist shrines in Java, or trace the ancient footsteps of pilgrims in Spain. For many of us, it is an attempt to uncover roots, or find the humanity which unites us all as world citizens. In modern society we feel disconnected from the traditional institutions of family and community and hope that in these "lost" places we can find something lost in us.

Sidebar 8-3
Two Methods of Organizing the Body of "About the Book"

Wide View First	Narrow View First
Inductive Method	*Deductive Method*
Establishes social, cultural, political, or other context. Builds case for timeliness—answering the question, "Why this book; why now?"	Introduces your book and its strongest feature and greatest benefit. States primary problem for which your book offers a solution and states that solution.
Uses statistics, authoritative quotes, and testimonials to explore context, problems, or needs.	Offers details about book—its features and corresponding benefits, using lists, summaries.
Points out shortcomings of existing literature.	Weaves in testimonials, case studies, and quotes.
Narrows "funnel" to offer your book as the perfect solution to the needs and times.	Widens "funnel" to offer the larger context—social, cultural, political, or other.
Introduces your book's strongest feature and greatest reader benefit.	Uses statistics, authoritative quotes to reinforce reasons for "why this book; why now?"
Uses lists, summaries, and hints to define unique features.	Integrates larger context with your specific book.
Weaves in author credentials, competitors, audience, market, and promotion throughout section.	Same.
Ends with upbeat conclusion that emphasizes most unique contribution of your book; why it is different and/or better.	Same.

Clearly, the author has presented a convincing case for her memoir by describing a current, universal need that most people have or will experience.

If you choose to begin this section with the wide perspective—the inductive method of organization—choose a current context within society or culture that is most relevant to your book. For instance, books about business could

> Make sure your "About the Book" section answers the two most fundamental questions asked by any editor or agent: "Why this book?" and "Why now?"

begin with a discussion of the economic climate. Books on parenting could begin with a discussion of social problems and changes in the family. For example, Susan Lloyd describes our "thirst for self-knowledge," how "we feel disconnected from...family and community," and how we hope "we can find something lost in us." All three identify problems that Lloyd considers part of the social and cultural climate.

Once you introduce the climate or context for your book and introduce the problem for which your book offers a solution, then, like the disappearing road in the painting, narrow the reader's focus to one topic—your book. You control the readers' perspective. Lead them from general to specific.

In the example in Sidebar 8-4, notice how Ralph Nansen accomplishes several important jobs on the first page of his "About the Book":

- Establishes the context for his book by acquainting the reader with the problem his book offers to solve.
- Uses statistics, a specific quote from a scientific paper, and a quote from a recognized scientist.
- Hook the reader's interest with a powerful paragraph of promises that, presumably, his book fulfills.
- Narrows reader perspective and introduces his book.

Sidebar 8-4

About the Book, from *Sun Power: The Global Solution for the Coming Energy Crisis*
Ralph Nansen

Last year, over 1,600 world scientists and Nobel laureates gathered to issue *A Warning to Humanity*. Their statement says, in part, that "...a great change in our stewardship of the earth and the life on it is required if vast human misery is to be avoided and our global home on this planet is not to be irretrievably mutilated." Among the actions called for is to reduce the use of fossil fuels and to increase the use of solar energy and other energy sources that are inexhaustible and environmentally benign.

"When you look closely, you find so many things going wrong with the environment. You are forced to reassess the hypothesis of intelligent life on Earth."

Astronomer Carl Sagan

Imagine a world with clean air, even in its largest cities. Imagine a world without the hazard of poisonous nuclear wastes. Imagine a world in which even the most remote jungle village has access to electricity for all of its needs. Imagine a world where the production and distribution of energy also helps to grow the food supply. Imagine a world in which oil-rich countries can't blackmail other nations. Imagine a world where the average monthly electric bill, including heating in winter, is only $30 a month. Imagine a world with quiet, affordable, nonpolluting transportation for everyone. [italics by proposal writer]

Now imagine that this scenario isn't some science-fiction fantasy but a reliable representation of the world within the foreseeable future; possibly within the next twelve years according to Ralph Nansen, author of *Sun Power: The Global Solution for the Coming Energy Crisis.*

The Deductive Method of Organization

This type of beginning for the body of "About the Book" boldly dominates the portrait. The proposal reader must focus on one subject—your book. In this method of organization, you introduce your book, at once emphasizing the promise it makes to readers and showcasing its unique features. After you've made the "sale," relax and introduce the sociological context that makes your book a well-timed endeavor and the problems for which your book offers a solution.

For the proposed book, *Act Like an Owner*, business owners Bob Blonchek and Marty O'Neill adopted the deductive method of organization for "About the Book." Their lead features three anecdotes followed by:

> What's going on here? How does a young engineer with just five years experience have the courage to say enough is enough? Why does a team, when given the chance to slow down, agree to do even more? Why does an employee go out of the way to find an answer to someone else's question? And, why is a new employee motivated to achieve tremendous personal and business objectives?
>
> *Act Like An Owner: The Power of an Ownership Culture* answers these questions. It is the first book to demonstrate that corporate culture, and specifically, an *ownership culture,* [bold in the actual proposal] can create an environment where ordinary people accomplish extraordinary things. It is the first book to elevate corporate culture to the stature of a business discipline.

If you use the narrow view, or deductive, method-of-organization approach, then plan to eventually expand your focus to address the larger context or climate for your book. Doing this supplies the needed persuasive context for your book.

THE CONCLUSION

A short, upbeat conclusion should end your "About the Book" section. Continue to generate enthusiasm, which you hope, by now, has infected the agent/editor. For instance, consider the inspirational conclusion crafted by Carolyn Cotter:

> *Stop Being Manipulated* can be read easily in a few hours. It leaves the readers with fresh ideas, tangible techniques, and hope. And with hope, everything is possible.

You may choose to end your chapter, like Rosemarie Ostler did, by summarizing the benefits to the readers and reiterating your primary audience:

> *The Hidden Life of Language* provides an illuminating look at that most human of skills, our ability to use language. This book is for everyone who has ever been curious (or flummoxed, misorderly, all adrift, or just plain bumfuzzled) about their or other people's ways of talking.

Your conclusion should continue to inform, dazzle, and persuade right to the end. Here is Dr. Lipman's conclusion:

> Aimed at the snorer and the "snoree," the medical waiting room and the hotel and motel night table, *The A-B-Z-z-z-z's of Snoring* finally offers snorers the possibility for silence and solace…and their long-suffering companions the opportunity to return from the spare room to the bedroom. It can't miss.

It's customary in "About the Book" to repeat the title of your "can't miss," proposed book often—at least one time per page. This may seem affected, but it is convention. In your conclusion, repeat your title one more time.

Five Categories of Information

You've already seen from the examples and Sidebar 8-3 how proposal writers include other specific types of information. For style as well as substance in your "About the Book," make sure you understand and include information in these five categories:

- Problems and Solutions
- Benefits and Features
- Personal Examples
- Specifics
- Hint-and-tease Items

PROBLEMS AND SOLUTIONS

Before writing your rough draft of this section, make a list of the problems that your book will address. Even if you simply want to share your personal experiences, you can usually link them with a larger social issue. For her inner-journey book, Susan Lloyd created a tie between the thirst for self-knowledge and an individual's lack of connection with family and culture.

Some books address one clear problem, such as Dr. Lipman's book on snoring. After his lead, where he quotes poets on sleep, he juxtaposes the non-poetic reality of snoring with a letter to Dear Abby:

Dear Abby:
I am desperately trying to find a cure for my husband's snoring. After being married for 27 years, I am convinced that there is no cure other than killing him, which is illegal in our country.

Dr. Lipman effectively introduces an agent/editor to the problem his book addresses. The personal testimony of a "Dear Abby" makes a powerful point, but Dr. Lipman continues to broaden his presentation of the problem:

Over forty million Americans snore. [This one-line paragraph makes greater impact than if he continued with the next two sentences:]

For some, it is no more than an occasional and innocuous habit. But for many, it represents a nightly disturbance that turns that "timely dew of sleep" into a disruptive and nerve-racking experience for those with whom they share their lives.

All right, I'm convinced, snoring is a problem. Even so, in his "About the Book," Dr. Lipman outlines other problems created by snoring, such as "adversely affect[ing] the quality of the snorer's waking life," and "represents a health condition serious enough to warrant medical attention." Several paragraphs later, he picks up the problem by offering a list of symptoms that could signal a snoring problem—just in case a person who snores does not have a spouse who is ready to kill him over her lost sleep.

After nearly a page of defining, developing, and presenting the problem of snoring, Dr. Lipman introduces his book and defines, develops, and presents his solutions in equal detail.

Take time to brainstorm all the possible problems your book addresses. What solutions do you offer through your book? Write both down and decide which problem is primary and which solution, therefore, is the focus of your book.

Look back at the sample "About the Book" by Lucy Hedrick in Sidebar 8-1. She highlights the problem through italicizing. What's her readers' problem? They want to get organized and stop floundering. They're not having much fun. What solution does her book offer? We don't really get the solution until later in her "About the Book" when she narrows our view to her book specifically. But then she tells us that her book "will provide a simple, uncluttered method for getting organized, getting going, and getting things done." Her title broadcasts her solution: *Five Days to an Organized Life.* If you think back to the list of slants in chapter two, you'll be able to identify her slant as both a promise and numbers slant. The title also portrays the solution to the readers' problem in the form of a promise.

BENEFITS AND FEATURES

If you'll recall from the discussion of concept statements, benefits describe what readers get from your book. They denote take-home value; benefits your readers can implement to make changes in their lives. Benefits can be tangible, like organizing your desk, stopping snoring, or writing a professional proposal. Or, they can be intangible, like gaining freedom, feeling more fulfilled, expanding understanding, or feeling self-confident.

Features describe how a book delivers those tangible or intangible benefits; they are the florist's car that delivers the dozen red roses.

Examples of features are: step-by-step instructions, diagrams, interviews, examples, questions, exercises, sidebars, maps, and bibliographic information.

> Make a list of your book's benefits and features and rank them by importance.

After Dr. Lipman finished outlining the problem of snoring, he introduced a solution in the form of his book's features, which I have italicized: "*The A-B-Z-z-z's of Snoring* [proposal title] solves this problem of misdiagnosis by providing *easy-to-follow diagrams and flow charts* that identify and classify snoring according to degrees *and symptoms*, as well as *treatment options*."

Present and emphasize your book's most important features first. Then work in the rest of your features as you progress through "About the Book." Features tend to appear in the narrow end of the body of this section, in the place where you introduce your book and title. If you begin inductively, with the wide perspective, they usually dominate the last part of the section, with benefits sandwiched in between.

Benefits and features offer ideal material for lists. When indented and bulleted, lists offer visual stimulation and relief from paragraphs. They draw interest and give a great sense that you are both organized and that you understand what your book really offers.

If you begin deductively, introducing your book and title first, benefits and features appear right away, mixed in with discussion of problems and solutions.

PERSONAL EXAMPLES

Personal examples add humanity to the discussion of your book and help your agent/editor identify with the real or created person's story and problem. Personal examples give you a chance to offer parallels to your reader demographics and, in effect, bring your targeted reader to life through carefully selected examples or anecdotes. They allow you to demonstrate how your readers' suffering will be relieved by your solutions. Personal examples lend testimony to the effectiveness of your solutions.

Dr. Lipman's example of the letter to Dear Abby is a great personal example. Later, he indents and offers what I call "an up-close-and-personal" example of one of his patients:

> Jerry Hamilton, a thirty-seven-year-old fireman, didn't know the meaning of a quiet night. Neither did his co-workers...until they banished him from the firehouse to a nearby trailer, which they equipped with an alarm system. At home, Jerry's girlfriend resigned herself to sleeping in the spare room. On the rare nights that she shared his bed, she would lie in the darkness surrounded by the frightening din of his snoring...fearful of the seemingly endless periods when he appeared to stop breathing, choke, and then revive himself with huge gasps while thrashing about with his arms and legs. Their relationship deteriorated, as did Jerry's health. He began to experience gradual loss of energy and took catnaps wherever and whenever he could.

Dr. Lipman uses this case study to tell his agent/editor about other sleep disorders for which snoring may be a symptom.

Some writers rely on short quotes as personal examples. In Susan Lloyd's proposal on *The Last Zapatista*, she wrote: "Zapata has become the *campesinos*' figurehead, role model, and inspiration. 'Zapata never died,' the people tell the author. 'He has come back!' "

You can use personal examples to "show" the problem and the solutions or benefits. Not only are they powerful because they humanize your topic, but they also demonstrate professional nonfiction writing, and the ability to "show" instead of "tell."

SPECIFICS

Specifics offer dashes of color and detail that transform a mediocre (though well-done) "About the Book" into a spectacular one. Specifics—facts, statistics, quotes by authorities, quotes by everyday people, and examples—support general statements and bring clarity and focus. Use as many of these as you can throughout your "About the Book" and throughout your proposal.

Notice the focusing effect of facts and statistics in Lucy Hedrick's sample "About the Book," featured near the beginning of this chapter. Recall her specific examples, such as, "laundry in the laundry basket, pencils in the pencil box, books on the bookshelf...learn to play an instrument, to operate a computer, or to make a tasty omelette."

Because you probably have completed some preliminary research on your subject by the time you get to this section, I hope you have jotted down some dazzling facts and figures that you can now include. Here's an example of some of the specifics I used for the proposal that sold this book to my first publisher in 1994:

> According to John Baker, an editor of *Publishers Weekly*, "Publishing is now a twelve billion-dollar industry....Over 50,000 titles are published each year; of them 85 percent are nonfiction." First-time authors comprise an incredible 75 percent of this group. According to Baker, writers may choose from among some 20,000 publishers, although 70 percent of all books published in the United States are produced by ten giant conglomerates.

Specifics add some of the excitement that keeps an agent or editor reading. Often, the main distinguishing point between good amateur writing and saleable professional writing is the writer's command of specifics.

HINT-AND-TEASE ITEMS

Hint-and-tease refers to tidbits about your qualifications, the competition, the market, production, and promotion. Just tidbits. Just enough to answer the emerging questions an agent/editor will have about each of these sections to come, but not so much that they won't feel excited and motivated to find out the full story. These hints are like coming attractions to moviegoers, just as the entire concept statement is a coming attraction for the proposal.

For instance, instead of using your book title to begin a sentence, reword it to say, "Teacher and researcher Juanita Garcia offers the reader..." Now you've hinted about your author credentials. When you begin to discuss the features that make your book unique, throw in some contrasting statement about a competitive book, such as, "In contrast to Fenh-Yu Chung's book on such-and-such,...(your title) includes the latest research about..." You've now planted a tease about the section on competition.

Look for ways to hint and tease in "About the Book" using items drawn from each of your subsequent sections. Not only will this pique agent/editor interest, it will begin to answer questions and quell anxieties.

STYLE OF PRESENTATION

Think graphically. Visualize your words on the page as a layout artist might. Be creative but don't overdo it. Consider putting your book's title in bold or caps, or both, rather than underlining it.

Although the "About the Book" sample on *Five Days* used fewer "visuals" than most proposals, notice how the author did make frequent use of italicized words and phrases.

Bulleted lists are another stylistic device used commonly in "About the Book" sections. They may highlight benefits, features, or the topics that make a book unique.

To keep your lists powerful in content as well as in graphic appeal, here are five guidelines:

1. List no fewer than three items. I prefer three to six. Longer lists tend to overload the reader with the feeling they'll have to sort too much data.

> Remember, this is your sales portrait; use your full palette:
> • bullets, indented quotes, *italics*, **bold**, CAPS, boxes, and S P A C E.

2. Keep marbles and eggs in separate lists. Benefits or features in separate lists will be clearer than benefits mixed with features.
3. Always set off your book's special qualities, or your special qualifications, using single bullets or bulleted lists.
4. Keep entries short.
5. Rank the contents of your lists, giving the strongest or most important element first.
6. Make lists parallel in grammatical structure; for instance, use active verbs like the ones in this list.

In the example that follows, freelance writer and stay-at-home mom Mary Jeanne Menna uses a list to highlight her book's benefits.

The greatest reader benefits of my book include:
• Moms get quick, real-life answers to their baby-care questions.
• Moms learn ways to solve their baby-care problems faster, better, easier.
• Moms lower their anxiety and stress levels during the emotionally charged first year.
• Moms don't feel quite so isolated knowing that they're not alone.
• Saves moms time and money.

Notice how Mary Jeanne did not have a parallel sentence start for her last bulleted item. She could have reworked it to be parallel as: "Moms save time and money."

Another stylistic element even more pronounced in "About the Book" than in the other sections, is repetition of your book title. It

---

Sidebar 8-5

Most Common Problems in "About the Book" and Solutions to Them

Problem	Solution
1. Lacks organization— wanders all over the place.	The solution to this problem is to plan ahead and outline. Decide on an inductive or deductive method and be clear about the problem, solution, features, and benefits. Sketch an outline and then rewrite.
2. Lackluster leads.	As a showcase for your writing, "About the Book" must sustain the excitement you've generated in the "Concept Statement." You've got to put out energy, show the editor you know what a lead is, and keep selling.
3. Section is too long or includes tangents. Almost reads like actual chapters.	Shorten. Outline.
4. Boring writing. Often this judgment corresponds to a lack of specifics and overuse of the to-be verb: is, was/were, be, and other inactive verbs, such as seems or appears.	Shorten sentences. All but eliminate adjectives and adverbs. Use concrete nouns.
5. No clear-cut benefit. Sometimes writers get so wrapped up in the proposed book's features, they fail to mention what their readers will get from it.	Specify audience, market.

(Continued)

---

6. Overly long lists. One client had over twenty items on a bulleted list. She had brain-stormed her book's contents and put these free-associations down without thought to groupings, order, parallelism, or quantity.

In general, keep to five or less, but have several group-ings, if you choose.

7. Includes a short chapter-by-chapter outline or table of contents in "About the Book." Since the agent/editor gets to read both of these later in the proposal, they shouldn't appear verbatim in "About the Book."

Pull out your strongest points—what makes your book contents unique, fasci-nating, and worth reading and feature them.

8. No sociopolitical or cultural context. No climate.

What helps establish your book's timeliness is provid-ing an overview of the times with regards to your sub-ject. Establishing context or climate for your book in-creases urgency. Make the agent/editor believe the world needs your book ASAP.

9. No mention of author name, qualifications, competitive titles, audience, or market.

Scant mention at least serves to answer questions and hint-and-tease about sections to come.

10. Diction too high, syntax too complex for the proposal. Academese is the kiss of death, unless you are plan-ning to write and sell to a university press or an aca-demic audience.

Study writing for lay readers and emulate. Watch TV.

Sidebar 8-6
Worksheet for Completing the "About the Book"

For each of the following types of leads, write one for your proposal, then choose the best: Anecdotes, Impressive Facts or Statistics, Quotes, Striking Statements, Narratives, Questions, Metaphors, or Analogies.

Choose an inductive method of organization (overview narrowed to your book) or deductive method (your book expanded to an overview) to structure this section.

1. Define the reader's greatest problem that your book will address.
2. Define the strongest solution your book offers.
3. List three benefits your readers should receive, beginning with the most important benefit.
4. List three features in your book that deliver the promised benefits.
5. Define what makes your book unique.
6. Define the context or "climate" that makes your book timely.
7. Determine what you can set off in bulleted lists, such as:
   • Reader benefits
   • Book's features
   • Topics that make your book unique
   • Any "plus" value—how your book will be the first, ways you are special or super qualified as the author.
8. Choose others to profile or create several personal examples.
9. List specifics you can use in "About the Book."
   • Statistics
   • Facts
   • Quotes from current magazines
   • Quotes from experts and authorities

should be highlighted by caps or bold in addition to Italics. While repetition of the title can be overdone—once every paragraph would be too much—if your title appears once or twice each page, you won't go wrong.

Last of all, "About the Book" sections typically run six to ten double-spaced pages. This allows you plenty of opportunity to develop your topic, without slipping into outlining the book (that comes later). In style, this section presents the book but doesn't dissect it.

Troubleshooting

By the time you've drafted "About the Book," you've accomplished a major task. *But*, expect to rewrite and revise this section many times—after you put it away for a while. Most writers revise this section half a dozen times. After I edit a proposal, the writer usually faces yet another revision or two. Sidebar 8-5 shows the most common problems I see in "About the Book" and possible solutions to those problems. Do the best you can; then move on to the rest of the proposal. When you return to this section, with a sharpened pencil and mind, you'll see it with new eyes.

Congratulate yourself, too. You've conquered a very difficult section to write. And, with the writing of "About the Book," you're about half-way done, if you don't count sample chapters. Celebrate!

CHAPTER NINE

Table of Contents and Chapter Summaries: Organizing Your Book

Chapter Goal: to learn how to organize your research and ideas, how to create a table of contents, and how to write a chapter outline in summary form.

    Concept Statement
    About the Book
    About the Author
    About the Market
    About the Competition
    Production Details
    About Promotion
  * Table of Contents
  * Chapter Summaries
    Sample Chapters
    The Appendix

The word "outline" is, for some people, like the word "plague," "internal revenue service," or "lima beans" for other people. Still others love outlining. Outlining is simply a way of organizing your material and assuring that a reader will understand. Your outline need not be complicated, confusing, or an object of loathing. On the other hand, without a good outline, your writing *will* go awry. The resulting cleanup edit will cost you far more time than you would have spent had you planned ahead and outlined first.

You may not have had a strong reason to outline anything you've written. Your book's table of contents is, in essence, a book outline. Chapter summaries carry through the overall plan of organization. The purpose of this chapter is to help you select an organizational plan for your book and carry it through in the chapter summaries required for the proposal. Your readers will be the ultimate benefactors of your organizational efforts.

> Outlining a book is more than necessity; it is the blueprint upon which your book—each chapter, each section, each paragraph—depends.

Definition and Purpose

A table of contents lists chapters by order of appearance and provides the page number where each chapter begins. An effective table of contents provides three reader services:

- Previews the book
- Projects its contents, depth, and style
- Provides easy access to each section

Agents and editors occasionally refer to "chapter outlines," which are one and the same as "chapter summaries." Although you need not create a paragraph-by-paragraph outline of your entire book, your chapter summaries must reveal clear organization to the book as a whole, as well as order and substance within each chapter. Think of your table of contents as the topic outline for your book and of your chapter summaries as a series of topic sentences.

Set-up for the Table of Contents

To develop your book's ideas into a table of contents:

- Review your audience and purpose
- Divide your research notes and ideas into groups of similar topics
- Assign working titles to these groups
- Select a method of organization

REVIEW YOUR AUDIENCE AND PURPOSE

The first steps of organizing your book are easy, if you begin with a review of your targeted audience and original purpose in writing your book. In chapters two and three, I discussed evaluating ideas and doing preliminary research. Recall your decision regarding your book's purpose: to inform, to entertain, or to persuade. Think again about the needs of your targeted reader.

DIVIDE YOUR RESEARCH NOTES AND IDEAS INTO GROUPS

After your preliminary research, you'll have some sort of files, note cards, or jottings. Divide this information into groups, putting all similar items together. These files or piles begin to form what will eventually become divisions. If you end up with only a few groupings, divide them again into smaller, same-subject units.

Chapter divisions will depend on your chosen subject matter and audience. Psychologist Dr. Kathleen N. McGuire, who proposed a book called *Moved to Tears: The Meaning and Joy in Learning to Cry*, might not have devoted the first *section* of her book to explaining why people cry had her targeted reader been therapists rather than the lay public.

My purpose (to inform) and my audience (inexperienced proposal writers) determined my chapter divisions. Most of the chapters in this book are organized to include one section of the proposal per chapter. How else could it be done? There is always a different way to organize a subject. Another book on proposal writing, reflecting a different author's vision about his readers' needs, packs all parts of the proposal into one chapter called "The Introduction." Be clear about your readership and purpose; they will lead you to a logical method of organization.

ASSIGN WORKING TITLES TO THESE GROUPS

Assign a working title to the different groups of identical topics. This label becomes a potential chapter title. A phrase will do fine. Make a list of these titles. While it's beyond the scope of this book to cover research methods, you may want to review this area to find your most comfortable style—computer files, sticky notes, index cards, etc.

SELECT A METHOD OF ORGANIZATION

For me, establishing a list of working titles and thinking about an organizational blueprint for my book brought great excitement. At last, the idea I'd carried in my mind began to take form on paper. I had to resist every temptation to begin writing chapter one, without a good outline. You should too. Channel your excitement into your first outline—the blueprint for your entire book. You accomplish this by selecting a method of organization.

A glance down your list of phrases of working titles for your chapters will reveal an inherent pattern. You may see

> Your chapter divisions suggest a table of contents, which in turn suggests an organizational plan for your entire book.

an affinity between your choice of one of the three purposes—to inform, to persuade, to entertain—and these six most common methods of organization:

- Chronological order
- Increasing or decreasing importance or complexity
- Order of need
- Classification and division
- Inductive and deductive
- Story order

Different subject matter lends itself to different organization. In a job as large as writing a book, you'll need several methods within a chapter, but for clarity's sake, choose just one for your table of contents. The following explanation for each of these six methods of organization, and examples based on them, should help you make a final selection.

Chronological Order

The chronological method of organization presents information based on the passage of time, usually from earlier time to later. Although only a few types of nonfiction books, such as histories, biographies, or travelogues, feature chronological order, many books use a chronological system of organization in at least one chapter, for instance, in a history chapter. Activists Emily Kay and Anita Saville used chronological order in their chapter summaries for the compelling biography of Molly Yard, former president of the National Organization for Women (NOW) in their proposal *We'll Remember in November: Molly Yard's Gift to Women's Rights*. Beginning with Molly Yard's early childhood in China, the book progresses through time to Yard's Democratic-party and civil-rights activism. It chronicles the history of her leadership of NOW and beyond.

Memoir and autobiography also rely upon a chronological method of organizaiton, but often in conjunction with, or secondary to, "story order."

Increasing or Decreasing Order of Importance or Complexity

For the right material, this method of organization gives readers a clear understanding of a book's idea. For example, Cotter and Green used this pattern for their book. From their concept statement, we learn that "... [readers] will learn five amazingly simple, increasingly potent levels for countering manipulation." This method of organization is an ideal map for their book's development.

If you believe a reader's understanding depends upon understanding simpler principles and information first, then you should organize your book according to an increasing order of complexity. That's what Mabel Armstrong did to create the table of contents for her book, *The Practical Woman's Guide to Real Estate Investment*. Before the novice can learn how to buy and sell to make money, she must first cover "Setting Your Goals...," "Identifying Your Team," "Learning the Ropes," "Analyzing Properties to Purchase," etc. The author introduces more complex ideas only after the reader has been exposed to simpler concepts.

Order of Need

In this method of organization, your reader's need determines your book's outline. Perhaps your book involves step-by-step instructions. Take a moment to look at the table of contents for this book. It's organized by a reader's need to create a proposal, rather than in the final order it will be presented to an agent or editor. Order of need also proved to be the best outlining choice for Carolyn Kortge. In *The Spirited Walker*, readers are introduced to material in the order they will need it.

Chapter 1: A Spirited Route: Whole-Body Walking
Chapter 2: First Steps: A Guide to Getting Started
Chapter 3: Spirited Walks: Words for Walkers
Chapter 4: Spirited Walks: Visions for Walkers
Chapter 5: Spirited Walks: Body Work for Walkers
Chapter 6: Daily Walks: A Practice of Commitment
Chapter 7: Out of Step: Stumbling on Resistance
Chapter 8: Motivation: Walker's Block to Starter's Block
Chapter 9: Healing Paths: Crossing Rocky Stretches
Chapter 10: A Spiritual Nature: Inspiration from Outside
Chapter 11: Pilgrimages: A Quest for Long Walks and Direction

Classification and Division

You can classify your book's material in two ways: You can divide the whole into classes, or you can place a thing into the whole of which it is a part.

Naturopathic physician Dr. Skye Weintraub created a book that lent itself perfectly to both classification and division. The first part of her book defines the eleven cell salts. In a "repertory," readers may look up symptoms or ailments, which are broken down into further divisions.

Linda Jean Shepherd chose classification and division for her book, *Lifting the Veil: The Feminine Face of Science*. After background chapters that define the broader classifications of "masculine principle" and "feminine principle," the author divides subsequent chapters into further divisions of the "feminine principle." Thus, the reader is led through chapters about qualities defined by the author as belonging to "the feminine principle"—chapters including: feeling, receptivity, subjectivity, egalitarianism, nurturing, cooperation, feminine intuition, and relatedness.

Inductive and Deductive

When an author's intent is to persuade readers to embrace his or her point of view, the primary organizing method should be similar to a formal argument. Because "argumentative writing" commands entire texts, review argument form before writing a book intended primarily to persuade. The two primary ways to organize an argument are either by inductive or deductive reasoning.

Ralph Nansen chose to organize his impassioned book on space-based solar energy satellites using an inductive method of organization. Early chapters of *Sun Power* establish the context for his book and lead the reader through existing policy and former energy "eras." Middle chapters explain how solar satellite systems and energy beams work. They overcome any reader arguments about technological limitations. Subsequent chapters argue for economic viability. The final chapters unveil Nansen's solar-energy development plan and leave the reader breathless regarding the potential for space development and a renewal of the earth-based environment. This is an example of a successful argument at its best.

Story Order

A variety of nonfiction subjects can be novel-like in form—biography, autobiography, and memoir among them. In such story form, generally an inciting incident introduces the author or subject and a problem that grows worse as the author/subject seeks to solve it. The story culminates in a climax where the problem is resolved and the person learns something fundamental about life and him- or herself. Memoir, autobiography, and biography gain cohesion and drama through this method of organization.

Two unusual members of the nonfiction family are true crime

and humor. Both require the preparation of a proposal, just like any other nonfiction book. Although true crime is classified as nonfiction, because it reports on actual life events and people, its overall structure is considered literary because it resembles that of a novel. Within a chapter, however, its structure relies upon analysis—the close examination of all theories and evidence.

Humor also fits within the order of a story better than common nonfiction methods of organization. Consider Bill Cosby's books, such as *Fathering* or *Turning Fifty*. The material is narrative. Most humorists tell stories, real and anecdotal, by organizing their material around single subjects—dogs, ex-husbands, parenting, growing old. Both true crime and humor, like novels, convey a "message," a theme for the reader to mull over. First-time authors of either humor or true crime can save themselves the heartbreak of endless rejections by studying the structure of fiction; in particular, how to craft a novel. In fact, I recommend that authors who believe that story order is the best method of organization for their books should read *The Writer's Journey* by Christopher Vogler. He gives a superb explanation of the mythic hero's journey as the organizational blueprint for stories.

After reviewing these six different methods of organization, select one as your "guiding light" for the duration of time it takes you to write your book. Your decision will inspire confidence in your proposed book's structure, and it will give you confidence that you are on track when you write your book. Now you can craft a table of contents and begin to write your chapter summaries.

Selecting and Writing the Table of Contents and Chapter Summaries

With basic decisions about the organization of the whole book, you're ready to move forward by doing the following:

- Establish a first-chapter hook.
- Rewrite working titles into chapter titles, and draft a table of contents.
- Choose subtitles or chapter descriptions.

- Find each chapter's main topics.
- Craft topic sentences and chapter summaries.

ESTABLISH A FIRST-CHAPTER HOOK

Each of the six methods of organizing a book dictates its own starting point, such as the earliest point in time for chronological order or gathering material and tools for order based on reader need. These natural starting points may, however, be less than exciting. Memoirs and autobiographies seldom succeed if they begin with, "I was born in...."

Your readers eagerly seek to receive the *benefits* that your book promises. Background, history, and developmental information rarely deliver these coveted benefits. For some books, the most compelling first chapter will be an exploration of the problem or problems for which your book offers some solution. Then, an exploration of the problem and its roots may draw readers in as they anticipate relief or answers from the rest of the book.

For the memoir genre, a most compelling beginning is often in the middle of a highly dramatic event, usually an event that became a turning point in the author's life and serves as the touchstone for the book's theme.

> All books should start with a lead chapter that hooks reader attention.

If your table of contents is a menu, your first chapter is the appetizer. Decide what will draw your readers into the book, will whet their appetites, then review the material on leads in chapter eight. Finally, select a chapter-one hook.

REWRITE WORKING TITLES; DRAFT A TABLE OF CONTENTS

Study the tables of contents from books similar to the one you plan to write. If you decide to vary your book's organization, chapter lengths, its style, or titling, be able to justify it. Other books in the same field as yours define a norm. Deciding to be different based on whim is not sufficient!

Chapter titles, like your book title, offer more opportunities for adding pizzazz. Some titles excite more than others. Consideration of this fact is especially vital when the subject matter for two published books is otherwise identical. For serious subjects, find evocative or provocative chapter titles.

Select firm chapter titles based on your selection of one method of organization for your book. Check your titles' grammatical structures and make sure they are parallel. Now, write down your chapter titles in order, beginning with your first-chapter hook. This is your table of contents.

CHOOSE SUBTITLES AND CHAPTER DESCRIPTIONS

Some books use chapter subtitles or chapter descriptions and some don't. Because no set rules exist for this decision, let convention guide you. Once again, review books similar in content to yours. Make your titles and subtitles parallel in length, grammatical structure, and style.

FIND EACH CHAPTER'S MAIN TOPICS

Review your research material for a given chapter and jot down main topics. Do the required research or brainstorm to fill in missing information wherever your research is too thin, or not yet begun. Weed out duplications and, in the order you've decided for each chapter, rank topics from most to least important.

CRAFT TOPIC SENTENCES AND WRITE CHAPTER SUMMARIES

Avoid the use of Roman numerals. Chapter summaries may be written in complete sentences or in fragments that begin with an active verb. For instance, some active verbs I used in my chapter summaries include: *explains, suggests, defines, shows, ends with, discusses, introduces, lists, offers, details, features, draws, gives, presents, and advises.*

Although editors and agents accept "This chapter explores… Next, this chapter relates…and, this chapter ends with…," sentences that begin with active verbs are terse and dynamic. You may use sentences without subjects, such as "Offers a new look…" instead of "This chapter offers a new look…" Where possible, avoid repetition of the verb, "will," such as "The author will explore…" Writers fall into this trap when they have not yet written the chapter. Drop the word "will" and use active verbs.

Summarize the topics for each chapter in *specific* terms. Include

---

Sidebar 9-1
Sample: Chapter Summary
Dr. Michael Rousell

Chapter Three: Constructing Our Reality

Children come into this world with a crude ability to interpret events in their lives. Through experience and guidance, they eventually construct a mental representation of the world and of themselves in it: "The world is scary—I'm vulnerable" or "The world is fascinating—I'm adventurous." These representations become their rose-colored spectacles for interpreting events in their lives. Their way of interpreting events also tends to be self-affirming, perpetuating itself. Victims see oppression and feel persecuted. Explorers see opportunities and feel adventurous.

Chapter Three Features:
- Illustrates how children instinctively interpret their experiences based on their own peculiar mental representatives of the world and of themselves.
- Examines how children actively interpret their experiences by imposing subjective meaning on objective events.
- Reveals how children's mental representations, whether correct or incorrect, generate self-affirming interpretations, which in turn frequently initiate self-fulfilling prophecies.
- Finishes by revealing why children are so susceptible to suggestions, particularly by parent figures such as teachers.

facts, figures, statistics, dates, and give specific names to terms, places, persons, and concepts.

Sidebar 9-1 shows an example of one chapter summary for Dr. Michael Rousell's book, *Breaking the Spell: Spontaneous Events That Shape a Child's Life.*

Limit each chapter summary to one manuscript page. Single-spaced or double-spaced summaries are a matter of personal choice, although you should always double-space sample chapters. Writers who elaborate beyond one page risk writing the chapter rather than summarizing it. On the other hand, if you provide too brief a summary, an agent or editor might question whether your idea has enough substance to warrant book-length publication.

Review Sidebar 9-2 to understand the steps that take you from idea to outline to chapter summaries.

Troubleshooting Special Cases

- Chapter summaries for simple books
- Chapter summaries for complex books
- Chapter summaries for memoirs and autobiographies

CHAPTER SUMMARIES FOR SIMPLE BOOKS

If you're a writer who leans toward brevity in your summaries, simply return to your stacks of research material for a particular chapter and see what you might have left out. Sometimes, you can integrate a less developed chapter with another one. More often, an inadequate chapter summary indicates a need for further research into the topics of that section. After all, most writers prepare a proposal in order to write a book. Major research looms ahead, as well as development of the basic ideas. Even so, if a particular chapter is too skimpy for purposes of a good proposal, you'll need to do more research.

Short chapters are common in step-by-step how-to books such as craft books. Most of the content of each chapter is likely to be how-to directions. No complex concepts or historical backdrops.

Sidebar 9-2
From Idea to Outline to Chapter Summaries

1. Review your purpose in writing a book and the profile of your intended reader.
2. Divide your book ideas and research notes into piles of similar topics.
3. Assign working chapter titles for these piles or files.
4. Select a method of organization to outline your book from the list of six types: chronological order, increasing or decreasing importance or complexity, order of need, classification and division, inductive and deductive, or literary order.
5. Study examples of tables of contents in books similar to yours, and create your own to correspond with the method of organization you choose.
6. Rewrite chapter titles for subject clarity, including a first chapter that hooks reader interest.
7. If appropriate to your book, choose subtitles and descriptions. Construct titles and subtitles so they are parallel in subject, grammar, and style.
8. List topics within each chapter beginning with a carefully selected lead topic.
9. Write a chapter summary for each chapter's material.

Aline Renauld Prince's book, *Cheapskate Decorating,* is one such example. When the chapter content is so straightforward, the summaries can only be brief. Here is her short paragraph on her second chapter, "Balloon Shades That Give Windows a Lift":

> Describes these shades and how to make and mount them. Detailed are two styles. Instructions included for each pattern, how to figure needed yardage, how to make the mounting and shades out of (eco)logical materials. Requires reader to use a cloth tape, do basic math, figure yardage, cut

fabric, do straight line machine sewing, cut two boards, nail them and install certain screws, attach pulling rings, and tie the cords.

Actually, most of this paragraph contains padding, pleasant padding. The entirety of her chapter could have been summarized as "Describes and details two styles of balloon shades, including how to make and mount them." However, the longer description should give the agent/editor a secure feeling that the simple tasks involved in making these shades are well within the capability of even a novice, so the "padding" serves a purpose.

CHAPTER SUMMARIES FOR COMPLEX BOOKS

Chapter summaries pose particular challenges for writers of books that are highly technical or filled with many levels of meaning. To present the details of a chapter in a technical book without swamping the reader with unknowns, consider the example in Sidebar 9-3 by the coauthors of *Act Like an Owner.* Because their book is divided into parts as well as chapters, this chapter summary was preceded with a two-paragraph summary of part two.

CHAPTER SUMMARIES FOR MEMOIRS AND AUTOBIOGRAPHIES

Writers of memoirs and autobiographies, including travel writers, face a special challenge in writing *succinct* chapter summaries. First, they must make clear to the agent/editor what is happening in the external environment of their stories. Second, they must bring out the personal meaning of their experiences. Each chapter summary must demonstrate that it supports a theme, delivers a pearl of wisdom, or offers a captivating insight to the reader. To satisfy this necessity, these authors face the job of braiding several strands into their stories. Doing so may take them into a second page for each chapter summary. They must resist the temptation of developing the actual chapter and just stick to a summary.

Even though memoirs and autobiographies are written in first person, many proposal writers prefer to write their summaries in

Sidebar 9-3
Sample: Chapter Summary
Blonchek & O'Neill

Chapter Two: The Ties that Bind

Chapter Two defines corporate culture and an ownership culture for the reader. It begins by looking at culture in society. The focus narrows as corporate culture is defined and examples of typical corporate cultures are presented.

Chapter Two then reviews the three types of corporate cultures identified by John Kotter in *Corporate Culture and Performance* including: a strong culture, a strategically fit culture, and an adaptive culture. Examples of each culture are provided, and an ownership culture is positioned as the ultimate adaptive culture—the type of culture that has the strongest, positive impact on company performance.

Next, the reader is introduced to the principles and values that define an *ownership culture* including:

- External focus—complete focus on understanding and serving the customer and not on internal policies and procedures
- Flexibility—quickly adapting to new customer priorities and market opportunities
- Leadership—the ability to motivate, inspire, and align people
- Trust—the entire organization believing in the vision and purpose of the business and each other
- Holistic view of business—everyone understanding and monitoring all aspects of the business including strategy, economics, processes, and people.

Examples and anecdotes expand the reader's understanding of an ownership culture.

(Continued)

Chapter Two concludes by tackling the issue of identifying the current culture at work in an organization. Through the use of real-life examples, Chapter Two illustrates how listening to the company's folklore can identify a corporate culture. It illustrates how a corporate culture is easily identified during times of difficulty—especially when a fundamental principle is broken.

Sidebar 9-4
Sample: Chapter Summary—Memoir Chanrithy Him

Chapter Four: When Broken Glass Begins to Float

We feel the early shudders as Phnom Penh crumbles to the Khmer Rouge. My uncle, a Cambodian Air pilot, flees the country. Thus begins the surreal forced evacuation of 2 million people. In one week, a nation's capital is emptied. I'm part of this strange exodus. My education with the new political regime begins when I find my schoolyard heaped with dead soldiers; we see men marched off at gunpoint; corpses float in the river as we walk across a bridge with other unwilling refugees. We walk for a week into the countryside, returning to the village where my father was born.

Chapter Five: There Are No Good-byes

While listening to a Voice of America broadcast, we are spied upon. The Khmer Rouge begin to systematically exterminate anyone who is educated. My father and uncles are tricked into revealing their identities and later executed. Women and children are sent to labor in the fields. Recent arrivals are shipped north in freight cars, a fearful cargo. Rumbling in the dark, cramped train cars, we wonder if we are being taken to our deaths.

third person. Avoiding first person helps some writers to summarize. Because chapter summaries seem to be the most difficult for the writer of memoir or autobiography, I've chosen a second sample chapter summary in Sidebar 9-4. It is written by author Chanrithy Him for her memoir, *When Broken Glass Begins to Float*. Notice the uncluttered and forceful way that she relates horrifying events.

Here is a small portion of the summary for chapter five, "Lucia's Kitchen, Clara's Restaurant," in Susan Caperna Lloyd's memoir, *No Pictures In My Grave*:

Back in Trapani, the author finds a contemporary "dark goddess" hidden in the white cloaks of propriety. She is Lucia, Carlo's mother, reminding the author of her grandmother. She is an ageless crone, cooks constantly like Car-

---

Sidebar 9-5
Seven Steps to Stirring Chapter Summaries

1. Avoid weak beginnings to sentences, such as "It is" and "There is."
2. Vary sentence beginnings, as well as sentence types and lengths.
3. Minimize use of "This chapter…" and "Readers will…."
4. Select active verbs; reduce use of to-be verbs: is/was/were/be/being/been.
5. Include topics, terms, facts, and other specifics.
6. Make sure each chapter summary includes at least one clear benefit and one specific feature.
7. Limit summaries to one page, single-spaced. (See "troubleshooting special cases" for exceptions.) Make sure that short summaries, one to two paragraphs, contain enough specific topics to display a well-defined chapter.

olina did, and teaches the author to make couscous. This grain staple's fertility symbolism is counterpointed by the deathlike dirge Lucia sings. She sifts the grain while shrieking countless verses of the Madonna's lamentation. Now the author hears the song of darkness, of longing that Sicilian women sing. Though Lucia is a formidable matriarch, she is a caged bird....

Chapter summaries for memoirs, autobiographies, and travel narratives require an extra amount of finesse because you must boil down everything into its strongest essence—blending description, action, information, and interpretation. Your goal is to convince the agent/editor that your reader will be so powerfully moved that he or she will share your insights and emotions.

For a final polish on your chapter summaries, read and apply Sidebar 9-5, "Seven Steps to a Stirring Chapter Summary."

CHAPTER TEN

The Heart of Your Proposal: Sample Chapters

Chapter Goal: To select and write sample chapters that will best showcase your book and sell your proposal package.

Concept Statement
About the Book
About the Author
About the Market
About the Competition
Production Details
About Promotion
Table of Contents
Chapter Summaries
* Sample Chapters
The Appendix

After learning how to write in the structure and style required for the proposal sections, now you get to change gears. Writing your sample chapters—or rewriting those you've previously drafted—requires the adoption of a different mind set and style than the one you assumed for writing the proposal. In these chapters, you must make good on all your promises and claims and satisfy the anticipation you've generated by writing an exciting proposal.

Definition and Purpose

Sample chapters are carefully written and thoughtfully selected excerpts from your book. While some agents and editors accept two chapters, or rarely just one substantial chapter, most agents/editors require at least three sample chapters. If you are writing a memoir or autobiography, expect to offer anywhere from six chapters to half the work. Occasionally, you'll be asked to supply the entire book before receiving a contract offer.

Well-written sample chapters convince editors that you can complete the book you propose. Sample chapters follow through on the promises you made in "About the Book." They showcase the contribution your book offers to make. Last of all, they give you an opportunity to display your unique style of writing, thereby proving you have the skill to craft a book—and the originality to make it interesting.

Criteria for Selection of Sample Chapters

If this is your first book, editors will expect a good chunk of writing, anywhere from thirty to sixty double-spaced pages. Put yourself behind an editor's reading glasses. Editors considering a previously unpublished author must be assured that you can finish such a big project and

> Choose to write the sample chapters that are most impressive and most representative.

not drop the ball halfway through. One would think editors would insist on seeing an entire book, as they do first novels. In contrast to nonfiction, fiction can go awry at any point in the process, regardless of a good outline. In this manner, memoir is akin to fiction. The proposal, including the chapter summaries and sample chapters, typically provides enough writing for editors to make an accurate judgment to confidently grant a contract.

Some editors prefer to see nonconsecutive sample chapters while others like consecutive chapters. Memoir or autobiography is always consecutive, beginning with chapter one or a prologue. An editor with St. Martin's Press expressed a widespread preference in saying: "While the chapters don't need to be from the beginning of the book, they do need to be substantive, rather than simply introductory." With the exception of memoir and autobiography, you should select your sample chapters to fulfill three functions:

- They should be the most representative of your originality or the unique contribution your book makes.
- They should be the chapters that best showcase your writing.
- They should include at least one chapter that is easier to write than others—for your sake.

Many times, chapters that capture your originality or your unique contribution are not necessarily consecutive. Introductory or first chapters rarely represent the book's originality or showcase your writing. Chapter one may be the hardest of all the chapters in a book to write. In my experience, most writers consider beginnings to be tortuous at worst, unpleasant at best. Beginnings also require more rewriting than any other chapter. Perhaps this universal phenomena has something to do with the specter of facing a blank page, and several hundred more beyond it, at a time when your brain is stuffed full of the entire book's contents. Or, perhaps you haven't truly been able to see the organization clearly and need to spend more time outlining. Most beginnings warm the reader to your ideas and lay down foundation material, background, definitions, or history. In middle and later chapters, readers encounter the material that conveys the core of the book's message.

Another form of insurance is to include the first two chapters, then writing and submitting one from later in your work. You orient the agent/editor to your ideas and then deliver a more complex, original application of them later. And, if your book is structured into larger parts or sections, I advise showing a chapter from each section.

The best way to select sample chapters is to read through your chapter summaries. Some chapters will look easier to write but may not showcase your writing or supply the requirement mentioned by the St. Martin's editor to be "substantive." Recall the ways in which you believe your book to be better and different from others in print, and choose the chapters that are most representative of that contribution.

Writing Your "Sample Chapters"

Once you've selected your sample chapters, you can be appreciative of the outlining work you did for your table of contents and chapter summaries. The good news is that your chapter summaries represent your hardest work in producing solid, well-organized sample chapters. The bad news is that well-written sample chapters require attention to several more details, namely:

- Craft a hooking lead for each sample chapter.
- Define terms and be clear about the purpose of each paragraph, section, and chapter.
- Plant a reader payoff, a benefit, on every page.
- Rewrite and edit for clarity, conciseness, and style.

CRAFT A HOOKING LEAD FOR EACH SAMPLE CHAPTER

In chapter eight, I introduced the different types of leads you could use to begin "About the Book." These same leads can be used to begin your sample chapters.

You may recall that your sample chapters will have two types of readers. These sample chapters will be read by agents and editors, who may not be as forgiving as the second group of readers, your book's purchasers.

Because you are in a competitive situation, vying with hundreds of authors for agent representation and then again for selection at the editorial committee, polish your sample-chapter leads. Study books like yours and determine which chapters obviously have been crafted with leads in mind. Then decide which leads seem most powerful and best suited for your material. Try several and select the best.

DEFINE TERMS AND BE CLEAR ABOUT PURPOSE

Define terms or words used in specialized ways. It's so easy for you, the expert on your subject, to forget that the reader doesn't know, for instance, what a sidebar is. A sidebar is a short article that accompanies the chapter, usually set off graphically on a page by itself, boxed within the text or otherwise distinguished.

As you select and write each sample chapter, remember that it has a purpose, as does each section and each paragraph within it. Sometimes the content will suggest two directions—an author's purpose versus a reader's need. For instance, I've collected a stack of great proposal examples. I'd like to supply you with six examples. That's author's purpose. You the reader simply want to understand the point I'm making and one example would do just fine. That's reader's need. It's a balance that must be struck in the interest of clarity. Cast yourself in both roles to better appreciate the problem; then give priority to your reader's need.

PLANT A READER PAYOFF, A BENEFIT, ON EVERY PAGE

Payoffs reward your reader for their effort. Payoffs are particular benefits that may or may not be the same as the ones you touted in "About the Book." They could be anything from understanding, motivation, an instruction, or an example, to a vicarious thrill.

Although one payoff per page may not be an average you maintain throughout your book, approximate it in your sample chapters for this one good reason: sales. When you are finished rewriting your book

> Make sure you plant at least one payoff on every page of each sample chapter.

to meet your contract, you can smooth out any differences in style. At the proposal stage, you're selling the sizzle of your book; in the sample chapters you're adding substance—your belief that you have something new, different, better than what has been previously published. Make sure your agent or editor can validate your belief on every page.

REWRITE AND EDIT FOR CLARITY, CONCISENESS, AND STYLE

Throughout these chapters, I've emphasized basic techniques of professional nonfiction writing. Here, in the sample chapters (the writing that you hope thousands or tens of thousands of readers will pore over), you want to present your very best writing. A strongly crafted lead gets your chapter started right. Ferret out other weaknesses in technique by reviewing books on professional nonfiction writing that are recommended in the Resource Directory. Two of my favorites are by instructor, novelist, and columnist Gary Provost— *Make Your Words Work* and *100 Ways to Improve Your Writing*. For a grammar review, try Val Dumond's *Grammar for Grownups*.

"Finished" is a word many writers never use. The nature of writing is such that it can always be improved. After you have written and revised your sample chapters until you can see nothing more that you can do, you're ready for professional editing. Once you've reached the limits of your ability to self-edit, the logical next step is to ask someone else to comment on your work. Unless your nearest and dearest are writing professionals, let a qualified person, outside of well-meaning family or friends, critique and edit your work. A lot can be said for having your material read by someone with no vested interest.

When you prepare your work for a freelance editor, be prepared to specify what you would like that person to accomplish. Of course, you'll want your editor to do copyediting—to catch your typos, grammar, spelling, and punctuation errors. Because poor organization tops the list of weaknesses in nonfiction writing, specifically mention this concern. To get the most help, supply chapter summaries and outlines of sample chapters.

Exceptions and Special Cases

Here are some exceptions and special cases to the guidelines laid out at the beginning of the chapter for writing your sample chapters:

- Cookbooks and list books
- Options for previously published authors

- Proposals that need more sample chapters
- When to include an introduction in lieu of a sample chapter
- What to do when you have a finished book before beginning the proposal process
- Handling artwork and photographs

COOKBOOKS AND LIST BOOKS

Because cookbooks and books of lists or other groupings may not have traditional chapters, it would make no sense to talk in terms of text-filled chapters. Instead, for these kinds of books, you need to supply a sample of the intended format and content. For instance, if a cookbook section begins with some author narrative and follows with twenty pages of recipes, it would be enough to supply the chapter leads plus three recipes from two or three sections. In a list book, or other collage of material, you want to supply a representative sample of what makes your collection so unique. Remember, you need to supply enough to convey your vision of the book and convince an agent or editor that you have come up with an idea and approach that is new, different, or better.

OPTIONS FOR PREVIOUSLY PUBLISHED AUTHORS

When you've already had a book published and are working with the same agent, you *may* be able to submit a proposal without sample chapters. There are some rewards in a writer's life! In fact, you may be able to get by with an abbreviated form of the proposal that hits the highlights of each section but offers much less detail. Why? Because you've demonstrated your ability to write and presumably have one or more successes to your credit. Regardless, be prepared for the possibility that a new publisher—not the one who published your prior book—may still require a full proposal.

PROPOSALS THAT NEED MORE SAMPLE CHAPTERS

Some editors believe that two chapters are enough to demonstrate writing ability and more won't make a difference. However, agents or editors may request that you produce additional chapters, if the samples you present are short, and if they feel unsure of your writing skill. This holds true especially for a writer whose qualifications might appear thin and who lacks publishing credits.

For instance, I worked with a psychologist who was writing a self-help book. John had solid credentials as a therapist, but no publishing credits and no history of public appearances. He'd been quietly doing a great job in his field for years and years. Now he wanted to go public. He'd never written articles. He lacked what agent Denise Marcil calls "national outreach," meaning a record of television appearances, radio shows, and seminars and workshops. Even if John wrote a third or fourth sample chapter, he was unlikely to secure interest from a major publisher. Instead, he would be lucky to see this first book published by a small to mid-sized publisher until he gained name recognition.

If you fall into a similar situation, don't wait for an agent to tell you to write a third chapter. You may simply get rejected, never knowing if more exposure to your writing and your book would have made the difference. You may also benefit through increased skill and confidence by writing more of your book during the proposal process. John had to write a rough draft of his entire book simply to learn how to write for the general reader.

When to Include an Introduction in Lieu of a Sample Chapter

Often, introductions explain where authors received the inspiration for their books. They may explain philosophies about the material and give quick overviews of the contents. Frequently, they tell the reader how to make the best use of a book. In other words, they offer introductory thoughts. Generally speaking, an introduction should not be selected as a sample chapter.

If your introduction begins with foundation material, and offers theories upon which the rest of the book depends, your introduction may be necessary for an agent/editor to grasp your ideas. If this is the case, you must offer the introduction as one sample chapter and provide chapters one and two as well. Perhaps, though, you should

consider renumbering your chapters and call your present introduction "chapter one."

WHAT TO DO WHEN YOU HAVE A FINISHED BOOK
BEFORE BEGINNING THE PROPOSAL PROCESS

My heart sinks when I get calls from writers who have been slaving
away without knowing the "rules" of publishing. "I've spent three
years writing my book," the writer might say. "I'm ready to get it
published. Can you tell me whether I should send it to an agent or
to a publisher directly?"

If you have finished your book, you have the luxury of really
knowing your material, having worked out changes and bugs from
your original vision. The "however" implied here is that you must
still write a proposal, and your proposal will only include two or
three sample chapters. No one wants you to send your entire manuscript—with a few rare exceptions. If you have an "in"—let's say
your brother-in-law is an editorial assistant at Scribners—well,
maybe he'll read the book or get it to the correct reader. Maybe
you're dating an agent and she says she'll read the whole book. If
you can't lasso an exception, then put the book aside, write a proposal, and select your best chapters to include as samples.

HANDLING ARTWORK AND PHOTOGRAPHY

If your book includes illustrations or photos created by an artist
whose contribution you deem important, then you should submit
samples of his or her work. If you have illustrated your sample
chapters, or purchased artwork or photography for your sample
chapters, include examples of these works—whether or not you
share co-authorship with the artist.

Submit copies (don't send originals) of illustrations on 8½" x
11" paper, and label where they belong in the text. When you reach
the place in your sample chapter where an illustration would be,
simply type a code, such as "illustration #1." Then include the illustration page after the text where it would appear. An additional clue

to where the illustration would appear is the page number on the illustration. Make sure it is the *same* page number as the page of text where it will ultimately appear. If you have more than one illustration (or photo) per page, you can go down the alphabet to label each one, using a page number plus a letter, such as 52a, 52b, 52c. This coding indicates that three different illustrations will appear on page 52 in the text. If your illustration will contain a caption when printed, for submission, make sure you type this underneath the illustration.

For color artwork and most photographs, submission of laser photocopies is fine. If you intend to include black-and-white photography, you must decide whether you believe laser copies are sufficient, or whether you prefer the more traditional 8" x 10" glossies. For slides, buy the kind of insert that allows you to slip them into pockets; these come often twenty to a sheet. On a paper behind the slides, include identification and caption details. The slides and the caption sheet are usually packaged in a folder pocket that holds the entire proposal, or at the end of the sample chapters.

If your artwork is something you generate with a computer program, some form of line drawings, graphs, tables, or figures, you can probably include these items in sequence within your text. If you're not able to integrate them into your text, put the text first and the artwork on the page that follows, as indicated earlier in this chapter.

It's perfectly acceptable to direct the agent/editor to your web site to see further illustrations, photos, or artwork.

Once you've written and revised your sample chapters to the best of your ability, and have shipped them off to a friend or editor for more input, forget about them. Use the time to zero in on writing the remaining sections of your proposal.

CHAPTER ELEVEN

Production Details: If You Had Your Way…

Chapter Goal: To specify your requirements and preferences about your book's format, production, and delivery.

Concept Statement
About the Book
About the Author
About the Market
About the Competition
* Production Details
About Promotion
Table of Contents
Chapter Summaries
Sample Chapters
The Appendix

By now, you should have a clear idea about how you want your book to look and feel in its finished form. This is the section in the proposal where you translate your wishes into specifications. Not that you can expect to get exactly what you wish. Although publishers have more to say about how your book is produced than you do, in the "Production Details" section of your proposal, you get to state your preferences.

Definition and Purpose

Simply expressed, this section of the proposal gives the physical specifications of your book. It lists everything you will include in addition to the text, information that helps the publisher estimate production costs and a retail price. How much your book will cost is a critical factor in whether a publisher will make an offer—and in determining the size of an advance.

From a writer's point of view, "Production Details" clarifies your vision of the whole, commits you to a delivery deadline, and gives you a chance to articulate how you would like your book to look in its finished form.

A Sample "Production Details"

This section of the proposal differs widely from author to author. In length, it may be as short as a paragraph or as long as two pages. For a standard example, in Sidebar 11-1, I've chosen Dr. Lipman's "Production Details" for his book on snoring.

STYLE

As you can see by Dr. Lipman's example, the style of this section departs from the narrative style of the rest of the proposal. A list replaces paragraphs. Sentence fragments are used more often than complete sentences. The typical order of information is: length and other format ideas, delivery date, front matter, back matter, and then anything unique to your book not covered by these categories.

LIST AND EXPLANATION OF PARTS

At most, your "Production Details" may include eleven different items. If listing three parts is all that your book requires, then your "Production Details" might be as simple as Val Dumond's for *Grammar For Grownups*: (note her departure from list style):

The proposed book is already researched, tested, and ready for writing. The manuscript could be completed in

four months. Book length will be about 200 pages, divided
into three sections:

Section 1, Parts of Speech (75 pages); Section 2, Punctuation
(75 pages); Section 3, Style (50 pages).

Sidebar 11-1
Sample: Production Details
Dr. Derek S. Lipman

Length:	30,000–35,000 words
Delivery:	6 months following delivery of first advance installment
Illustrations:	25–30, b&w
Sidebars:	5–6
Permissions:	Being sought for material in Chapters 1 & 7 (see enclosed letter)
Front matter:	Foreword offered by Melvin Belli, attorney (had UPPP operation; see enclosed letter)
Introduction:	Offered by Jack Gluckman, M.D.
	— Professor of Otolaryngology and Director of the Head and Neck Surgery Service, University of Cincinnati
	— Examiner for American Board of Otolaryngology
	— Author/coauthor of numerous medical articles and textbooks
Back matter:	Appendix: names/addresses of U.S. sleep centers
Bibliography	
Index	

Select from the following list of eleven possible specifications,
and include only those items that apply directly to your project.

- Length
- Delivery date
- Computer system (optional)
- Format (optional)
- Sidebars
- Permissions
- Front matter
- Back matter
- Photographs and Artwork
- Endorsements
- Resources Needed to Complete Your Book

LENGTH

Since you haven't written your entire book, how can you know how long it will be? Make an educated guess. It has to be a fairly reasonable guess, because you could be held to it.

Your best gauge for estimating total length is to take the average number of pages in your sample chapters and multiply by the number of chapters you decided upon in your table of contents. To fine-tune your estimate, reread your chapter summaries and decide whether some chapters might end up longer or shorter than your average sample chapter. If so, make an adjustment to your estimate.

Agents and editors prefer estimates that have a rounded-off number of manuscript pages, versus a guess at final printed pages (about which you cannot know). Most authors give a range within 25 pages, such as 250–275 pages or 200–225 pages. Authors who have already written their books may give the word count from their computers (rounded off) such as 65,000 words.

Even though you don't really know if your book will end up within the range you project, you must express a firm figure. Part of this goes back to sales. You want to convey confidence and certainty. After all, you are the authority on your book. Therefore, make a calculated guess based upon the standard 250 words per double-spaced page.

DELIVERY DATE

If, at the time you market your proposal, you truly have a finished, polished manuscript, put "upon receipt of advance" as your delivery date. If you're half done, or one third done, you can make an estimate based on the time it has already taken you and on the demands in your life.

Delivery dates are typically expressed in three-month increments: 3, 6, 9, 12, or 15 months. If you've only written your sample chapters, don't commit to a delivery date earlier than 9 months. In general, even short books require months to write and rewrite. Don't cut yourself short. On the other hand, publishers don't favor estimates beyond 12 to 15 months, because many acquire books to fit publishing slots within 12 to 15 months from the date of acquisition.

> Ultimately, specify what delivery date you can reasonably and comfortably fulfill.

In contrast, smaller publishers may be able to publish within six months of acquisition and would prefer delivery as soon as possible. Unhampered by bureaucracy, smaller publishers can get your work into print more quickly.

COMPUTER SYSTEM

Now that most computers can translate nearly any electronic file, it is no longer mandatory to specify what kind of computer software you use, or which PC type—IBM, IBM clone, or Macintosh. However, you are expected to be able to deliver your manuscript in an electronic form, on floppy disk or via e-mail, depending on your publisher's preference. You must also supply, assuming your publisher wants it, a hard copy of your manuscript. Haven't things changed!

In *Three Cats, Two Dogs, One Journey Through Multiple Pet Loss*, author David Congalton supplied this short but concise entry in his "Production Details": "Manuscript available on disk or via electronic transmission in Microsoft Word."

FORMAT

Format refers to the preferred size of a book and its binding. Most writers *don't* include this in their "Production Details," because publishers decide, if not control, this decision. You may be accustomed to thinking that the best books come out in hardback first, then in trade paperback, and finally in mass-market paperback. Times have changed, though, and anything goes. Especially with the large publishers, they may opt for one, two, or all three formats at the same time. Many publishers, especially small publishers, may publish all of their books in trade paperback. The actual dimensions often depend on the sheet size used by the printer and the amount of waste that different trim sizes produce. These are not author decisions.

That said, you may still express your vision for your book. For her biography, *The Last Zapatista*, Susan Lloyd created a section called "Format," as follows:

FORMAT
Size: 6" x 9"
Pages: 290
HARDBACK/TRADE PAPERBACK: Prefer the book to be published both in hardback and quality trade paperback.

If your book includes large photographs or special charts, it may need a specific size or binding, so make sure to specify this under "Format."

SIDEBARS

Sidebars, those short articles that supplement a chapter, sometimes involve production set-up for graphics—for instance, to enclose in a box or to shade with a shadow or other effect. Sidebars may add production time, which translates into additional production cost. State or estimate the number of sidebars you anticipate. In the proposal for this book, for instance, I created a heading for sidebars and gave an estimate of ten to fifteen.

PERMISSIONS

When you use other people's copyright-protected, printed, or published material, or the essence of their original ideas, you must give them credit in your book. Anything you find on the Web, including e-mail correspondence, belongs to the person who wrote it. Credit means quoting or paraphrasing the creator's words and giving attribution; that is, citing the name of the author. You may provide this credit in the text, in a footnote, or in a bibliography.

> Your agent, and later your editor, can help you decide if you must seek formal permission to use someone else's material.

For small amounts of credited material, the "fair use" language of the Copyright Act states that use without permission (but with attribution) is legal. The criteria are: nature of use (commercial or noncommercial), proportion of work used, and whether or not the use denies the holder of sales. In other words, the "fair use" language is sufficiently vague to keep lawyers steadily employed.

If you suspect or know that you will need to ask permission of others to use their words (or photos, or illustrations), then you must do the following:

- Send a permissions form to the author.
- Develop a permissions section in "Production Detail."
- Hope for free use but be prepared to pay a fee.

Send a Permissions Form

The *Chicago Manual of Style*, a reference book available in most libraries, includes a standard form for requesting permission to reprint published material. Or, you may create your own. I combined and adopted several forms to match my needs on various projects. Because the proposal examples used in this book represent copyrighted material belonging to their creators, I was legally bound to request permission from every author whose proposal I used. The form I used is included in the Sidebar 11-2. Adapt it to your needs; you have my permission!

Sidebar 11-2
Permissions Form

I am preparing a book tentatively entitled *Nonfiction Book Proposals Anybody Can Write*, which Blue Heron Publishing, i.e. A Concept Inc. (Portland, Oregon), is planning to publish in the summer of 2000.

Please give me permission to reproduce the material listed below in any or all editions of the book, or in any part thereof and in any and all derivative works based thereon throughout the world, and in the advertising, promotion, and publicity thereof. Full credit will be given in the form of your name as author and copyright holder, title of your book, and publisher or agent, whichever is appropriate.

Please grant permission for use of excerpts from your proposal with the working title of:

Proposal Copyright (c) _____ by _____
                                                 Copyright Holder
All rights reserved.

Your signature above and below on this form, returned to me as soon as possible, will be greatly appreciated.

Signed: _____ Dated:_____

If you are writing memoir/autobiography, biography, or exposé, you will probably need to have permission to write about other individuals. You'll find another permissions form in this book's appendix that you may use or adapt for this purpose, although I recommend that you consult with your agent, editor, or possibly an attorney.

Because these forms can sound intimidating to the recipient, always include a friendly cover letter that explains your book, indicates why you need permission, and gives your timetable. Enclose a self-addressed, stamped envelope (SASE). Follow up with a thank-you note.

Develop a Permissions Section

Here's how Carolyn Kortge entered her request for permissions in her "Production Details."

> Permissions will be sought as needed, including rights to reproduce poetry in Chapter XI, George Sheehan column in Chapter VII, and excerpts from *Real Moments* by Barbara DeAngelis in Chapter VIII.

Hope for Free Use, But Be Prepared to Pay a Fee

Some authors ask payment, usually in the form of a flat fee, for use of their material. Others are happy to be credited, satisfied with the compliment and the increased exposure for their books and names. Generally speaking, the more famous the author or quote, the more likely it is that you will have to pay a fee. Be aware that acquiring permission to use song lyrics, for instance, typically involves payment of a tidy sum. While you cannot know ahead of time how much you may have to pay, "Production Details" allows you to itemize costs involved in writing your book. If permissions end up costing you $500 per author or more, they will take a bite from your advance, so weigh this against the advantages of using the material.

FRONT MATTER

Front matter includes everything that goes in the front of a book. It begins with the half-title page, title page, copyright page, and table(s) of contents. The only parts you need to list in your production details, if you have them, are the preface, foreword, and introduction. You may also plan a dedication and acknowledgments page, but they require no special listing. You may also choose not to have any front matter. It's unlikely that your book will include everything on the list of front matter, although looking at other books like yours will give you an idea of what to consider.

Preface

A preface may include a brief explanation of a book's slant, the author's philosophy, a description of the book's creation, and an explanation about the book's organization or sources, and the genesis of the book's creation. The preface, like the introduction and the foreword, needs to sell the book's benefits by creating a bridge to the readers' needs.

The first two paragraphs of the preface in *Act Like an Owner* by Blonchek and O'Neill demonstrate this "soft sell":

> The business model presented in this book, which we call *act like an owner* (ALO), grew out of our experience in building information-technology service businesses. When we started our first business, our goal was to create an environment that we would enjoy working in, an environment based on trust and team spirit. Having spent many years working for a large, international, management-consulting firm, where teamwork was frowned upon and where internal competition took precedence over customer satisfaction, we were committed to a new approach.

> Early on, as a company of just six people, we wrote a corporate creed that documented our principles and values—our culture. This creed simply stated that we would build a successful business by focusing on the customer, encouraging entrepreneurial spirit, empowering everyone, and sharing both success and failure. We call this culture an *ownership culture*.

Foreword

A foreword (check your spelling; it's not the same as *forward*) contains short introductory remarks written by an authority your readers will respect—usually not your mother. The idea is to have this person say kind and exciting things about your book to whet the reader's appetite and snare a sale at the bookstore. If you can line up a recognized authority in your field, a published author, or a celebrity, state this in "Production Details." Sometimes you have to pay a fee to this person; if so, note that here or under a later itemization of your expenses.

Notice in the sample "Production Details" how Dr. Lipman let the editors know they could count on the famous attorney, Melvin Belli, for a foreword. Here's how mythologist and counselor Demetra George listed her only front matter:

> Foreword: Written by Vicki Noble, author of *Motherpeace* and *The Shakti Woman*

If you haven't yet contacted authorities to write your foreword—or to provide you with a few superlatives as an endorsement—then indicate to the agent/editor that you intend to pursue their services. Make sure to state the expertise for which these people are known. Avoid making a long wish list. It begins to look like a fishing trip, rather than a carefully selected list of individuals who really might respond positively to your request. And did I mention the most frequent error in "Production Details?" Remember, foreword is spelled: f-o-r-e-w-o-r-d.

Introductions

If you are writing an introductory chapter to your book, you should not list it in "Production Details." Instead, include it in your chapter summaries.

Although authors usually write introductions while VIPs write forewords, introductions may be written by luminaries. If this is the case, mention who will write your introduction in "Production Details." The person need not be a household name or even known by your readers. Nevertheless, this person should have some authority to lend importance, and an endorsement, to your book. Dr. Lipman's "Production Details," in sidebar 11–1, offers a good example. Dr. Gluckman is a stranger to us, but as a medical doctor, his comments reflect what is called "warranty," a seal of approval to the author's ideas. His credentials and words of praise will increase some readers' respect for the book even *before* they begin to read it.

If you decide to write an author introduction, be aware that your words may be the first ones read by your readers. You must hook your reader here *and* in chapter one. Therefore, remember to begin your introduction with a lead that draws readers into your book based on their needs to discover your book's benefits. If you begin with what led you to write the book, you may lose reader interest.

BACK MATTER

When your reader finishes your last page of text, everything after this is called back matter. You might decide to include a bibliography, appendix, glossary, or index. Although less common, you could have an addendum (for late, additional information), author's notes, an afterword, or a colophon page (giving details about type style, design, kind of paper and other production details).

PHOTOGRAPHS AND ARTWORK

If you plan artwork or photographs other than what is included in your word-processing program, list them under "Production Details." Photographic reproduction adds expense to a book's costs—color much more so than black-and-white. If your book demands "plates" for the photographs, the cost can run even higher. For example, a coffee-table book with dozens of color photographs may retail at $35–$50 per book or more. You must supply the publisher with sufficient information to create an accurate budget.

Because Susan Lloyd is a professional photographer and teaches photography, photographs are an important addition to her books. For her biography, *The Last Zapatista*, she detailed exactly how many, what kind, and what placement she envisioned for the photographs in her book, as follows:

Photographs
Approximately ten, black-and-white photographs, printed full-frame and appearing on the title page of each new chapter. Each photograph, made by the author, who is

a professional photographer, will illustrate the theme of the particular chapter: for instance, a photograph of Diego Rivera's mural at Chapingo, depicting Zapata buried in the ground with corn sprouting from his body (Chapter 1); a portrait of Ana Maria Zapata, in her home surrounded by memorabilia and photographs of Emiliano Zapata (Chapter 2); an image of campesino bull-riders (Chapter 3); the Zapata family at Cuahuixtla hacienda ruins (Chapter 4); a portrait of Martin Balderrama holding his young son (Chapter 5); a portrait of Emeterio Pantaleon husking corn in his adobe hut (Chapter 6), etc.

You need not go into such specific detail (I would have placed her "etc." after Chapter 3); however, such detail leaves no room for confusion about her preferences.

ENDORSEMENTS

If you do not list your endorsement hopefuls in with your foreword and front matter, then list them as a separate item. Under "Endorsements," name anyone whom you can guarantee (because you have spoken with them) will write an endorsement for your book. Also list those persons whom you "plan to contact" or from whom you "hope to secure" an endorsement. Don't forget to indicate their connection to your book, or how they are publicly known.

RESOURCES NEEDED TO COMPLETE YOUR BOOK

While every book costs you money to write—for paper, printer supplies, postage, and general office overhead, you are expected to absorb or deduct these costs from your advance. If you do not get an advance, you must bear the costs on your own. When completion of your book necessitates expenses beyond these usual ones, add a budget of these projected expenses to your "Production Details." You could gain a greater advance *if* the publisher is willing to cover some of your expenses—always a matter of negotiation. The primary areas that may produce additional costs are travel expenses, photographic supplies and development, long-distance telephone calls, permissions, endorsements, forewords, professional typing, and editing.

When listing expenses, round off figures and begin with the most costly item first. Here is an example of Susan Caperna Lloyd's "Resources Needed to Complete Book" for her proposal on *No Pictures in My Grave*:

> Research for the book has been completed and four chapters have been written. I would like to utilize a residence grant I have received from the Wurlitzer Foundation in Taos, New Mexico, for a three-month stay (use of writing studio) during May–July 1991, to work on the remaining chapters. The manuscript will be finished and delivered nine months after receipt of an advance.

Itemized resources are:

Travel & Board in New Mexico	$2,700
Payment for Foreword	750
Clerical Expenses	800
Editing	500
Photographic Printing Supplies	300
(if photographs are used)	
TOTAL	$5,000

Itemization of your expenses in no way guarantees an advance sufficient to cover them. Advances are not based upon your expenses, even though the philosophy behind them is to provide monies for completion of the book. You may recall that the advance is figured, in part, based on a formula: Retail cost of one book times the number of books in the print run times the author's royalty percentage. For example: $20 times 10,000 = $200,000 times 10 percent = $20,000. Often, a small publisher will only be able to capitalize a first print run that is half this size, about 5000. You can see using this formula why a small press might not even offer an advance; they might offer one that is quite small.

Sidebar 11-3:
A Summary of "Production Details"

The "Production Details" section of a proposal is where the author lists specifications and preferences for the book's physical look and layout. From these details, the publisher estimates costs, including the advance, and learns when the author can deliver the finished manuscript.

Make sure your "Production Details" include the following details:

1. Book length, rounded off in double-spaced manuscript pages or in a word count.
2. Delivery date—usually expressed as "upon receipt of advance," or "in 3 months, 6 months, 9 months, 12 months, or 15 months."
3. Format—if you have any special preferences in size, binding, treatment of text.
4. Sidebars—estimate number.
5. Permissions—how many you will seek, sometimes naming the cited authors, and indicate actual or estimated fees.
6. Front matter—whether you plan to have a preface, foreword, or introduction.
7. Back matter—whether or not you plan to have an index, bibliography, a resource directory, glossary, or appendices.
8. Photographs and artwork—details about type styles and any special treatments of photos or artwork.
9. Endorsements—who you've arranged or hope to contact for endorsements.
10. Resources needed to complete your book—itemized expenses, such as: travel, photographic supplies, long-distance calls, permissions, editing, foreword fee, editing, or professional typing.

On the subject of itemized expenses, an editor at St. Martin's Press expressed his ambivalence as follows:

> I often feel that the writer itemizing expenses is positioning me. My job is to pay an advance that reflects what the publisher thinks the book is worth; that number is based on a projection of earned royalties, not on the author's expenses.

Every publisher is as different as every book deal. Many factors, other than "projected earned royalties," can weigh in the awarding of an advance, such as the financial condition of the publisher, production costs versus retail price, the perceived selling power of the book, the author's reputation, the skill of your agent, and how much excitement your proposal engenders in the editor and the committee.

CHAPTER TWELVE

About Promotion: Good Morning, Springfield. Good Morning, America.

Chapter Goal: To outline a workable plan for promoting your book.

Concept Statement
About the Book
About the Author
About the Market
About the Competition
Production Details
* About Promotion
Table of Contents
Chapter Summaries
Appendix

When you watch Oprah, *Today*, or C-SPAN's "Booknotes," you may begin to imagine yourself on those shows, answering questions about your book for an audience of millions. You may imagine what it will be like when your publisher sends you on a coast-to-coast promotional tour—all expenses paid. You may even think of the adoring crowds, the book signings, the luxury hotels, perhaps even the chance to see favorite Aunt Betty in Dallas whom you haven't talked to in years.

You're dreaming.

I won't deny that your book *could* be high-zoot enough to warrant this kind of treatment, at your publisher's expense. If so, they'll call you, *they* being your publisher's publicity department. However, a high-rolling media blitz is reserved for relatively few authors and even fewer first-time authors.

In general, publishers have suffered more than a decade of belt-tightening mergers, and madness! Most have jettisoned promotion of what they call "midlist" books. "Midlist" refers to those books that are not bestsellers; they may or may not earn back the monies paid in advance to the author. They are books that few people recognize by name, yet they comprise the largest number of titles in a publisher's catalog—the big hump in the bell-shaped curve.

> Make sure you have a strong plan to promote your book, and you'll be more likely to secure publisher assistance.

Even though the production budget for your book includes a percentage earmarked for promotion, publishers are not obligated to spend that money on *your* book. It's not fair, I know. In fact, it has been a subject of discussion in the Book Division of the National Writers Union. If publishers have a hot title that begins to soar in sales, they can, and will, draw from the general, promotion slush fund, holding promotions' monies from all of their titles to push the hot seller.

The marketing members of the editorial committee have powerful voices in the selection of books. No matter how much an acquisitions editor loves your book, if someone in marketing makes a convincing case for why your book would be hard to sell, his no vote will override the editor's yes vote.

Where are you in this picture? You had better have a strong plan to promote your own book. As literary agent Denise Marcil commented, "This is the most important part of the proposal; the more details the better."

Your efforts as the author may make the difference between your publisher soaring into the black or plunging into the red. In some cases, what you offer in "About Promotion" may make the difference between a contract offered and a proposal declined. Be specific and detailed to get the committee to believe in you as well as in your book. Offer a credible plan that demonstrates your marketing ability and willingness to travel and promote for at least a good year after publication. Show how you will devote your own time to help sell your book, or state your intent to hire a publicist. Then, when you propose your next book, you'll have a sales history that will make all the difference.

Sidebar 12-1:
Sample: About Promotion
Demetra George

Publicity

There exist three major ways that the author can help to promote *Mysteries of the Dark Moon*: 1) by presenting lectures and workshops, 2) by writing magazine articles and arranging for book reviews, and 3) through media appearances.

The author, Demetra George, can promote *Mysteries of the Dark Moon* at the many workshops she presents across the United States and Canada on mythology, astrology, and women's issues. She is a popular speaker in the women's spirituality community, and teaches on a regular basis in the San Francisco Bay area. She has been invited to present the *Mysteries of the Dark Moon* teachings in Australia and New Zealand in January–February 1990.

She will commit to presenting one to two workshops per month in the six months following publication of *Mysteries of the Dark Moon*. Some possible places for presentations are the Omega Institute and the Open Door Center in New York, Joy Lake in Nevada, Breitenbush Retreat Center in Oregon, the Feathered Pipe Ranch in Montana, Women's Alliance Summer Camps in California and Maine, School of Shamanic Healing Arts in Berkeley, and individual sponsoring organizations.

(Continued)

Magazine articles and book reviews are a powerful way of informing the public about new publications. Magazine articles on *Mysteries of the Dark Moon* have appeared in *Woman of Power* and *Snake* magazine. Additional articles and book reviews can be arranged with new-age magazines, such as *New Age Journal, East-West, Magical Blend, Shaman's Drum, New Realities*; women's journals, such as *Woman of Power, Snake Power, Circle Network News, Seattle Feminist Times*; and psychology journals, such as *Psychology Today* and *Brain-Mind Bulletin*.

Media appearances on television and radio talk shows is by far the most powerful way of reaching large numbers of people with whom to share the *Mysteries of the Dark Moon* insights.

Ms. George has appeared on several television and radio programs, including *AM Northwest*—a Portland TV talk show, *Quest Four*—a Los Angeles, metaphysical, TV interview show, and *Woman's Magazine*—KPFA San Francisco radio program. She has been asked to film a one-hour interview on *Mysteries of the Dark Moon* for an LA cable-TV series entitled *The Goddess in Art* with Starr Goode.

Return visits with the above programs can be arranged. With the help of a publicist, many other interviews on radio-talk programs and possibly television talk shows like *Sally Jessy Raphael* would greatly enhance the popularity of the book.

Definition and Purpose

Promotion refers to what you, and your publisher, do to draw sales of your book. *Publicity* is what you get for your promotional efforts, all the better if it doesn't cost you or the publisher a dime. *Advertising* is promotion that someone pays for. The best marketing plan is one that yields maximum publicity for minimal time or money. Having a lot of money for promotion helps, but does not guarantee lots of publicity or sales. Sometimes writers think advertising is the answer to selling more books. There is much debate over the utility of ads, since it is usually difficult to assess results and the origins of bookstore orders are unavailable. You're unlikely to get your publisher to spend their precious-little promotional monies on costly advertising.

Successful marketing requires knowledge and skill. In the "About Promotion" section, you must demonstrate that combination. The agent/editor will read this section for three purposes:

- To assess your willingness, enthusiasm, and cooperative attitude toward promoting your book
- To evaluate your connections and therefore how many sales you might be able to generate
- To provide the marketing department with ideas on how to best reach the market for your particular book

No one cares about your book's success as strongly as you do. You know idiosyncratic ways that you can help promote your book. You must inform the publisher of these. The promotional section in Sidebar 12-1, by Demetra George, is one example. It is shorter than most promotion sections, because she is an established author with several prior books to her credit. Most of the first-time authors with whom I have worked have developed "About Promotion" sections that are six to ten pages long. This increase in detail corresponds to changes in the industry that have put greater pressure on authors to meet more demanding bottom-line expectations than in the past.

Structure and Content

STRUCTURE

Like most proposal sections, "About Promotion" should have a lead, a body, and a conclusion. Your lead should indicate your willingness to help promote your book. Be enthusiastic; sell yourself. In her promotion section, Susan Caperna Lloyd wrote a first sentence that showed her willingness and cooperative spirit: "I hope to work closely with the sales and publicity team of the publisher of..."

In the body of your "About Promotion," you can use Demetra George's example as a model. Use either third person or first person. You may also use a numbered list rather than paragraphs. Make your "About Promotion" graphically appealing. For instance, I would have preferred that George have added bold or underlining to her headings for the three ways to promote her book. Remember that agents and editors are busy, overworked, and fatigued. They have hundreds of other proposals they could be reading. Make their job easier! Organize your material well and make it visually appealing.

Organization by Activity

As shown in Sidebar 12-1, George organized her section using three promotional activities: presenting lectures and workshops, writing magazine articles and arranging for book reviews, and media appearances. With the explosion of Internet commerce, you should add Internet resources as an activity.

You may also create your own headings tailored to your promotional activities. In his book about surviving multiple pet loss, David Congalton first described his local connections and prior experience as a radio talk-show host, television show host, and journalist in his community, San Luis Obispo, California. Other headings in his "About Promotion" include: Relevant Professional Organizations, Internet Resources, Specialized Media (related to pets and animal welfare), Mainstream Media, and Other.

An entirely different way to structure the body of your promotion section is geographically.

Organization by Geography

You may use geographic headings, such as "local," "regional," and "national." Since one would assume you can do your greatest promotion locally, this organization system can be an advantage for a writer who doesn't yet have experience in lecturing, or many publishing credits, or media connections. The disadvantage is that you can end up repeating how you'll present and teach, write, or make media appearances under each geographic heading.

Finish your promotion section with a conclusion that reiterates the same enthusiasm and willingness to work that you projected in your lead.

CONTENT

Your promotional activities should be described in depth, no matter how you organize the section. Remember, too, "About the Market" directed the publisher to special markets for their staff to pursue: book clubs, foreign translations, course adoption, or specialty bookstores. This information does not belong in "About Promotion." The promotion section is all about what you will do. Make sure you develop in depth each of the following promotional activities:

- Presenting and teaching
- Writing
- Making media appearances
- Internet resources
- Using publicists

PRESENTING AND TEACHING

Think of clubs, organizations, schools, universities, or conferences where you could teach or make presentations. I'm not talking about being a keynote speaker (unless you can pull those strings). Instead, presenting and teaching encompass giving lectures, leading workshops, or facilitating seminars on the subject of your book. Ask your reference librarian for help in finding specific school programs, lecture series, and appropriate organization names. For a listing of 7500 conferences, look through the *National Trade and Professional Associations of the United States*—or select from the 20,000 listings in the *Encyclopedia of Associations*. From these sources, quote several good matches to your book's subject. Don't overlook your own organizational memberships and affiliations. They hold the most promise, because you are already an insider by virtue of your membership. When you list potential organizations where you might present or teach, include membership figures. The more specific and detailed you can be in your suggestions, the more you will be able to convince a publisher that you can, in fact, actively sell your book.

WRITING

You can promote your book by writing articles, flyers, and pitch letters. The sole purpose of pitch letters is to persuade someone to buy your product—your book—or to use your services—as a lecturer, for instance. Most of your promotional writing will be aimed at newspapers, newsletters, magazines, and direct mailing.

Demetra George mentioned, by name, thirteen possible magazines or journals where she would pursue publication of magazine articles and book reviews. Rosemarie Ostler suggested that a direct-mail flyer be sent to the Linguistic and English departments of colleges and universities.

Make an inventory of your own subscriptions, memberships, and prior publishing successes, and identify specific people to whom you can send material; or find media outlets where you can seek others to write book reviews. If you can't name names, then be specific in a general way, like author Susan Lloyd did in this section of her "About Promotion":

> I will also be able to utilize numerous connections I have in the Latino community—a growing force in the southern Oregon area. Venues in the area include three Spanish-language newspapers, two Latino television programs, and several Latino and farm-worker organizations.

Be realistic about where you believe you can get articles published or printed. If you're going to list *The New Yorker*, *Atlantic Monthly*, or even *Redbook*, indicate prior successful publication with these magazines or some personal contact; otherwise you'll lose credibility.

If you are short on publishing credits and doubt whether you can get articles published in major magazines, concentrate on newsletters. Their editors are often crying for material. Nearly every organization has a newsletter. When you search for names and

---

Sidebar 12-2:
Internet Resources for Author Promotion

Web Authoring Resources:
www.wwwscribe.com/resource.htm

Internet Promotions:

www.bookmarket.com

BookWire (extensive links, including to publishers, publicists, and online bookstores):
www.bookwire.com

Mining Co.:
www.miningco.com

Suite 101:
www.suite101.com/WritingCenter/

Top Ten Mistakes in Web Design:
www.useit.com/alertbox/9605.html

---

membership figures for organizations where you might present and teach, jot down names of the newsletters and any trade magazines. In fact, trade magazines—publications sent only to members—are far easier to make a sale to than publications written for the general public, which get deluged with material.

Although Carolyn Kortge, the author of *The Spirited Walker*, was an established journalist with many publishing credits in nationally circulated magazines, in her "About Promotion," she combined potential speaking opportunities with writing opportunities, as follows:

- International Association of Fitness Professionals (IDEA) 23,000 members

- IDEA Fitness Manager
  IDEA Today (Magazine/10 year)
- American Council on Exercise (ACE)
  ACE Fitness Matters (bimonthly newsletter/30,000 circ.)
- Aerobics and Fitness Association of America (AFAA)
  80,000 members
- *American Fitness* (bimonthly newsletter)
  ...and three more listings.

If you don't want to commit to writing magazine articles or to seeking reviews, perhaps you wouldn't mind sending flyers on your book to people on your personal mailing list. Many writers have now become adept with graphics and art software. If you've got the skills, offer to work with your publisher on developing a flyer and a pitch letter. If appropriate, offer to pursue direct-mail contact with suppliers of a retail item—cookware for a cookbook or garden equipment for a gardening book—with the expectation of establishing retail outlets for your book.

MEDIA APPEARANCES

Perhaps your book will sell well enough for your publisher to send you on a limited, nationwide, promotional tour. For instance, the five coauthors of *Mothering Twins* were sent to a national twins convention by Fireside, publishing imprint of Simon & Schuster. Whether or not a publicity tour is in the offing, include a sentence indicating your willingness (if you are) to "travel, speak, and promote anywhere in the country at the publisher's arrangement" or "to participate in any publisher's author's tour."

In addition to book signings and tours arranged by your publisher at their expense, this proposal section allows you to suggest media events or bookstore appearances by your own arrangement or with some publisher. For instance, you could offer to arrange book signings locally or regionally with independent bookstores or with superstores such as Borders, Chapters (Canada), or Barnes & Noble.

You can plan interviews on local or regional television and

radio stations for talk and interview shows. Consider following the example of author David Congalton, who offered to purchase a display listing in *Radio/TV Interview Report* (circulation: 4000), a primary source used by talk-show hosts and producers across the country to book radio and TV guests.

Plan to contact newspapers about reviews and interviews. Don't, by the way, state that you will write book reviews. Authors don't write reviews of their own books! If you know someone or have made prior appearances on a station, name the show, station, and/or show host. An agent or editor is not going to believe that you can get yourself on *Oprah*, unless "About the Author" suggests it, or unless you can offer proof of a believable connection.

Giving a lecture or saying a few words to a club is different than being a professional speaker. Professional means that you get paid for being a speaker and that you know how to give a speech. Speakers' bureaus exist to help match organizations with proven professional speakers. Authors, of course, can make interesting speakers, but only if they are professionals in public speaking. If you qualify, include in your promotion section how you will use this skill.

INTERNET RESOURCES

As much as the Internet can ease the most unwieldy task of research, its potential for use as a promotional tool is expanding, if not exploding, every day.

Many web sites allow writers to become online journalists in their subject specialty. One such site, The Mining Co., calls their 600 contributing writers "guides." Essentially, their guides write short articles for a pittance (30 percent of net ad revenues). The writer holds the copyright on content. The main benefit for any book writer is exposure to a large audience and a publishing credit.

A second web site for writers who are subject authorities is called Suite 101. With about 500 "contributing editors," the site continues to expand its staff. Again, the pay is low (about $25 a month for weekly articles, less for monthly articles), but you're gaining exposure and credits.

All proposal writers should seriously consider creating their own web site. While you could offer in "About Promotion" to establish one after your book is published, you'll reap a greater advantage if you get a web site up and running for marketing your proposal to agents and editors.

The ability to use the Internet is a skill increasingly expected of writers, agents, and editors. Offer your Web address in "About Promotion," (and in your query); this gives you yet another place to sell yourself and your ideas.

Before you rush to throw up a site or hire the first tech person who offers such a service, stop. What you don't want is an amateurish, error-filled, boring, home page. Read books on the subject of web design and construction. Interview half-a-dozen businesses that offer such a service before hiring one. My favorite book on Internet resources that's slanted for the unique perspective and needs of writers is *writing.com* by Moira Anderson Allen.

An important aspect of your web site is developing links to your publisher, online bookstores, online clearinghouses and directories, and to other web sites related to your subject. Sidebar 12-2 shows some Internet resources for promoting yourself, your subject, or your book.

PUBLICISTS

The job of publicists is to secure publicity for your book. Like any consultants, they vary in skill, in fees, and in their connections. I have heard of fees ranging from hundreds of dollars to thousands of dollars. Obviously, hiring a publicist can eat up your advance, when so much promotion can be done by yourself and your publisher.

List your intent to hire a publicist only if you anticipate selling your book to a larger publisher, or if you expect an advance substantial enough to absorb this cost. If you foresee publication with a small, regional, or specialty publisher, you may not receive an advance, or your advance will be low—excluding extra money to hire a publicist and negating the need for one.

If you don't know a publicist to put down by name in your "About Promotion," then merely state your intention to hire a publicist from a portion of your advance monies.

The best way to find a publicist is by word of mouth. When the time comes, ask your agent or other published authors for the names of accomplished publicists. If you belong to an organization for writers, such as National Writers Union, they will have lists or recommendations of trusted publicists. Avoid making a commitment to the first one with whom you talk. Interview several and select the one whose plan, personality, and fees you find most agreeable.

An advantage to working with a publicist is that a good one knows how to approach major-network talk shows. They have connections you can't easily make. Every book and every author is unique, and good publicists will customize their services to your needs.

Troubleshooting

Two considerations about promotion deserve special mention. They involve:

- Writers who prefer not to promote or are cash short
- Writers who plan extensive promotion from independent resources

Prefer Not to Promote or Are Cash Short

If, for whatever reasons, you prefer not to promote your book, begin the promotion section with a general statement indicating your willingness to cooperate with the publicity department. You can say no later to specific requests not to your liking.

Even if you are unwilling to make public appearances, perhaps you would have no objections to offering your personal or professional mailing list to the marketing department. Perhaps you can offer to write letters requesting reviews or suggesting articles.

If you want nothing to do with promotion but your advance allows it, plan to hire a publicist. Although George Green indicated willingness to promote his book in the usual ways, he and coauthor

Carolyn Cotter learned of a publicist who would handle all of their book's promotion with press releases, radio spots, and book reviews. They hired her.

Many writers tend to be cash short, time short, or both. The expectation for promoting any book involves at least some monies and time, and time translates into money.

If you anticipate being short of cash by the time your book enters production and is released, suggest ideas in "About Promotion" that primarily involve time. Then begin to mentally prepare for, if not physically budget, a percentage of your work week—after you've finished writing your book—toward promotion. In the appendix of his bestseller, *The Self-Publishing Manual*, Dan Poynter, has a great month-by-month checklist of promotional ideas that can help any author. Two books where you can glean great ideas from every page are: *Jump Start Your Book Sales* by Marilyn and Tom Ross, and the virtual classic on the subject, *1001 Ways to Market Your Books* by John Kremer. You can do an amazing amount of promotion with a small outlay of money—mostly for the cost of office supplies and postage.

One writer I met orchestrated the promotion of his self-published book entirely by appearances on radio talk shows. His expenses included postcards and postage for mailing his pitch to talk-show hosts across the country, and later for setting up an 800-line and credit-card billing for the orders that flooded in. His method of promotion became so successful that he eventually hired a telephone service with multiple 800 lines to handle the large influx of calls. This writer had the gift of gab. He tallied 650 radio interviews, all secured at the cost of postcards and long-distance follow-up calls. He never left his easy chair to promote his book.

If a radio-talk-show forum sounds like your bailiwick, offer to pursue this in your promotion section and study how to do it from books mentioned in the Resource Directory.

Don't make generous offers to promote your book in other regions or nationally at your own expense, if you can't do so. Transportation costs, food, and lodging can mount up, even for travel within your state. On the other hand, you may have friends or family in many locales who can offset lodging and food costs. Perhaps you're intending to make a recreational trip to another state. Offer only what you can deliver.

PLAN EXTENSIVE PROMOTION FROM INDEPENDENT RESOURCES

Some writers have financial backing from corporations which, independent of the publisher, have their own marketing, sales, and publicity departments. Other writers possess the means and funds to hire a public relations firm. You may be in a position to buy a large number of your books for resale or giveaways. You may be able to buy advertising or obtain it through connections. You may know the "right" people, who have power and access to print and television media.

If you were a member of an editorial committee, how would you react to a writer with independent resources or backing? Such writers' ability to promote increases the likelihood of a higher advance or better book contract, for obvious reasons; they can absorb a publisher's promotion expenses and, to some degree, guarantee sales. If this describes your situation, make your "About Promotion" reflect these abilities. Also, make sure you broadcast your connections, financial resources, and influence in "About the Book," "About the Author," and in your query letter.

CHAPTER THIRTEEN

Last But Not Least: The Appendix

Chapter Goal: To assemble exhibits that enhance your credibility and the importance and timeliness of your book.

Concept Statement
About the Book
About the Author
About the Market
About the Competition
Production Details
About Promotion
Table of Contents
Chapter Summaries
Sample Chapters
* The Appendix

"The Appendix" contains materials that supplement and "dress up" your proposal. It should deliver a positive, first impression of your proposal. This may seem strange since "appendix" implies something at the end of more important information. However, the appendix serves an important function that is both decorative and functional.

Definition and Purpose

"The Appendix" is a collection of publicity exhibits about you and your book's subject. By exhibits, I mean articles, letters, photos, artwork, and other items. Its purpose is to show off your past accomplishments in order to further persuade an agent/editor that you are qualified to write your book. Secondly, "The Appendix" provides ancillary support for the worthiness and timeliness of your book, and shows how you intend to sell it. Its scope is limited only by your imagination.

Contents

"The Appendix" may contain an assortment of documents and exhibits. What follows is a list and description of possibilities from which you may select.

DOCUMENTS

1. Published writing samples. These clips, photocopies of articles, ads, or anything else you've written and published, are among the most important documents. If you have many credits, or if the clips are for subjects unrelated to your book's subject, include a bibliography of your published works.
2. Published material about you. This might include newspaper articles about you, your hobby, or your business. Have you been written up in a *Who's Who* or a trade biography? Photocopy your entry. Has someone else given you acknowledgment in his or her book? How about Web bookstore reviews of prior books? Include a copy in "The Appendix."
3. Published material about your book's subject. Remember that your proposal must answer the questions, "Why this book? Why now?" Photocopy half a dozen (or fewer) recent newspaper articles or magazine features on your subject to show its popularity or timeliness.
4. Copies of promotional material about yourself or your busi-

ness. These might include flyers about workshops, brochures, or advertisements related to your book's subject.

5. Copies of award certificates or letters of commendation. Make sure they are related to your book or your writing.

6. Copies of reviews about your prior books, artistic creations, or technical inventions not necessarily related to this book.

7. A complete résumé. While a résumé is inappropriate in "About the Author," you may include one in "The Appendix." Do so only if you have had to omit significant or substantial background in your author section.

8. A written summary of television, radio, and movie coverage of your subject, citing programs or movie names and dates (only if this seems relevant to your book).

Exhibits

1. Sample illustrations, cartoons, photographs, charts, and graphs. Send copies or photocopies, never originals. Label everything.

2. Videotapes. You may send a videotape of yourself speaking in a television interview, giving a lecture on your book's subject, or promoting yourself and your subject commercially. Cliché that it is, a picture is worth a thousand words.

3. Audio tapes. If you have a clear audio tape of a radio interview, or an audio tape as part of your promotional material, or even one recording a lecture you've given, label and send it—but only if it is a flattering and relevant representation of you and the book.

4. Author photograph. While it may be useful for promotion, the photo is at first unimportant, although it's a common addition to most proposals. If it's a mug shot, make sure it's professional quality, either black-and-white or color. A high-quality laser copy is sufficient. If you have good-quality photographs of yourself posed in an action related to your book, use them too. Avoid shots of you and Furface-the-Cat or of you and the kids on sum-

mer vacation. If your book is on kayaking and someone took a shot of you plunging into a class-six rapids on the Yangtze, that's a different story. Send it.

Presentation

Most agents package proposals in double-pocketed folders or as loose pages stacked in a manuscript box. An agent may place some of your appendix material on top so that it is the first thing an editor sees. Even if "The Appendix" is left at the end of the proposal after an editor has read through your manuscript, it offers a contrast, both visually and in style, to the proposal itself.

Presentation is important. Avoid the impression that your agent/editor is rifling through a musty shoebox collection of your past. Take odd-sized copies of articles, reviews, ads, or other printed documents and photocopy them onto 8½" x 11" paper. If you need to, make enlargements or reductions of this material. Cut and paste and rearrange until you have visually appealing documents.

When a published article has appeared on page thirty-eight of a magazine or in section F of your newspaper, cut it out and eliminate competing articles or advertisements. Consider placing this clip under the masthead of the magazine or newspaper—still providing the header that shows the date and page number where it originally appeared. This dresses up your articles, improves their presentation, and makes them easier to read.

When it comes to reproducing your flyers, workshop notices, or brochures, if the originals are blah, copy them onto colored paper—simply for the visual stimulation this provides. If your entire appendix material is on white paper, consider adding blank sheets of color papers as separators between different types of material. Think presentation as well as organization.

For photocopies of articles or features about your subject that include color photographs, make color copies for their visual appeal. This adds cost, especially if your agent requests ten copies of your proposal for marketing, but doing so makes the whole package more attractive. It is one of the "plus" values that's easy for you to achieve.

You know why you've included particular exhibits in "The Appendix" but will an agent/editor? Use a highlighter to circle or mark what you want them to notice. Glue a typed caption over an article or feature to explain its relevancy to you or to your subject. Make it easy for your reader. Add a cover sheet, as page one of "The Appendix," with a table of contents of your documents and exhibits (with or without page numbers).

Some writers go to even greater lengths to make an impression by sending T-shirts, baked goods, or other "promo hype." I don't recommend it. In answer to my question about whether he had received unusual items with proposals, one New York editor said, "I've received t-shirts, coffee mugs and bags of coffee beans, baseball cards, signed author photos, and other stuff. It doesn't influence me at all."

Problems With "The Appendix"

Rarely will a writer have too much material for "The Appendix." Include more rather than less items, knowing that your agent can eliminate what he or she considers "too much," or "irrelevant." A greater problem exists for writers who have little or nothing for "The Appendix."

If you believe you have nothing to put in an appendix, double-check the possibilities listed above. Nearly everyone can do research and find something written about a book's subject in magazines or journals. However, let's suppose that you are writing original material, never before described in print.

Have you ever spoken on the topic? Could you speak or lecture: if so, can you make an audio recording or a videotape? Can you generate some visuals—some graphs or charts that translate your written ideas into some kind of display? If this isn't your forté, ask a teacher friend to help you (many teachers are geniuses at creating visual displays). Or, employ a copy or print shop that has a graphic artist who can help.

What Not to Include

Don't include any document or exhibit that would devalue you or trivialize your book's worthiness. Also, eliminate rejection letters from other agents or publishers, even if their letterhead is embossed, and even if they had kind words to say about your writing. Rejection letters plant the thought of rejection. If your agent or editor asks where else you've sent your proposal, then you can supply an accounting of your rejections.

Evaluate carefully any letters of commendation or recommendation. If the person writing them is unknown or working for a local company, agency, or institution, the letter may convey a "small-time" image. Including them may make you seem provincial, not a quality considered charming—or marketable. Exclude documents of a controversial or politically incorrect nature, unless they relate directly to your book's subject. Perhaps you were one of the protesters at a campus building featured by a newspaper during a demonstration. Put these clips away to share with your offspring.

Materials that would reveal your age, religion, sexual orientation, or racial group might not be relevant to your book, but they do reveal private information about you. Agents and editors are people first, and they too carry biases. Supply only information that is relevant to your book and will enhance its sale.

Last of all, if you have nothing for your appendix and choose not to create material, you haven't forfeited all chances for seeing your book published. This is, after all, the *appendix*, the postscript, to your proposal. If the rest of your proposal is well written, fully developed, and professionally presented, you're going to get a sincere reading, with or without "The Appendix."

Now it's really time to celebrate; you have a complete, first draft of your proposal. "Put it to bed," meaning lay it aside. In the next chapter, you'll learn how to revise it from a fresh perspective.

CHAPTER FOURTEEN

Marketing Strategies: Queries and Responses, Agents and Editors

Chapter Goal: To write a compelling query and to develop a marketing strategy that leads to a request for your proposal.

Many years ago, I taught a series of mini-workshops covering everything from writing novels and magazine articles to proposals. A few weeks after the series, I received a call from an excited student.

"It works!" she proclaimed. "I kind of didn't believe it would, but I followed your instructions for writing a query letter. I sent it out as a multiple submission to twenty editors, and guess what?"

"An editor wants it?" I guessed.

> When you can follow up a request for your proposal with no more than two weeks delay, begin sending queries.

"No, seventeen want it," she told me. "And I haven't even started my proposal."

My student did one thing right: She started her marketing process with a query letter. As mentioned in chapter one, agents and editors prefer a letter describing a book project and offering a proposal. In fact, her query yielded exactly what a writer hopes. What she didn't do according to Hoyle is have her proposal nearly finished and ready to send out in response. To her credit, she sacrificed all of her free time for the next two months and blitzed a proposal together.

Later, when you've written a proposal or two and know how long it will take you to write one, you might test the waters with a query letter, knowing that you have the skill to quickly bang out a proposal.

The Query Letter

On a basic level, a query is a business letter asking an agent/editor if he or she is interested enough in your book idea to see a proposal. However, it is much more than a trial balloon. It is the first evidence of your writing. The query letter becomes a showcase of your writing—of your command over organization, style, grammar, punctuation, and spelling. Because the marketplace is flooded with correspondence from writers seeking publication, the query letter is also your sales pitch, your first foot in the door.

In a response to a student of mine, literary agent Denise Marcil reported that she receives an average of 100 query letters each week, and gives a yes to ten or less.

By now, having written a rough draft of your proposal, you're an expert at writing sales' documents. After all, every section of your proposal is a sales pitch.

Like every section of your proposal, the query letter has a lead, a body, and a conclusion. It may also have enclosures.

LEAD

You can craft an arresting lead by drawing from the list of possibilities offered in chapter eight. For instance, try a short anecdote, a startling statement, a statistic, or a comparison. You may be able to pirate your lead from "About the Book," or the "Concept Statement," and use it verbatim for your query. Here's a lead for a query letter written by the five authors *Mothering Twins*:

"Help!" is the first thought in the mind of the woman facing the frightening/exciting prospect of having twins. She wants to know firsthand what it's *really* like. Five mothers are filling a publication void by joining their stories in a book titled *Mothering Twins: From Hearing the News to Beyond the Terrible Twos.*

An equally acceptable query lead rejects the bells and whistles of a clever lead in favor of a clear, concise statement of purpose. A straightforward lead might begin: "I am writing a book for writers on ...." Or, it might start with your author credentials: "I am a blah-blah-blah with fifteen years experience..." If you have been referred to the agent or editor by someone who knows them, your letter should start with that referral. The higher that person is held in repute by the agent/editor, the more weight it will carry in consideration of your query.

BODY

In the body of your query letter, you should expand upon the subject of your book, the market, and its competition. Does this sound familiar? It should. You've done all of the research and writing to know precisely what makes your book better or different than others. You identified your strongest market and you researched the competition.

Because query letters are meant to be short—no more than two pages, better if one—you must address the subject, the market, and the competition in a few paragraphs. Some writers "lift" portions (or all) of their concept statements to supply the brevity and pizzazz it takes to capture the agent or editor's attention.

Don't forget, within the body, to rely upon specifics to focus your query on the need for your book. That's a mark of professionalism as a writer. Use specifics, such as quotes from a leading magazine or famous person, a statistic that provides evidence of your market, and authors and titles of one or two competitors with a few words about their shortcomings.

The five authors of *Mothering Twins* used specifics to shape and polish their query to editors, which yielded an interest in their proposal and eventual publication. I've picked items out of their query letter to give you an idea of how specific information can be used.

Specifics	Its Purpose
An article on twins in *Newsweek Magazine*, Nov. 23, 1989, stated, "Sometimes, the best advice comes from twins and their parents who have been through it all."	Supports their book's unique approach offering personal accounts from five mothers.
Other books on the market address the "how-to's" of parenting multiples... [ours] provid[es]...practical knowledge and validation for the feelings and work.	Describes need that their book addresses and contrasts theirs with competition.
TWINS Magazine, circulation 40,000... 33,000 sets of twins born each year... 4.5 million twins and their families	Gives indication of size of market for the book

A final paragraph or two in the body must supply author credentials, unless you opt for attaching a page of author biography. This is perfectly acceptable and a route I recommend if you have substantial qualifications for writing your book. Even if you attach a bio, write a line or two, or a small paragraph, in case the agent/editor doesn't want to take the time to read an enclosure.

When you select from your many credentials for use in the query, pick the strongest ones and those most relevant to your book. Review what you selected for "About the Author" and you may find lines or a paragraph you can simply copy into your query. Pretend you are your own public-relations person and talk yourself up as a client.

CONCLUSION

Wrap up your query letter with a strong handshake. In other words, offer to send your proposal, give thanks, and affirm your desire for a speedy response. Here is one generic close to a query that includes these three items:

I would be happy to send you a proposal on _____ (your book's title). Thank you for your consideration. I look forward to hearing from you at your earliest convenience.

Sometimes, I've added a P.S. to a query. I am more personal in a postscript, adding a comment or two regarding how I learned about this agent or editor—perhaps from reading about them in a directory or hearing good things about them from a friend. It is one way to acknowledge a human connection. It's also good sales. Here is a postscript written by one of my students in her query to Jean Naggar Literary Agency: "I have long heard wonderful things about your agency from writer P.H., and especially liked what you had to say in Jeff Herman's *Writer's Guide* [*to Book Editors, Publishers, and Literary Agents*]."

If this student had a stronger connection to Jean Naggar— having met her at a writers' conference—I would have suggested mentioning that connection in the lead paragraph.

Enclosures

If you plan to send anything with your query letter, then add "enc:" below your letter signature and list your enclosures. You may enclose an author biography, as mentioned. I recommend including a table of contents of your proposed book and a photocopy or two of some articles or features relevant to your book or your author credentials. In other words, you don't want to load down the query package, but you do want to select what will make the best first impression.

After you've written your query letter, plan to revise it again and again. I know some writers who have spent as many as twenty hours on this one- or two-page document. They examined every word, every sentence, every paragraph. They played with order; they substituted one approach for another. They asked an eagle-eyed editor or a critique group to help them proofread for mistakes and weaknesses. I'm a believer in the theory that you can't spend too much time on a query letter, or have too many critics review it.

You won't get to impress an agent/editor with your proposal unless they say yes to your query. Nevertheless, you can only do what you can do. If you follow these instructions, your query letter will succeed.

At a later date, you will probably come back to the query you sweated over for hours and decide it can be improved. If the agents or editors to whom you first sent it have rejected it, take the time to rewrite it before sending it out again.

The point is not to dash off a letter, like you might for simple business correspondences. Instead, polish your query as if it were a contest entry with a prize of $20,000 to the winner—the average investment capital spent on a book by some publishing houses.

Two Sample Queries

The first query letter in Sidebar 14-1 was written by Carolyn Kortge, author of *The Spirited Walker*. It succeeded in attracting an agent who phoned her to request her proposal and subsequently offered her representation. About 60 percent of the agents she queried requested her proposal, but everyone, other than this one agent, used the mail. Agents, too, use strategies. Clearly, the agent who called her expected that she would receive many positive responses. Believing this, he acted quickly and beat out his competition. I consider Carolyn's query to be a superb model. If I have any criticism, it would be of its length. I would have advised her to

> Remember, your query and your enclosures have only one purpose: to gain a request to see your proposal.

shorten it by one-half to one-third. However, every writer has his or her own style of writing, and book subjects differ in complexity. Remember, your goal is to get a high percentage of positive interest from agents and editors, not to get stuck worrying about whether your letter is too short or too long.

In Sidebar 14-1, I've added my comments pointing out what job Carolyn Kortge accomplished in each paragraph. Use this fine letter as one model.

Sidebar 14-1
Sample: Query Letter
Carolyn Scott Kortge

Comments on the query are inserted between paragraphs in italics.

Dear Agent:

"Walking is the nation's most popular fitness activity, five times as popular as jogging," *New York Times* health writer Jane Brody reported in an April 17, 1996, article. Pollsters tell us that anywhere from 36 to 60 million Americans walk for exercise. *The Walking Magazine* labels 16.2 million of those people "frequent walkers" who exercise more than 100 days a year.

The query lead uses a quote from an authority that establishes the popularity of walking for fitness. Statistics support the size of the market and why this book meets the needs of our society at this time. Notice the powerful case made by authoritative sources and statistics.

This enormous body of walkers represents a vast market for a walking book that goes beyond heart rates and calorie counts. My book, *The Spirited Walker: Fitness Walking for Clarity, Balance, and Spiritual Connection,* takes off where other fitness walking guides end. It places care of the soul on equal footing with care of the body and transforms workouts into active, walking meditations. As readers learn to still mental distractions and connect with the spirit within, walking workouts become a route to increased clarity, self-awareness, and personal strength.

This paragraph introduces the proposed book and its breadth, stating how it is different and identifying the primary reader benefits.

I would like you to represent this book because of the respect Natalie Goldberg has expressed for you in her books. When I read *Writing Down the Bones*, I'd already collected quite a few national journalism awards. Writing was my work, my passion. I'd never considered that it could also be a spiritual practice. As that awareness stretched into my daily life, it transformed not only my journal but also my workouts. Thank you for seeing the power of her work.

This paragraph personalizes the query to a particular agent. The author substituted similar paragraphs personalized to each agent

(Continued)

she queried. She also introduces her author qualifications and the origins of her interest in the topic.

The Spirited Walker: Fitness Walking for Clarity, Balance, and Spiritual Connection emerges out of a solid base of journalism, walking experience, and spiritual exploration. In 1990, the American Association of Sunday and Feature Editors called me one of "The Best" in a national competition. The award echoes opinions of newspaper readers, editors, and journalism judges who have praised my work during a twenty-year writing career. In 1989, I entered my first athletic event, a 10K race walk for athletes aged thirty-five and over. By 1992, I ranked in the top five women walkers nationally in my age group. Two years ago, I stepped back from competition and found my stride in aerobic, walking meditations.

This paragraph features author qualifications. Notice how specific she is and how she asserts her accomplishments with confidence.

Typically, walking books tuck references to the mental or spiritual components of walking into chapters on relaxation and stress management. Meditation books tend to leave walkers at stroll. But the continued popularity of walking for fitness has brought increasing awareness of its impact as a mind-body workout. In his current bestseller, *Timeless Healing* (1996, Scribner), Herbert Benson, M.D., introduces the concept of "focused walking" for relaxation. The authors of *Walk Aerobics* (1995, The Overlook Press) conclude with a chapter on "inner walking." Linus Mundy's pocket guide to *Prayer-Walking* (1994, Abbey Press) encourages walkers to connect with God. These books, along with magazine articles that recommend walking to combat stress, suggest that it is time for a walking book that lifts body-mind awareness out of the back pages and makes it the focus of an invigorating new approach to America's leading fitness exercise.

This is a substantial paragraph introducing competitive and similar titles, but showing how her book is the right book for the emerging readiness in the culture. Kortge establishes her book as fulfilling the needs introduced but not developed by prior authors.

With a powerful blend of polished journalism and compelling personal essays, *The Spirited Walker: Fitness Walking for Clarity, Balance, and Spiritual Connection* leads fitness walkers along a path of mental and physical exercise that transforms aerobic walking work-

(Continued)

outs into an active, spiritual practice. It engages walkers of any age or fitness level in an exploration of moving meditations that combine walking with words of inspiration, with affirmations, visualizations, and breath work.

This paragraph combines more author qualifications with a reminder of reader benefits. It begins to introduce The Spirited Walker's features.

Anecdotes from the author's experiences as fitness walker, competitive athlete, and walking instructor weave warm, intimate threads through the book. Profiles of walkers whose steps have led to similar, whole-body experiences broaden its range. Supporting material from sports psychologists, physicians, physical therapists, fitness trainers, walkers, athletes and researchers assists readers in developing personal, whole-body walking programs. In each chapter, a blend of interviews, practical how-to's, and personal examples leads readers into workouts that strengthen muscle, mind, and spirit. Suggested exercises, grouped in "Moves for Spirit and Soul" sections, introduce simple walking or meditation techniques. Sidebars and charts supplement the text with capsule information on walker basics including location, target heart rates, motivational resources, and walking with pets.

This whopper of a paragraph details the features that comprise the book. Such a detailed list conveys that the author has either written a substantial portion of the book or has thoroughly thought out its structure and contents. Through the features, the author telegraphs the depth of the work and the fact that it will be richer through the inclusion of wisdom and knowledge from others.

The Spirited Walker: Fitness Walking for Clarity, Balance, and Spiritual Connection is both practical and inspirational. It maps a route to awareness and wholeness, to re-connection with self, with nature or with a higher power one step at a time, on the sidewalks outside our homes. It invites us to discover in our own neighborhoods what Peter Matthiessen, author of *The Snow Leopard*, learned while walking in the mountains of Nepal: "The purpose of meditation practice is not enlightenment; it is to pay attention even at unextraordinary times, to be of the present, nothing-but-the-present, to bear this mindfulness of *now* into each event of ordinary life."

(Continued)

This paragraph emphasizes reader benefits and draws upon a quote by a bestselling inspirational author to further indicate the meditation aspect that echoes the author's philosophy and can be expected in the writing.

Thank you for considering this request for representation. I am enclosing additional background information and clips of my writing. A complete proposal and sample chapters from *The Spirited Walker: Fitness Walking for Clarity, Balance, and Spiritual Connection* are available at your request. Please call or FAX to ask for a copy. I look forward to talking with you.

This closing paragraph offers the conclusion to the query, informing the agent of a completed proposal. Notice, too, the many repetitions of the book's title.

Cordially,
Carolyn Scott Kortge

Because short is sweet in the land of query letters, try to keep your letter to one page. Often, the top of letterhead stationery consumes the quarter top of the first page. In this case, it's worth the professional presentation, even if your query spills over onto a second page.

The second query example in Sidebar 14-2 features an impressive query for a memoir written by Chanrithy Him to agent Meredith Bernstein. Her book is *When Broken Glass Floats: A Memoir of the Khmer Rouge Years in Cambodia.* As an exception to the rule, the author tells me that she was able to secure agent representation and a contract on the strength of this query, a chapter summary, reference letters, and three sample chapters. When you read the query, I think you'll see why.

Marketing Strategies

Once you've finished drafting and polishing your query letter, you face five tasks before sending it. You must:

- Choose between agents and editors
- Decide whether or not to market to agents and editors simultaneously
- Find an agent or editor
- Evaluate agent/editor qualifications
- Develop a marketing strategy.

CHOOSE BETWEEN AGENTS AND EDITORS

Every book demands a different marketing strategy, and every writer has a unique set of values and preferences. Agents sell proposals to editors, and editors pitch proposals to publishing committees. Some writers look at this chain of sales and decide they will be one step ahead if they market directly to editors of publishing houses. This may or may not be to a writer's advantage. Others decide to play both hands and market to agents and editors simultaneously. Sidebar 14-3 shows some differences between marketing to an agent versus marketing to an editor.

With the exception of the special cases I will discuss at the end of the chapter, I recommend seeking an agent to help you market your proposal *only if* your market is mid-sized or large. Agents do much more for writers than find publishers and finagle higher advances. They are publishing experts. As literary agent Natasha Kern expressed in an article for *Writer's Northwest Handbook*:

> Agenting requires understanding sales and marketing (they are not the same thing); literary law; editing; publishing business practices; industry standards; requirements and protocols; publicity and promotion; counseling and career development; international and film-rights markets; arbitration; and a myriad of other things including the rapidly burgeoning opportunities in high-tech publishing.

Practically speaking, agents can't make a living selling books to small publishers. Remember how advances are figured (print size times retail cost times author's royalty rate). Now subtract the agent's 15 percent of author monies. Let's review: A common print run for a small or regional publisher is 5000. A trade book about the size of

Sidebar 14-2
Sample: Query Letter for a Memoir
Chanrithy Him

Comments analyzing what the author accomplishes are supplied in italics following each paragraph.

Dear Ms. Bernstein:

I consulted with Ms. Elizabeth Lyon about sending book proposals to literary agents and she recommended me to query you.

If you have been referred, always begin a query with mention of the person who referred you.

When I spoke at a 1991 conference at Portland State University, I was introduced to the audience, made up of educators and counselors, as "the Cambodian Anne Frank." While there are similarities in our stories, there are also differences, not the least of which is that the Cambodian holocaust is still underreported. In particular, the story of Cambodia's children has not been fully told. Recently I have completed the final draft of my memoir entitled, *When Broken Glass Floats*, which consists of 450 pages, including the epilogue. It won a 1996 Oregon Literary Fellowship, and a chapter from it ("When the Owl Cries") has been reprinted in an anthology (compiled by Mr. Dith Pran) from Yale University Press entitled, *Children of Cambodia's Killing Fields: Memoirs of Survivors*. Since it has been out, I have been contacted by readers who are interested in reading it.

This paragraph introduces the author as a public speaker and offers a terrific selling handle, "the Cambodian Anne Frank." The second sentence appeals to a larger reason for publishing the memoir—letting others know about the "underreported" holocaust of Cambodian children. I would have begun a new paragraph after this. However, the rest of the paragraph offers impressive publishing credits, awards, and the fact that the book is finished. With this paragraph, the author has already answered most of the questions in an agent's mind.

When Broken Glass Floats recounts my experiences from age four, in 1969, when my house in Takeo was destroyed, through the invasion of Cambodia by the Viet Cong, the witness of the covert American bombings near my uncle's home, the fall of Phnom Penh in 1975,

and the years during which the Khmer Rouge attempted to exterminate the entire educated population. While we were held prisoner in
our own country, my father and uncles were executed; my mother
and three siblings died of starvation-related illnesses; and I lost
twenty-eight members of my extended family in similar ways. Two of
my brothers, two older sisters, and I survived; today, we are United
States citizens.

*I doubt anyone could read this paragraph and not be moved. The
author describes the historical events and span of time included in
the memoir and how she personally experienced them. The horror
and tragedy are so great that Him wisely does not add any emotional embellishment. The facts speak for themselves. The closing
sentence of the paragraph offers some emotional relief and tells
that the author is a survivor and an American citizen.*

All who have read my manuscript have responded with praise
and encouragement. They have also told me that the events of my
childhood are not only heart-wrenching, but they also raise important questions about how human beings treat each other in times of
political conflict. The events of Bosnia, Rwanda, Northern Ireland,
and Iraq all point to the compelling necessity of the human family
finding ways of resolving conflicts without inflicting such suffering
on innocents. The story of my experiences in refugee camps and my
eventual immigration to the United States will help many people to
understand those who have followed similar paths.

*In this paragraph, the author describes the transcendent theme and
universal reach of her story. She widens the scope and describes the
difference she hopes her work will make for all readers, and especially for greater understanding of other refugees' experiences.*

Last December I presented a twelve-year follow-up study on
Cambodians who were young children during the Khmer Rouge
regime at the International Conference on Cambodia: "Power,
Myth, and Memory," in Melbourne, Australia, as well as at a conference called "Consolidation of the Cambodian Family: The Past, the
Present, and a Version of the Future," at California State University,
Long Beach. For a number of years, I have worked as a research
associate at the Division of Child Psychiatry at Oregon Health Sci-
ences University, on the study "The Khmer Adolescent Project on

(Continued)

Post Traumatic Stress Disorder in Victims of the Cambodian Holocaust," and have been a coauthor of several papers, which have been published by various psychological and psychiatric journals.

This amazing author now reveals her depth of involvement and commitment, as well as expertise. Any agent/editor would recognize that she can speak as an author who experienced what she has written about and as an expert who knows the latest research.

I met with Ms. Sarah Pinckney, the Trade Division editor at Simon & Schuster at the 1997 Pacific Northwest Writers Conference. She suggested that my memoir would appeal to publishers because of its timeliness, since horrible, poignant news has been escalating in Cambodia and has made news internationally. There has been fighting, many innocent people are dying, and thousands are dodging bullets and escaping to Thailand again, just as my remaining family and I, and thousands and thousands of others did eighteen years ago. Ms. Deb Futter (a friend of a friend), an editor at Random House, has been interested in seeing my manuscript. Although I have considered sending her a book proposal, as well as one to Ms. Pinckney, I have not sent it to them. Also, I have had inquiries from Mr. Neal Miller, a film producer and director and president of the Rubicon Film Productions, Ltd., with whom I met in April 1996. Other literary agents have read the manuscript and two have considered representing it. However, I would like to query more agents before I make my decision as to whom would be best representing me.

In this paragraph, Him offers the agent leads to editors she has already talked with, as well as to one film producer. She also draws from current events to highlight the timeliness of the book and the implied idea that "underreporting" might be contributing to history repeating itself in an awful way. She definitely offers a carrot on a stick to the right agent.

I am asking Mr. David Hawk, former head of Amnesty International, former director of the Cambodia Documentation Commission, and head of the Center for Human Rights at Columbia University, to write the introduction to my book and am enclosing a copy of Dr. William Sack's letter recommending that he do so. Mr. Sydney Schanberg of New York *Newsday*, and Mr. Dith Prah of *The New York Times*, whose experiences were portrayed in the film, *The*

(Continued)

Killing Fields, have agreed to write a jacket blurb and to do a book review, respectively. I will also ask Mr. William Shawcross, bestselling author of *Sideshow: Kissinger, Nixon, and the Destruction of Cambodia;* and the 1984 winner of World Hunger Media Award for the book, *Quality of Mercy*, the sequel to *Sideshow,* to write a foreword.

The author's passion is evident in her thoroughness. The author contacts and qualifications also speak to her ability to promote the book, to having "national outreach" and "international outreach." It is also a testament to how well respected she is.

I am also sending a letter of reference from my editor, Ms. Barbara Branscomb. I appreciate your careful consideration and look forward to hearing from you soon.

The editor to which Him refers is a freelance editor. Because English is not among Him's native languages, she sought help with her project from a well-respected literary book doctor. This also offers assurance to any agent/editor, although the writing in the query, whether the author's own or produced with assistance, is an example of her full competency with the language.

Best regards,
Chanrithy Him

Note: *Literary agent Meredith Bernstein did represent Chanrithy Him, selling her memoir to W.W. Norton.*

this one retails for about $20. Typically an author royalty would be about 7–8 percent of that price; let's say 8 percent. From the $100,000 the publisher would gross on that first print run, author royalties would ring in at $8000 (and publisher's net would be about the same). Let's say this publisher gives advances, perhaps $4000. The agent would see 15 percent, or $600 up front, and if the book sold through all 5000 copies, the agent would receive another $600—eventually. Since it takes the same effort to sell another book to a large publisher who plans to print 15,000–50,000 copies, if you were an agent, which project would you represent?

Sidebar 14-3

Pros and Cons of Marketing to Agents and Editors

Advantages With Agents

1. Ninety percent of all published books were represented by an agent. With an editor, you may get a lower priority reading. Most large publishers refuse unagented material.

2. Agents know which houses and editors are buying. Your work could get lost or rejected by the "wrong" editor.

3. Agents can reach editors with more clout. You may have to work up through readers to a senior editor.

4. Agents can make multiple submissions and arrange auctions. Generally, you may submit only one proposal at a time to editors.

5. Agents work for you; they usually negotiate for more money, subsidiary rights, and protection clauses.

6. Editors work for publishers. They may use a poorer contract for writers without agents.

7. An agent can act as a buffer between an editor and writer. Agents absorb rejection and act as mediators on your behalf. You're blessed or stuck with dealing with your editor, and they've got the power.

8. Agents help sculpt your career. They can market future works to other publishers. Editors work to save money. Their first concern is the bottom line, not you.

9. Agents receive letters of explanation for rejected materials. Writers more often get form rejections.

10. Because editors have long-term relationships with agents, editors respond more quickly to agent submissions than to those sent by writers.

11. Editors come and go; an agent works for the long-haul.

12. Through publishers, monies from the sale of subsidiary sales are applied against the advance. Agents can reserve many subsidiary rights, so the writer receives those monies before the advance is earned out.

(Continued)

Advantages With Editors

1. You receive all advance monies and royalties as specified in your contract. Agents deduct 15 percent commissions on all monies you receive.

2. Editors read for free. Some agents still charge reading fees.

3. You pay for marketing that your agent does on your behalf. After you have a contract, the publisher pays for any mailings on your behalf.

4. You reach "The Source" directly and enjoy a relationship uncomplicated by a person in the middle.

5. Marketing time is on your side. You are active, not passive. Months or years may go by waiting for an inefficient agent to market or respond to you.

6. With one book to market, your research can find appropriate publishers. Agents have favorite editors and houses. If your book doesn't fit these, it may never be sent to the right house or editor.

7. You receive more money dealing directly with an editor. On a first book, an agent may not secure a better contract or get you more money, yet you pay their 15 percent commission on all royalties you receive.

8. Time and effort to find an editor shortcuts the process. It's easy to find an agent after you've got a publisher.

9. You spend time and effort just to find an agent. You must still wait while they market to publishers.

10. Agents often don't handle specialized books, books too small, or books for a regional publisher.

DECIDE WHETHER OR NOT TO MARKET SIMULTANEOUSLY TO AGENTS AND EDITORS

If your book is aimed at a market large enough to warrant agent representation, you can query agents and editors at the same time. However, first pursue any referrals or requests—agent or editor. If you have no referrals and must rely upon a list of unfamiliar names in directories, then market to both groups, unless you have a strong

preference otherwise. By querying editors at publishing houses, you
could eliminate the long passages of time while waiting to find an
agent who in turn will approach editors, in which case you must
wait again. If you are offered a contract from an interested publisher, you'll have no trouble finding an agent. You've done the marketing and found a buyer, and this indeed makes you an attractive
client to an agent. You will even be in a position to interview agents
and choose your favorite.

Why get an agent if you've already found a publisher, especially
if you feel comfortable working directly with your editor? In the
Resource Directory, I've listed some books that offer guidance for
negotiating your own contract. However, agents are contract
experts; for all of the reasons mentioned previously, and in Sidebar
14-3, agents have many more functions that may be helpful to a
writer.

One more reality that weighs in on the side of seeking agent representation for your book is that, increasingly, the giant conglomerates with their hundreds of imprint publishing houses may only
consider inquiries or manuscripts submitted by agents. In fact, several of my agent friends complain that they, too, must often wait three
to five months to get decisions from editors whom they know well.

FIND AN AGENT OR EDITOR

Several matchmaking methods exist for connecting writers with
agents and editors. Successful "marriages" have blossomed from
each method. The primary goal is to find one that works for you.

You may find an agent/editor through:

- Face-to-face contact
- Word-of-mouth recommendations
- Directories, listings, or Web sites

Face-to-face Contact

In an ideal universe, you would meet face to face with one hundred
agents and editors. Then you would select each other based upon
personal chemistry, shared goals, and the merits of your proposal.

For most writers, it is not possible to ring up one, much less 100 agents or editors, to suggest that you "do lunch." Even if you live in the same city with a literary agent, don't expect a warm response to your invitation to get together. Agents don't have the time and, to tell the truth, with a 99 percent rejection rate, it would be unprofitable for them to meet most writers. As a result, agents and editors prefer query letters.

> Every writer I know who has gone to a conference and met with agents or editors has returned with at least one request to send material.

Regardless, a great way to gather first impressions is to go to writer's conferences where agents and editors attend. These publishing professionals not only attend because it is good public relations for their firms; they hope to meet new writers. They really are talent scouts, hoping to meet the next Dr. John Gray (*Men Are From Mars Women Are From Venus*), or Elizabeth Marshall Thomas (*The Hidden Life of Dogs*), or Thomas Moore (*Soul Mates*).

In their May issue, *Writer's Digest Magazine* publishes a list of some of the hundreds of conferences that take place each year. A terrific Internet site is the Guide to Writers Conferences, www.shaw guides.com. You may also find out what conferences take place in your region by contacting local arts associations, local or regional chapters of writers' organizations, and through directories stocked by most libraries (See Resource Directory). Or ask your local reference librarian to help you find conferences that take place near you.

The benefit of face-to-face meetings with agents or editors is that you can get a lot accomplished instantly. While both of you are recording your impressions of each other as people, you'll be discussing your book project. Best of all, you'll get an on-the-spot yes or no to your book idea, without having to wait weeks or months for your proposal to reach the top of someone's backlog.

Word-of-Mouth Recommendations

Word-of-mouth remains the best sales tool in existence. Everyone in business builds a reputation. You can get name referrals, especially for agents (but also for editors), by asking anyone with a connection to the publishing industry. Go to book signings and presentations and talk with authors. Call or meet with your friendly manager of Barnes and Noble or an owner of an independent bookstore. If you get an editor interested in your book, ask him or her for referrals to trustworthy agents. Talk with freelance editors and writing teachers, or with a book-review editor at your newspaper. Call editors or publishing consultants listed in your yellow pages. Pretty soon, you'll hear a repetition of names, know who to avoid, or receive a resounding recommendation.

Directories, Listings, or Web Sites

Even if you live in an igloo hundreds of miles above the Arctic Circle, you can find an agent or editor by letting "your fingers do the walking" and your mouse do the clicking. Instead of the telephone book (unless you live in New York where over one hundred agents are listed), consult the directories shown in Sidebar 14-4. Also realize that the majority of publishers and agents now have web pages. Many of these sites also list their nonfiction book interests and guidelines for writing and submitting nonfiction book proposals.

EVALUATE AGENT/EDITOR QUALIFICATIONS

Most writers have a difficult time evaluating whether or not an agent/editor is qualified and the right match for their books. Agents and editors, like any other professionals, come in three categories: great at what they do, good at what they do, and not so good.

Literary Agents

A literary agent may be great for one author and so-so for another. Just like trying to find a good dance partner, sometimes you can't tell about someone until you get out on the floor.

Directories and web sites will help you make an initial judgement. For instance, you can find out how long an agent has been in business and whether or not she belongs to the AAR (Association of

Author's Representatives) which, as a membership requirement, demands agreement to a code of ethics and demonstration of success. Look closely at the types of books an agent prefers, titles of recent sales, and the percentage of nonfiction represented.

While the directories often list recent sales by title and publisher, you can write to an agent and request a client list or a list of recent sales. (Do enclose an SASE.) Postpone this step, however, until an agent has accepted your proposal.

From their agency brochures, web sites, or directory examples, check recent sales by agents of books like yours. Determine the size, variety, and location of the listed publishers. Are they large houses or obscure small ones? Do you see a predominance of sales to the same publishers, implying agent familiarity with only a few favorites?

While no one charges to read query letters, a small number of agents charge a fee ranging from $25–$75 to read and evaluate proposals, even though the AAR agents have agreed as an organization that reading fees are unethical. If you see any fee higher than this amount, consider it a red flag.

Some agents sidestep the issue of reading fees by charging an editing fee. Writer beware. Most proposals and books do, in fact, need revision and polishing before they are ready for the eyes of an acquisitions editor. Ethical agents handle this need for editing in one of two ways. Either they edit the manuscripts themselves, at no charge, or they recommend the editorial services of several freelance editors whom they know and trust.

For instance, half a dozen agents occasionally refer writers to me for editing. This is ethical and an example of networking. But, even a system of referral can be abused. A few years ago, hundreds of unpublished writers were exploited by one large editing company who set up a kickback arrangement with agents, while giving lower than average editing advice for the high amounts of dollars they charged. Fortunately, the company was indicted for mail fraud. There is nothing new about this arrangement. Every year, this same hand-in-glove, money-making operation shows up in many smaller forms. Since the most common agent directories don't screen their

Sidebar 14-4
Agent and Editor Directories and Web Sites

Note: While a majority of agents and publishers are legitimate and honest, some of the bad eggs slip into these directories. Always check backgrounds.

- *The Literary Market Place*: Lists several hundred agent and editor names, addresses, and preferences. www.*literarymarketplace.com*
- LiteraryAgent.com: A web site devoted to helping authors find agents, including links to agent home pages. *www.literaryagent.com*
- *Guide to Literary Agents: a Paperback Directory* published annually by Writers Digest Books: Lists about 500 agents, their basic credentials, memberships in AAR (Association of Author's Representatives), and what they are looking for. It also identifies agents who represent books for children.
- The Association of Author's Representatives (AAR), the only professional organization for literary agents: Offers a members' list and a code of ethics, if you will send a legal-sized self-addressed-stamped envelope (SASE) with two first-class stamps and $5 in check or money order to: AAR, PO Box 237201, Ansonia Station, N.Y., N.Y. 10003. Or go to their web site: *www.bookwire.com/AAR/*
- *Writer's Market* (about 1,200 publisher listings and 50 agents) and *Children's Writer's and Illustrator's Market*: Lists and describes publishers, their needs, and the editors to whom you should address your query. Available in CD-ROM as well. *www.writersdigest.com*
- *Writer's Handbook*, published by The Writer, Inc.: Lists and describes publishers and offers about 200 agent listings, though the description for each is sparse.

(Continued)

- *Writer's Guide to Book Editors, Publishers, and Literary Agents* by Jeff Herman (Prima Publishing): The only guide (other than *LMP*) that gives in-house editor names and their specialties. Describes about 500 North American publishers and about 200 agents.
- *How to Get Your Teaching Ideas Published: A Writer's Guide to Educational Publishing,* (Walker & Co.): Helps connect the teacher/writer with an educational publisher.
- *Writing for the Ethnic Markets* by Meera Lester, (Writer's Connection): Out of print, but available on used market. Provides names and descriptions to publishers who seek books targeted to ethnic audiences or with multicultural emphasis.
- Predators and Editors: Listings of agents who are "not recommended." *www.sfwa.org/prededitors/peala.htm*
- Agent Research and Evaluation: A company that monitors literary agents and will check on a specific agent for you without charge. *www.agentresearch.com*

listings, each year I recognize a few of these bad apples at the bottom of the barrel.

You may be wondering what the issue is. After all, other businesses routinely send a gratuity to thank companies that refer customers. And writers should expect to pay editorial fees for editorial services.

Here is the problem: Since most manuscripts are rejected by agents, you must ask yourself if an agent is making money from editorial services or from cuts on referrals, and not from selling works. In the case of editorial services—ranging from several hundred to several thousand dollars—literary agents risk a conflict of interest. The problem with a financial relationship between a particular agent and a freelance editor is that the two businesses appear objective and separate from one another. If an agent always recommends

"Acme Editing Services" with every response letter sent out, once again, the writer might draw conclusions that are not based in fact. They may assume that it is this agent's professional opinion that the manuscript needs editing, that this one editing service is the very best, and after using this particular service, the agent will consider representation. With these arrangements, the agent does not typically disclose the comfortable financial arrangement, and may never personally read any of the author's work.

The gray areas abound. After all, those of us in this business happily refer writers to other professionals whom we know. But we do so freely, no strings attached—if we are ethical. You can protect yourself from exploitation by asking any agent who suggests that you could benefit from professional editing services to recommend three to five independent editors. Make sure that no money passes hands for these referrals. Then, interview the editors as you would any other professional offering a service. Ask for names of satisfied customers and what goes into a typical manuscript evaluation.

Although many background facts can be researched before you commit to an agent, you should reserve some crucial questions of qualifications and compatibility until your manuscript has been accepted. Sometimes writers feel so relieved to have found an agent who likes their work and wants to represent them that they fail to ask other important questions that could make the difference between a good partnership and a bad one. I'll introduce these questions later in chapter fifteen.

Editors

It's much easier to get information about the performance of agents than of editors. Many marketing directories provide editor names and titles, and some offer an editor's specialty, but I haven't heard of a directory that spells out how long an editor has been in the business, or in a position. I doubt you will find a source that reports how many of one author's books an editor has shepherded from acquisitions to publication. The problem of evaluating an editor's skill is complicated by the revolving door changes in personnel in most houses. An editor who acquires your book may not be employed with your publisher when it is published.

Your best hope of getting some impressions about editors is to meet them at writer's conferences and to track them through the ardent reading of *Publishers Weekly*. A reference librarian can also initiate a computer search to find every time an editor's—or agent's—name has appeared in print. One particular technique for finding a "hungry" editor—or evaluating one—is to read the columns in *Publishers Weekly* called "People" and "Rights." You'll pick up the rumors and reports of who has moved where or sold what to whom.

> Phone queries are almost universally inappropriate. E-mail queries must be decided on a case by case basis.

Here's where agents once again prove invaluable. Good agents listen to the talking drums of the Big Apple. They hear stories and add their personal experience with editors to the rumors. If you work with an agent, he or she is your best barometer for measuring an editor's skill and compatibility with your project; conversely, an astute editor can steer you toward a qualified agent.

DEVELOP A MARKETING STRATEGY

Let's suppose you've culled through directories and web sites, received various word-of-mouth recommendations, and have even met some agents or editors at a workshop. From this, you have identified several dozen agents or editors to whom your project could be sent. What's next? What will further your goals?

First, you must be sensitive to the issue of "simultaneous submissions." This refers to mailing a submission, meaning a query or proposal, to more than one agent or editor at a time. Simultaneous submissions contrast with "exclusive submissions," in which the writer is expected to submit to one agent/editor and wait for a response before marketing to anyone else.

It is universally agreed that writers may send simultaneous submissions of queries, and not mention this fact in their letters. Policies about simultaneous submissions of proposals and book manuscripts, however, differ widely from one agency and publisher to another.

Some agents make their preferences known in the agent directories. Others tell you what they prefer in the same response with policies they have with the same response letter that requests the proposal. The best way to be clear about an agent or editor "rules" is to ask about their policy is after you get their requests to see your proposal or manuscript. In fact, at this point, a phone call might be expedient. Everyone in the industry recognizes the insufferable passage of time while manuscripts are being processed. Many editors and agents find nothing wrong with writers submitting simultaneously, *as long as they are so informed.*

A strategy that puts you in control of the waiting process with an agent or editor who requests exclusive consideration of your proposal is to inform the person that you will allow the "exclusive" for six or eight weeks, after which you'll begin to send it elsewhere. Be specific and include a date. About two weeks before the end of the exclusive time period, call or send an e-mail or note reminding the agent or editor of your continuing hope that they will want to represent or purchase your manuscript, and politely remind them of the deadline. Believe me, most of us work to a deadline and not a moment before.

From an agent or editor's point of view, instructions to you about what to submit and how constitute a kind of test. Agent Natasha Kern said that if a writer doesn't follow her agency's instructions, it makes her wonder if she would have problems with communication later. When a writer doesn't submit what an agent or editor requests, it plants an image of unreliability. On the other hand, writers are so used to kowtowing to agents and editors, these professionals may have forgotten that communication is a two-way street; writers can make requests as well.

In the past, I've recommended that writers send a query or requested proposal as an exclusive to any agent or editor they've met or been personally referred to. However, exclusive submissions can put you in the uncompromising position of having no choice. If that agent or editor accepts your manuscript, do you then say "No,

I want to shop around"? In the end, a writer's strongest option is to send simultaneous submissions.

Send simultaneous queries to as many or as few agents and editors as you wish. I suggest mailing your material in batches of ten. Although you could theoretically mail queries to all 800 agents in North America and be done with marketing, this might hinder your chances of success more than help. Ten queries allow you to test the market and receive feedback. You'll find out whether your query will yield multiple requests for your proposal, form rejections, or rejections with reasons that could help you adapt your approach for the next batch.

The late Gaines Smith—a writer, teacher, and editor to whom this book is dedicated—introduced me to the idea of staggered submissions. He noticed in directories that some agents and editors stated they responded to queries within six weeks. Others listed four weeks, two weeks, or one week. He staggered the mailing of his queries in order to receive all responses back at the same time— theoretically giving him maximum choice and allowing for the least amount of lag time between an agent request for his manuscript and acting upon that request.

Reading fees may also factor into your decision about who to query. Although no one charges to read a query, you may decide to exclude agents who charge a fee to read your proposal. Of course, editors of publishing houses never charge reading fees.

While marketing your book, first with a query and then with your proposal, only one taboo exists: Never query an agent or editor over the phone. When asked, these publishing professionals universally expressed a loathing of phone interruptions from writers wanting to pitch their ideas. *Send a query.*

That said, here's the inevitable exception: You may call a publisher in order to get the appropriate editor name. Occasionally, this will put you in touch with a senior editor in charge of your book's subject, instead of with a secretary. Be prepared to describe your project. Remember your selling handle. Have your concept statement close by. The editor may invite you to submit your proposal. If so, you've just upgraded your submission from unsolicited to solicited. Last of all, increasingly, more agents now list their e-mail addresses in directories and on web sites. This is not an open invitation to send an e-mail query. While some agents prefer the e-mail query, you must read their instructions and follow them. Let me reiterate, never—almost never—call or e-mail an agent or editor.

Interpreting Responses From Query Letters

You can expect one of three responses to your query letters.

- A form rejection letter
- A personalized rejection letter
- A go-ahead letter

A FORM REJECTION LETTER

Form rejections are a curse to everyone in the publishing industry. Editors and agents don't enjoy sending them, and writers hate receiving them. Even a small publisher can easily spend ten hours per week saying no to unsolicited submissions and queries with SASEs. That's more than most can afford. But every query, no matter how tersely rejected, is first considered seriously. A competent editor is always hoping to find that one in a hundred. But most queries are not even targeted to the right publisher. That's one of the problems for which this book is a solution.

Most active agents receive 3000–5000 queries each year. If you were a one-person agency, perhaps with some clerical help, how would you respond to 50 to 100 queries each week when only half a dozen or fewer sounded interesting?

Take a form rejection at face value. A refusal from one agent/editor may be a blessing to try another, better-suited one. A refusal from a publisher might signal a need on your part to make sure you're sending your query to appropriate publishers for your subject and approach.

A PERSONALIZED REJECTION LETTER

Let me save you a beginner's error in judgment: Don't dwell on the rejection in a personalized response letter and fail to recognize the encouragement. Agents and editors don't write personal letters or notes for the exercise. Pay close attention. If an agent or editor goes to the trouble to explain why your query was rejected, you may be able to make adjustments, rewrite, and then resubmit to the same agent or editor. Because they often do not have the time to explain how closely your work came to supplying their needs, a resubmission may still meet with rejection. You can't know ahead of time, so go ahead and resubmit. Your problem could be as simple as inexperience in crafting a good query. The agent/editor might feel unsure of your market; you can clarify or expand it by changing your slant. The agent/editor might feel uncertain about your author qualifications; you can send an expanded author biography and clips of articles about yourself or your subject.

You may get rejected a second time, but you will have earned respect as a writer willing to write and rewrite. You've actually begun a relationship. On the other hand, you may get accepted the second time. Your rewritten query may lead to a request for your proposal. Bull's-eye! In this case, the initial rejection has been transformed into an acceptance.

Although all agents and editors have their own biases and tastes, any comment by one of these professionals is worth your serious consideration. You may be tempted to discard the reason for rejection, but more likely, you'll find some kernel of critique that will help you adjust your approach.

Last of all, you will occasionally get a personalized rejection letter that completely disagrees with your sensibilities. It may be written in what seems to be an insulting choice of words. The reasons for rejection express one opinion, and the source may have had indigestion or personal problems that had nothing to do with you. Remember, these editors or agents may write things that irritate you, but not *to* irritate you. You, the writer, make the final decision of what comments or criticism you accept or reject. If something written seems mean-spirited or untrue, be Teflon-coated and let it slide out of your life.

A GO-AHEAD

Savor the exciting moment when an agent or editor says, "Yes!" You may even receive a phone call to your query, especially if the editor or agent is excited about your project and wants the kind of impressions that can only come from some kind of personal contact. He may call in order to gain assurance that someone else hasn't beaten him to the acquisition. It's great to be sought after. Stay on your toes, however. If the agent or editor asks you for exclusive consideration of your proposal, or any other kind of terms, be ready to express delight in a request for your proposal, but keep all your options open. You can suggest that you've already promised to let another agent or editor read the proposal, or you can grant exclusive consideration but only if you get a quick response, say, within four weeks.

If you have the opportunity of such a phone response, gather your wits. This is an appropriate time to ask further questions about your prospective agent or editor. Some of these questions are offered in chapter fifteen.

Based on a phone acceptance or a letter of acceptance, do not send your proposal prematurely. You have a window of two weeks or so in which to finish polishing and packaging your proposal. Use this time to make final rewrites. Two weeks is nothing in this industry of hurry-up-and-wait, at least not at this stage.

When you get that yes, it's time to polish, package, and send your proposal.

CHAPTER FIFTEEN

The Perfect Proposal: From Final Edit to Contract Offer

Chapter Goal: To polish your proposal and secure agent representation and editorial acceptance.

Polishing Your Proposal

While your query letters are zipping through the mails to their destinations, turn your full attention to revising, polishing, and packaging your proposal. You must edit your proposal at least three times for three different purposes: for content, for copy mistakes, and for format.

CONTENT EDIT

Playing the part of an editor, look at your proposal objectively for three content-related problems:

1. A good title
2. Correct organization
3. Clear definition and purpose

A Good Title

Although you've had a working title throughout the creation of the proposal, reexamine the title now. How well will it serve as a selling hook? Two guidelines may help.

- Market tests show that book purchasers respond most favorably to titles that are five words or less.
- Choose a descriptive title over a clever title. (*Cheapskate Decorating* is both!)

When your main title is literary or poetic, you should use your subtitle to modify or better explain your book. For example, *We'll Remember in November: Molly Yard's Gift to Women's Rights*. Remember, too, your first customer is an agent/editor.

Correct Organization

One of the most important aspects of content editing is to diagnose how clearly, logically, and appropriately a writer has organized each section of the proposal. Confusing structure shows up as the most common "disease" in the proposals I "treat." For a high-energy manuscript, repair and reorder sections, paragraphs, sentences, and words that are misplaced. Check each section against your outline and review the instructions in this book for organizing each section.

Clear Definition and Purpose

Another aspect of content editing is to make sure that each section of your proposal accomplishes its intended purpose. Review the statements of chapter goals in this book and those sections marked "definition and purpose."

COPY EDIT

Copy editing is like giving your manuscript a face-lift. It refers to corrections of grammar, spelling, and punctuation. You've probably become so accustomed to your work that you may not even see those unsightly blemishes. Seek outside help for editing. It's a manifestation of Murphy's Law that once you send off your proposal, you'll look over your copy and find at least one typo—usually on page one.

> Clarity and consistency in format increases clarity of content.

Some of the most effective editing involves tightening, which means revising nearly every sentence, every paragraph, and every page. Clarify muddy thoughts and you'll find extra words to delete. Shorten a work and it becomes better.

FORMAT EDIT

Although many writers know about content and copy editing, proposals are specialized documents that also require editing for format. Two aspects of format that you must check are:

- Order of the proposal parts
- Graphic consistency

Order of the Proposal Parts

Because this book has led you through the construction of a proposal in the order that is most helpful to writing it, you must now reorganize the sections for consideration by an agent or editor. A complete list of proposal parts in standard order is:

Title Page
Concept Statement *
Proposal Table of Contents *
About the Book
About the Author *   *Asterisk refers to sections*
About the Market *   *that may be moved around*
About the Competition *   *for emphasis or marketing*
Production Details *   *reasons.*
About Promotion *
Table of Contents
Chapter Summaries
Sample Chapters
The Appendix

In earlier chapters, you learned about all the essential sections of the proposal. Now is the time to draft a title page and table of contents for your proposal.

TITLE PAGE

You may use a larger font size to dress up your title. Use caps or bold or both. Don't use an underlined title, even though that is the grammatically correct way to show manuscript italics for a book title. This is a sales tool, not an English term paper. You're allowed to take certain liberties to enhance your product.

PROPOSAL TABLE OF CONTENTS

The proposal table of contents looks like any other table of contents. Even so, think appearances, not just content. Line up indents, spaces, and periods to create a subtle but powerful graphic feeling of order and beauty. Seriously. For example:

GRAPHIC CONSISTENCY

In your editing for format, check the following items:

1. Consistent labeling
2. Consistent font, size, and emphasis
3. Consistent space and overall format

Consistent Labeling

Throughout this book, I have used the same name for each of the proposal parts. The industry has no standard template for proposal design; nor is there one set of titles for each of the parts. One of my hopes is that this book will introduce a guideline for proposals that could serve as a prototype for an industry standard.

Regardless, no two books or authors are the same. The proposal must be flexible enough to accommodate individuality and creativity, but it must remain clear to the reader. Where a different section heading better matches your subject or personality than the ones I've used, know that you can make a change without breaking some rule.

Sidebar 15-1
Title Page

[start one-third to one-half down]

THE BEST BOOK EVER

by

Jane Doe

Jane Doe
1111 Main St., Town, ST. 00000
541-555-1212
email: jane@janedoe.com
www.janedoe.com

Inconsistent section headings, however, are as distracting as loud commercials. Because headings emphasize important divisions within your text and formulate "meaning bytes" (my term), it's important to think about their construction.

Check your headings according to the following guidelines:

- Make them brief, half a line or less
- Use parallel syntax for same-level headings
- Avoid using a long series of nouns or adjectives
- Eliminate double-meanings and confusing terms.

Consistent Font, Size, and Emphasis

I owe Stew Meyers, a brilliant technical editor and a wonderful friend, a debt of gratitude. He first brought to my attention "little" details that I had previously ignored. Technical writers like Stew are light years ahead in making written material accessible to readers. He pointed out to me that consistent headlines enhance accessibility and aesthetics.

Headings increase reader accessibility by their content and by the way they break up text, visually. Make sure you use the same font, size, and emphasis for the headings at each level across all proposal sections. By level, I mean the heading that would correspond, in an outline, to the large Roman numerals I, II, III, then the A, B, C, and then to the 1, 2, 3, and so forth. If you look back over the headings in this book, you'll see an example of consistency in headings by font, size, and emphasis for each level or hierarchy of information.

> The standard type size is still 10-12 points, no smaller. Use an attractive, non-compressed font with serifs.

In this age of increasingly sophisticated software and printers, many writers have the capacity to create whatever size of type they choose. Twelve-point font size often corresponds to the standard ten characters per inch, but not if you use a compressed font like Times New Roman. If you are unsure about your type size, get out a ruler and count! You can depart from standard size, but only if you go slightly larger. You may also select a font of your choice (Courier is still acceptable but not required), but always choose one with serifs for easy readability.

Size and emphasis (bold, uppercase, underline, etc.) correspond to levels of organization (hierarchy), giving your reader easier access to your material. The following guidelines may help you make those decisions about these "little" details:

- Indentation shows more importance than non-indentation
- Larger type shows more importance than smaller type
- Upper case shows more importance than lower case, though studies show that upper case is slower to read
- Bold shows more importance than non-bold
- Bold and upper case show more importance than either alone
- Italics and underlining show more importance than using neither; however, both are considered harder to read.

Consistent Space and Overall Format

While checking your headings, also check your spacing. Make sure your right margin is *un*justified. Drop down the same amount of space from the top of each page to begin typing. Use the same spacing between text and the headings that follow it and between headings and the text that follows it. Also use the same spacing between items on a list, and between lists and text. This may seem like extraordinary measures; but consistent format, including use of space, creates a subtle but powerful impact of order and professionalism.

> Consider overusing space rather than underusing it, since agents and editors spend most of their time looking at the printed page.

Released from the confusion of inconsistency, the agent/editor can focus on the content of your proposal.

Most agents and editors prefer double-spacing throughout the proposal, as well as for the sample chapters. Others accept single-spacing (with spaces left between paragraphs), as long as the sample chapters are double-spaced. You may find that a mixture looks best—double-spacing for most sections and single-spacing for a few. I like to use lots of graphics to create organizational units, both for visual relief and for reader stimulation. These graphics simply don't look as good with double-spacing as with single-spacing. Indented and bulleted lists, for instance, look best when single-spaced. If your proposal is mostly text, use double-spacing. For clarity's sake, always double-space sample chapters. Your agent will let you know her or his preference.

Be generous with your margins. While professional specifications demand a minimum of a one-inch margin, studies show that readers prefer a print density of 40 percent. You would not want to go as far as having pages that are 60 percent blank; however, you do want to make it easy to read your proposal.

Use a 1" to 1.25" margin for all sides. It's standard to drop down six line spaces (or half an inch) before you begin your header—your name, title, and page number. However, you could drop another 0.75" to 1" in line space *after* the header, before you print your first section title.

Among the many changes in format since many of us attended high school and college is the amount of space left after a period. Use one space, not two. The reason for the change has to do with the proportional spacing of computer fonts that make every typed page look as if a typesetter has prepared it for print.

Page numbering in your proposal should, by the way, be consecutive from the first page of "About the Book" through the last page of your chapter summaries. Start over with page number one for the first page of your sample chapters.

If you'd rather be writing your book than editing for format, hire a perfectionist to edit it for you.

Packaging Your Proposal

You could mail in your typed proposal with no special effects and you'll still have a more professional presentation than most. But why stop there? Imagine your proposal as a shop filled with treasures. Agents and editors have never been inside this store before. Their first impressions begin with the display window. What's there should draw them in, from title page to "Concept Statement" to the last page of the sample chapters.

Depending upon the proposal, the display window might be something from the appendix, such as your photo, a color photocopy of an article, or perhaps a clearly labeled videotape. Or, the display window might be an attractive title page on one side of a folder and the first page of the sample chapters on the other side—both with clear, dark print on white paper. Arrange your material in the way that makes the best first impression.

Depending upon the length of your proposal and the additional bulk provided by material in your appendix, you may need to package your proposal in a standard manuscript box. These are available at most office-supply stores. If you do have a large proposal, stack it in the box in the following top-to-bottom order:

- Self-addressed, stamped envelope (SASE)
- Cover letter
- The proposal

In some cases, you may want to put your photograph, or some impressive bit of publicity about yourself or your book, after the cover letter. If you don't like your photos, slip in one of Jennifer Lopez, Eddie Murphy, or some other favorite movie star. No—I'm not serious.

If your proposal does not require a manuscript box, then buy a simple, double-pocket folder. Two typical ways of packaging the proposal: the main proposal and appendix material on one side and the sample chapters on the other side, or the main proposal and sample chapters on one side and the appendix on the other. Either way, lay your cover letter on top of the right pocket, to be seen and read first. Put your SASE (with the correct postage for the return of the manuscript) under the cover letter. Remember, any package weighing over one pound (for U.S. only) must be taken to a post office, as a security precaution, for hand stamping.

Interpreting Responses to Your Proposal

While a go-ahead response to your query represents a foot in the door, the real test comes with an agent or editor's reaction to your proposal. If you've secured agent representation, most of the time you'll receive editorial-committee response too.

As with responses to your query, you can expect to receive one of three types of responses to your proposal:

- A personalized rejection
- A qualified acceptance
- An enthusiastic acceptance

A PERSONALIZED REJECTION

When an agent/editor has requested your proposal based upon a query and spent the time to read it, you're unlikely to get a form rejection. Explaining why the proposal was rejected is an understood courtesy. The explanation may be brief: "sales potential too small," "not quite right for our list," "the proposal was strong but the sample chapters disappointed," or "seems written for an academic audience." Rarely can you re-interest an agent/editor by attempting to improve your proposal based on these comments. Your best strategy is to accept the rejection and try elsewhere.

> Every agent is part editor, and every editor edits! Expect to revise your proposal.

If an agent or editor tells you that your book's sales potential is too small or its market is too specialized or competitive, you may have misjudged your book's potential. Perhaps you sent your query to the wrong type or size of publisher or to an agent when you don't need one.

A QUALIFIED ACCEPTANCE

An agent/editor may ask you to rewrite or rethink some aspect of your proposal or book before he or she offers you representation or a contract. This kind of acceptance offers encouragement but no guarantee against subsequent rejection. You have every reason to be excited. You're close. Read the criticism and address the problems, then resubmit.

An Enthusiastic Acceptance

Whether you get this response to a first reading of your proposal or to a subsequent one, bask in the moments, or if you can make it last, the hours of glorious acceptance. Often an agent/editor phones you to offer a personal acceptance. It's an equally special moment for an agent or editor. After so much searching, he or she has finally discovered another worthy book. For most, it's a joy to announce "I like it. I want it. I believe in you."

Your new agent or editor may have phoned for other reasons as well. Be prepared for discussion of strategies or terms. Take good notes, but don't commit to anything important; instead, insist on time to mull over everything.

> In publishing, verbal agreements are legally binding.

Questions For Your Agent/Editor

If an agent has accepted your proposal and wants to represent you, now is the time to articulate concerns about his or her range of experience, business methods, and communication style. For instance, here are some questions to ask an agent, on the phone or in writing, prior to agreeing to representation:

1. Which publishers are you thinking about contacting? How many proposals do you send to start with? How many publishers do you try, on average, before you give up?
2. How often can I expect to hear from you? Will you send me copies of rejection letters as you get them? Will you apprise me of your marketing strategies and, in general, keep in frequent contact?
3. What fees, if any, can I expect to pay? How is this handled?

How do you manage the receipt of advances and royalties? Do you set up separate accounts for each author? Do you pay immediately upon receiving monies from the publisher?

4. May I have a list of your recent sales in nonfiction? May I contact several of your current clients? Do you have any brochures about your agency? Are you a member of AAR? If not, why not?

5. Do you have a written contract that spells out each of our rights and responsibilities and explains how either of us can terminate this relationship? Will you send me a sample contract?

If you have been offered a contract by an editor directly, you may want to ask these questions and others.

1. What advance are you offering? What royalty rate? When will the advance be paid out?

2. How big of a print run do you plan?

3. How much will my book sell for? Will it come out in hardback, trade paperback, or mass market?

4. Will you recommend three to five agents whom you hold in high regard?

If you intend to use an agent, refrain from any discussion of an advance, even if an editor brings it up and pushes you for a decision. Contract negotiation is the domain of your agent, whose hands are tied if you've agreed to any terms. An agent, can nearly always secure a better contract, including a higher advance or better royalty. An agent can also protect you from unscrupulous publishers who take advantage of the moment to gain your verbal agreement.

To protect yourself, prepare a script for the day you get your acceptance call. Say something like, "I'm truly excited by your offer. You've given me a lot to think about. I'll get back to you within forty-eight hours." The consequences are too serious for you not to postpone your decision. Your best defense against ignorance or gullibility is to become informed. Once you have an agent, he or she can answer your questions. Even so, learn as much as you can. One of the best ways is to read books on the subject, talk with published authors, and meet editors and agents at conferences. Check the Resource Directory at the end of this book for other helpful books on the industry.

Special Considerations

The greatest problem faced by writers in deciding whether or not to seek agent representation comes with accurately assessing the size of the market. To a great extent, the type of book you are writing will aim you toward either an agent or an editor. Books written for a narrow audience, books of a specialized nature, such as this one, typically require no agent help. Nor do instructional guides for teachers, most religious book, or most nonfiction books for children.

AN AGENT'S EXPENSES

Some agent expenses averaged over all clients produce a cost per author of $600–$800. If you step into an agent's shoes, you'd evaluate each book based upon whether you can recoup that $800 in expenses and make a profit. Since narrow-interest books usually involve modest print runs, the arithmetic produces a grim picture from an agent's viewpoint.

Because of financial reality, most agents sell only to the mid- to large-sized publishers, and they take on only books that support a strong market. The staple sales for any agency are solid and large markets, such as books on business, parenting, how-to, self-help, celebrity biography, and other wide markets.

ASSESSING YOUR BOOK'S PLACE

One of the most difficult decisions for many writers is determining whether their book idea is too specialized to seek an agent and expect publication with a major house. It's not an easy judgment call. Your best insurance in judging correctly is to follow the advice in chapter two about evaluating your idea; talk with booksellers and compare your book against the competition; and to do an in-depth assessment of your market.

TESTING THE MARKET

Initially, I believed that Jan Jett had a large market for her book on profitable tour escorting. I considered the cresting tsunami of baby boomers as evidence of an up-and-coming large market. After all, as they retire they'll use their leisure time to travel more. Jan agreed and queried mid-sized and large publishers. Only one, a vocational book publisher, considered her proposal seriously enough to hash it over in an editorial committee. In the end, she earned praise for the proposal and for the book concept but a rejection because of the perceived narrow market. Jan's solution? She became an independent publisher selling her tour-escort book through direct mail.

When Dr. Kathleen McGuire, author of a proposed book, *Moved to Tears*, secured agent representation for her book, the agent believed they would find a large market and editors eager to publish it. Although editors were positive about Dr. McGuire's ability to write, they were lukewarm about the book's concept. "Women believe they know how to cry, and men aren't interested," said many editors. Dr. McGuire and her agent concluded that she might be ahead of the culture; however, to publish now, she would have to broaden her book's scope beyond the importance and meaning of tears.

For every rule in publishing, exceptions abound. Perceived large-market books might not sell well and perceived small-market books might become bestsellers. The five authors of the book on twins feared their book would be seen as serving a small, specialized market. They decided to test the possibilities by sending a query to ten large publishing houses. One requested the proposal but ultimately rejected the book as "not quite right for us." However, the editor was enthusiastic enough to recommend agent Carol Abel, whom she knew had particular interest in the twin topic. Ms. Abel became their agent and made the sale within three months to Fireside, an imprint of Simon & Schuster, just as the company was planning the development of a birthing-related line of books. They needed *one* book on twins. The book sold out its first 10,000 copies and went into a second printing. It's still a special-interest book to a highly targeted audience, but it found a large enough market to sustain itself. Their book is evidence of the maxim, "In publishing, timing is everything."

Reclaiming Perspective

Once you sign a contract, you can shift your perspective from the book's potential, what it might do once it comes out, to the necessity of writing it to the best of your ability. In the contract-negotiation phase of a book deal, it's easy to be swept into the bigger world of profits and praise. Now is the time to narrow your focus on the reason you did all this: to write your book.

You have much to look forward to, including the satisfying moment when a reader lets you know how he or she has been helped, persuaded, or entertained by your book. I enjoyed that moment with the book that launched my own publishing career, one that I had self-published. In 1980 I wrote about Mabel Dzata, a midwife from Ghana, Africa, who had delivered my two children by home birth. The book began as a thank-you and memory book and ended with birth stories of a dozen families spanning 158 pages and a first print run of 2600 copies.

Ten years after its publication, I attended a reunion picnic for Mabel, attended by dozens of families. The children ran and played, unaware of their parents' gratitude to the woman with healing hands who had "caught" the children during birth. I saw a mother twenty years younger than myself, clutching a much-used copy of my book. I didn't tell her who I was, but couldn't resist asking her about the book. She said, "It got me through the birth of my girl. I want Mabel to sign it." Her words were payment beyond any royalty; they were satisfaction that filled my soul.

I couldn't wish you more.

Appendices

Appendix 1

Proposal Writers Who Contributed to This Book and the Status of Their Books

Act Like an Owner: Building an Ownership Culture
(business)
Robert Blonchek and Martin O'Neill, business owners, The Capstone Group.
John Wiley & Sons, Inc.; Professional/Trade Division, $29.99.
Literary agent: Natasha Kern.

The authors' book was sold, but the finishing touches were not yet completed on their contract when their publisher merged with another. Unsure of where they stood, the authors simply had to wait most of a year until the merger's reorganization was completed. Fortunately, their book was retained and has since seen enthusiastic sales.

Body Salts: A Way to Health Naturally
(holistic medicine, reference)
Dr. Skye Weintraub, N.D.
Complementary Medicine Publishing Co., Portland, OR. 1993, $20.
No agent.

Sold through retail outlets that sell natural foods and supplements and through direct mail to other holistic practitioners. In 1995, Dr. Weintraub's second book, *Minding Your Body: A Comprehensive Guide to Natural Living in an Unnatural Environment*, was published.

Cheapskate Decorating
    (craft, how-to)
    Aline Renauld Prince, decorator and instructor.
        Finished as a proposal; the author was unable to find
    an agent or publisher.

Creating Eden: The Garden As a Healing Space
    (self-help, nature, ecology)
    Marilyn Barrett, Ph.D., psychotherapist.
    HarperCollins, 1992, $18. pb, 1997.
    Literary agent: Natasha Kern.
        Although *Creating Eden* was successful enough to be
    reprinted in paperback in 1997, the author's most success-
    ful book was one published by Bullfinch Press in 1994 that
    is still in print. Using her talent as a professional photogra-
    pher, Marilyn produced a book titled *Aggies, Immies, Shoot-
    ers, and Swirls: The Magical World of Marbles.*

Five Days to an Organized Life
    (business)
    Lucy H. Hedrick, time management and business consultant.
    Bantam Doubleday Dell Publishing Group Inc., 1990, $8.95
        U.S., $11.95 Canada; over 80,000 sold.
    Literary agent: Denise Marcil.
        Subsequent books: *365 Ways to Save Time* ('92, '95)—
    first print run of 35,000 sold; *365 Ways to Save Time With
    Kids* ('93)—first print run of 25,000 sold; *365 Ways to Save
    Money* ('94): published by The Hearst Group. Now out of
    print.

Grammar for Grownups
    (grammar, how-to, reference)
    Val Dumond, business writing consultant and freelance editor.
    HarperCollins, 1994. $8, pb, $20 hc.
    Literary agent: Denise Marcil.
    Previous book: *Elements of Non-Sexist Usage* (Prentice-Hall,
        1991, $4.95)

The Hidden Life of Language
  (language education)
  Rosemarie Ostler, Ph.D., linguistics educator.

  Although this book's proposal gained representation from a literary agent, it did not sell. The author's subsequent book, *Abandoned Slang,* was represented by Sheree Bykofsky and sold to Oxford Press.

The Iron Butterfly: A Trip Through the Twentieth Century
  (autobiography)
  Doris Colmes, wise woman.

  Publish America, 2002. This fascinating story of a German-born Jew whose family fled Nazi rule and settled in 1930s Harlem becomes the story of an American woman who leaves the "perfect" life of a suburban housewife/mother. Feminist, hippy, Vietnam and civil rights protester, Doris Colmes also experiences communal living, becomes a homeless person, an initiate to a female shaman, and a girlfriend to an African-American gangster. Midlife years find her as a bridge-tender, ski-patroller, mediator, New-Thought minister, counselor to troubled youths, hospice worker, and Reality-Therapy counselor. Now in her early 70s, Doris says, "The trip is still a trip."

The Last Zapatista
  (Latino history, travel, personal experience)
  Susan Caperna Lloyd, author, photographer, filmmaker, lay
    historian.

  Read by a dozen publishers in the mid-nineties, the proposal found no buyers. Editors and her agent advised the author to revise to widen scope to the Zapatista uprising, not just to its namesake. The author also completed a documentary film on Zapata. This is another book that may have to wait for cultural readiness to be re-marketed. Certainly, interest by mainstream publishers in serving the growing readership with ancestry in Spanish-speaking cultures may make this book of greater interest now than in the mid-nineties.

Lifting the Veil: The Feminine Face of Science
  (new science)
  Linda Jean Shepherd, Ph.D., biochemist.
  Shambhala Publications, 1993, $14.00 pb.
  Literary agent: Natasha Kern.
    First edition of 6,500 copies nearly sold out. Book cap-
  tured 1994 Washington State Governor's Literary Award.
  The author is at work on a novel!

Mom to New Mom: Practical Tips and Advice for the New Mom
  (birth, parenting, family)
  Times Books/Random House, 2001, pb.
  Mary Jeanne Menna, journalist, at-home mother.
  Literary agent: Anne Hawkins.
    Although the author queried agents and publishers,
  she received an offer of publication from the publisher and
  then sought an agent. The Internet organization Author-
  link! recommended several agents. Mary interviewed them
  by phone and selected Anne Hawkins of John Hawkins &
  Associates. The author is hard at work on the next book in
  her series on parenting.

Mothering Twins: From Hearing the News to Beyond the Terrible Twos
  (birth, parenting, family)
  Linda Albi, Deborah Johnson, Debra Catlin, Donna Florien
    Deurloo, Sheryll Greatwood.
  Fireside, Simon & Schuster, 1993, $13.00 pb.
  Literary agent: Carol Abel.
    Having sold out the first 10,000 copies, the book
  enjoyed a second printing and is now out of print.

Moved to Tears: The Meaning and Joy in Learning to Cry
  (how-to, psychology)
  Dr. Kathleen N. McGuire, Ph.D., psychologist.
    At first, her proposal was enthusiastically represented
  by an agent and circulated to large publishers. Because of
  feedback about the book having a shaky market because of

its focus on crying, this version of the proposal was turned back to the author.

Mysteries of the Dark Moon: The Healing Power of the Dark Goddess
(self-help, women's psychology, astrology)
Demetra George, counselor, mythologist, and astrologer.
HarperCollins, 1992, $15.
Literary Agent: Natasha Kern.

Strong sales as the author's third book, and accompanied by a workbook published and sold separately by A.C.S. Publishers: *Finding Our Way Through the Dark* was published in 1995. It is an astrological companion to *Mysteries of the Dark Moon*. Previous books: *Asteroid Goddess* (A.C.S. 1986) and *Astrology for Yourself* (Wingbow Press 1987).

No Pictures in My Grave: A Spiritual Journey in Sicily
(memoir/inner journey, travel)
Susan Lloyd.
Mercury House, 1992, $12.95 pb U.S.; $16.95 Canada.
Literary agent: Natasha Kern.

In addition to this literary, travel memoir, the author produced a documentary on her experience: *Processione: A Sicilian Easter*, which won the 1990 American Film Festival award, the American Anthropological Association Society for Visual Anthropology award, the Vitas Film Festival of Folklore and Popular Culture 1991 Best award, and the Bronze Apple with the National Educational Film and Video Festival.

Organic Parenting: Raising Real People Through the Art of Human Relating, Birth to Six

(Parenting)
Dean Walker, counselor and child development specialist.

Proposal was represented by agent Bobbie Segal but did not sell.

The Practical Woman's Guide to Real Estate Investment
   (real estate)
   Mabel Armstrong, real-estate investor and instructor.
      Author's agent felt the slant to a woman's audience was too narrow, but has recently thought the timing may again be right to reconsider this work. In the meantime, the author is completing a series on women scientists for young readers.

Profitable Tour Escorting: A Comprehensive Guide
   (travel, how-to)
   Jan G. Jett, tour-escort instructor.
   Fox Hollow Press, 1992, $14.95 pb, unbound edition.
      Jan founded her own press and successfully sold her book through direct mail.

The Spirited Walker: Fitness Walking for Clarity, Balance, and Spiritual Connection
   (fitness, self-help)
   Carolyn Scott Kortge, award-winning journalist, walking instructor.
   HarperCollins, 1998, $15.00 U.S., $21.50 Canada.
   Literary agent: Jonathon Lazear.
      From query to representation to sale involved about four months. While the author worked to complete the manuscript, HarperCollins downsized and her acquisitions editor, Thomas Grady, was laid off and has since become a literary agent. As over 100 HarperCollins authors' contracts were terminated, Carolyn's newly purchased book was assigned to a new editor. Carolyn made sure to meet with her new editor and the sales staff. One week before her book's release, she was informed that the promotional budget for *The Spirited Walker* had been slashed due to fewer presale orders than was originally hoped for. Carolyn mounted an aggressive author promotion, making hundreds of speeches, book-signings, and author-led "spirited

walks" across the country. She also wrote articles for half a dozen national-circulation magazines, and many others reviewed her book or published features on it. By the end of her first year, the book had sold 12,000 copies. Not satisfied with her relationship with her agent, she has terminated their contract. Due to staff changes at HC, no one who had direct involvement with editing and promotion of her book now remains with the organization.

Stop Being Manipulated: How to Neutralize the Bullies, Bosses, and Brutes in Your Life
(self-help psychology)
Dr. George H. Green and Carolyn Cotter, M.B.A.
Berkley Publishing Group, 1995, $4.95 U.S., $6.50 Canada, mass pb.
Literary agent: Denise Marcil.

From writing the proposal to finding an agent to securing a publishing contract spanned a period of five years, testimony to the importance of persistence. Unlike most mass-market paperbacks, which may have a life of a few months, this book has seen six printings and has been translated into several languages for foreign sales.

Stop Your Husband From Snoring: A Medically Proven Program to Cure the Night's Worst Nuisance
(medicine, how-to)
Dr. Derek S. Lipman, M.D.
Rodale Press, 1990, $7.95, out-of-print.
Literary agent: David Morgan.

Although a success by any measure, with over 30,000 books sold and sales in four foreign countries, including two translations, Dr. Lipman was nevertheless disappointed by his publisher's choice of titles, which he felt was "narrow, politically incorrect, and downright offensive." The book is presently out-of-print and the rights reverted to the author. With the resurgence of public interest in sleeping disorders and with new research, Dr. Lipman secured another agent and received substantial offers from two big New York houses for a revised edition. The publishers withdrew their offers when it was discovered that a remaindering company had purchased those rights from Rodale and was still selling the prior book. In essence, Dr. Lipman's new book would be competing against his old one. Undaunted, he updated the book, which was published in 1997 by Diane Publishing, a small press specializing in health-related and socially responsible books. His new book, well reviewed and available in hardback and paperback, is: *Snoring From A to ZZzz: Proven Cures for the Night's Worst Nuisance.*

Breaking the Spell: Spontaneous Events That Shape a Child's Life
(education, psychology)
Dr. Michael Rousell, Ph.D., teacher, psychologist, hypnotist.

Represented by several different agents over a period of years, this book is still looking for a home. Dr. Rousell has revised it substantially, not only to add new research but to find and polish a reader-friendly writing style. The ideas in this book are cutting edge and he may have to wait for the culture to catch up. An agent with strong successes in psychology and health now represents the book.

Sun Power: The Global Solution for the Coming Energy Crisis
(science, energy technologies)
Ralph Nansen, former Boeing Solar Power Satellite Program Manager.
Ocean Press, $14.95 pb. PO Box 1812, Ocean Shores, WA 98569

The proposal was at first represented by an agent and marketed to large publishers. When it did not land a large publisher, the author decided to independently publish rather than market to small or specialized publishers. With his contacts and reputation, Ralph has not only seen good sales of his book, but more importantly, he has found investors for a plant that is being built to implement his ideas. You may reach the author at the above address for his book or to inquire about securing this visionary scientist for a speaking engagement.

Tales From Coon Creek Farm
(autobiography/literary)
Barbara Stevens-Newcomb, storyteller and artist.

Through the author's personal memories, this literary nonfiction book seeks to awaken the reader's own sense of place, allowing the reader to recapture the fundamental questions of youth.

Three Cats, Two Dogs, One Journey Through Multiple Pet Loss
(animal welfare, pets, memoir)
David Congalton, journalist, radio talk-show host, television talk-show host.
NewSage Press (Portland, Oregon), 2000. $12.95 pb.

At first, the author queried several literary agents, many of whom had represented books too similar to take on David's. One of the agents recommended that he query NewSage Press. His query and proposal met an enthusiastic response. He felt a strong rapport with the editor/owner, who also outlined a detailed plan for promotion. David feels like he found the very best publisher for his book, which was selected by Dog Writers Association of America as year 2000 Human-Animal Bond Award for Best Writing. David and his wife, Charlotte Alexander, coauthored a second book, *When Your Pet Outlives You*, 2002.

We'll Remember in November: Molly Yard's Gift to Women's Rights
(biography, women's history)
Emily Kay and Anita Saville, activists and members of N.O.W.
Literary agent: Natasha Kern.

This book was never published, even though the authors received an offer for publication from Prometheus. The advance offered was inadequate for the authors' needs.

When Broken Glass Floats: Growing Up Under the Khmer Rouge
    (memoir, biography)
    Chanrithy Him, researcher for Khmer Adolescent Project. W.W.
        Norton & Co. (New York) 2000. $23.95 hc.
    Literary agent: Meredith Bernstein.

    When Broken Glass Floats, the title referring to a time
when evil dominates over good, was the 2001 Oregon
Book Award Winner in literary nonfiction. It was a finalist
in the 2000 Kiriyama Book Prize.

    The author is working on a sequel.

Appendix 2

Resource Directory

On the World of Publishing

Author's Note: I've included some out-of-print titles because many books are being resurrected and made available in electronic databases for "on-demand" printing. Out-of-print titles are also frequently available on the used market.

Balkin, Richard. *A Writer's Guide to Book Publishing,* third edition revised by Nick Bakalar and Richard Balkin. New York, NY: Plume/Penguin Group, 1994. Out-of-print but worth searching for a used copy. As the author says, "This book presumes to contain most of what...a potential author might want to know about publishing." Clear and well written, this book does exactly that.

Beren, Peter and Brad Bunnin. *Writer's Legal Companion: The Complete Handbook for the Working Writer.* New York: Perseus, 1998. Two lawyers offer explanations of publishing law, including contracts, copyrights, permissions, libel, subsidiary rights, agent agreements, and more.

Collier, Oscar and Frances Spatz Leighton. *How to Write and Sell Your First Nonfiction Book.* New York, NY: St. Martin's Press, 1994. While the proposal process is swept over in a single chapter, the rest of the book offers good advice on the world of agents, editors, and selling. The authors also offer practical advice for how to write your book once you have a contract.

Grants and Awards Available to American Writers, 21st edition. PEN American Center, 2000

Gross, Gerald, editor. *Editors on Editing: What Writers Need to Know About What Editors Do,* third edition. New York, NY: Grove Press, 1993. Comments by many of the most prestigious editors in the business. Addresses all aspects of editing—structural, theoretical, practical—with wit and insight. This anthology is incomparable in building a historical understanding of this complex and arcane industry.

Jassin, Lloyd J. et al. *The Copyright Permission and Libel Handbook: A Step-by-Step Guide for Writers, Editors, and Publishers.* New York, NY: John Wiley & Sons, 1998. Invaluable resource for answering questions about those gray areas, including everything from interview releases to derivative works, old copyrights, "fair use," locating copyright holders, and which circumstances you don't need permission for use.

Kirsch, Jonathan. *Kirsch's Guide to the Book Contract: For Authors, Publishers, Editors, and Agents.* Venice, CA: Acrobat, 1998. Written by a lawyer who is also a novelist, this handbook clarifies your rights and responsibilities as a writer. It explains contracts, documentation of research and sources, legal protections of confidential sources, copyright and "fair use" laws, defamation, and invasion of privacy. It also covers electronic and subsidiary rights, and often overlooked rights that occur with the end of your book's life. Kirsch includes a model contract and breaks down the "boilerplate" contract that is used most often.

Mandell, Judy. *Book Editors Talk to Writers.* New York, NY: John Wiley & Sons, Inc., 1995. Covering every aspect of publishing that would interest nonfiction or fiction writers, this book's question-and-answer format grants accessibility of the information and feels like the editors are talking directly to the reader. This book features penetrating interviews with forty-four experienced editors. By now, its discussions about "new media" are out of date, but the rest of the book is helpful.

Poynter, Dan. *The Self-Publishing Manual: How to Write, Publish and Sell Your Own Book,* thirteenth edition. Santa Barbara, CA: Para Publishing, 2001. Although written for the self-publisher, this classic offers easy-to-understand and up-to-date information on promotion, publicity, distribution, and online bookstores for book sales.

Ross, Marilyn, and Tom Ross. *The Complete Guide to Self-Publishing,* fourth edition. Cincinnati, OH: Writer's Digest Books, 2002. Even though you may not wish to self-publish, this comprehensive guide offers good information on selecting a marketable topic, "product development," promotion, and organizing and editing your manuscript.

Shindler, Jason, et al. *The First-Book Market: A Writer's Resource.* New York, NY: Macmillan, 1998. The slant of this book is "first book." You'll find authors discussing their publishing experiences with their first book, publishers most favorable to first books, awards favorable to first books, and planning a first book's promotion.

Stengl, Jean. *How to Get Your Teaching Ideas Published: A Writer's Guide to Educational Publishing.* New York, NY: Walker & Co., 1994. Out of print. A specialty guidebook offering the steps and resources to connect teacher/writer with educational publishers.

Web Resources

Copyright protection in Electronic Publishing:
  www.press.umich.edu/jep/works/

Copyright and Fair Use:
  www.fairuse.stanford.edu/

Writers Resources:
  www.zuzu.com
  www.tipsforwriters.com

REFERENCE BOOKS TO FIND OTHER BOOKS ON YOUR SUBJECT

Book Review Index. Detroit, MI: Gale Research Inc. Master Indexed by author and title. Cumulations from 1965–1984 and from 1985 to present. Nearly 2 million review citations from about 500 periodicals. A great way to look up books that might be competitors for "About the Competition." Also look for *Book Review Index Cumulations.*

Books in Print. Annual. New Providence, RI: R.R. Bowker. Indexed by author, title, and subject, these volumes index over 1.5 million books in the U.S. from over 60,000 publishers and distributors.

Books Out of Print. Annual. New Providence, RI: R.R. Bowker. Important to check by subject and cross-reference by synonyms so that you can find other books published on your subject within the last five years—for "About the Competition," and to keep abreast in your field.

British Books in Print. Annual. London: J. Whitaker & Sons (distributed in the U.S. by R.R. Bowker).

Business and Economics Books and Serials in Print, published irregularly. New Providence, RI: R.R. Bowker.

Canadian Books in Print. Annual. Toronto, ON: University of Toronto Press. Indexed by author and title and with a subject index.

Children's Books in Print. Annual. New Providence, RI: R.R. Bowker. An author, illustrator, and title index to some 150,000 children's books available in the U.S. and written for children.

Computer Books and Serials in Print, published annually. New Providence, RI: R.R. Bowker.

Forthcoming Books, published bimonthly, New Providence, RI: R.R. Bowker. Use this index to nab books for your "About the Competition" that will be published in the next six months.

Paperbound Books in Print. Semiannual (spring and fall). New Providence, RI: R.R. Bowker. Author, title, and subject indexes to all in-print and forthcoming paperback books: trade and text, adult and juvenile, scholarly and mass market. Although *Books in Print* includes some paperbound books, this index will supply missing books in print on your subject.

Religious Books and Serials in Print: An Index to Religious Literature Including Philosophy. Biennial (in fall). New Providence, RI: R.R. Bowker.

Small Press Record of Books in Print. Annual. Paradise, CA: Dustbooks. Editor, Len Fulton. Offers full in-print listings of 50,000 books in more than 5000 of the world's small, independent, education, and self publishers.

Subject Guide to Books in Print. Annual. New Providence, RI: R.R. Bowker. As a companion volume to *Books in Print*, this volume indexes nearly a million in-print nonfiction books from over 45,000 U.S. publishers and distributors, using 72,000 Library of Congress headings and 60,000 cross-references. You may also find a *Subject Guide to Children's Books in Print,* and a *Subject Guide to Forthcoming Books in Print.*

Young Adult Book Review Index. Gale Group; 1988.

Web Resources

Bookstores online:
    www.amazon.com; www.bn.com (Barnes & Noble);
    www.bookfinder.com; www.borders.com
Children's Literature Web Guide:
    www.acs.ucalgary.ca/~dkbrown/

www.childrenslit.com
www.write4kids.com

ON RESEARCH

Allen, Moira Anderson. *writing.com: Creative Internet Strategies to Advance Your Writing Career.* New York: Allworth Press, 1999. As far as I'm concerned, this book is the beginning and the end of everything a writer needs to know related to his or her use of the Internet. Completely tailored to our needs to pursue research, find publishers and agents, set up web sites, improve our craft, meet other writers, and best of all, to get answers as technical novices and not have to take courses to be able to do so. This book is your one-stop guide. Indispensable.

Bennett, William. *The Index of Leading Cultural Indicators: American Society at the End of the 20th Century.* New York: Broadway Books, 1999. Provides facts, statistics, and interpretation of context related to crime, the family, education, youth behavior, popular culture and religion, civic participation, and international comparisons of the same areas. This insightful book is made to order (and in an inexpensive paperback) for the proposal writers' needs for supportive hard data in their queries, "About the Book," and "About the Market" sections.

Berkman, Robert I. *Find it Fast: How to Uncover Expert Information on Any Subject,* fifth edition, updated and revised. New York: Harper Resources, 2000. This book streamlines the research process. You'll learn not only how to locate and interview experts, take notes, and evaluate information, but you'll also find solid introductory information on using library resources, finding government sources, using automated CD-ROM systems, and consumer online services and the Internet.

The Gale Directory of Publications and Broadcast Media. Annual. Detroit, MI: Gale Research Inc. Arranged by state, province, and city with demographics given for each city. This directory provides information on periodicals and broadcast media, but not books.

The Reader's Guide to Periodical Literature. I've included this only to suggest that you exclude it from your research. This guide is probably the one you are most familiar with from school research. However, it only indexes about 180 magazines. Nowadays, there are so many indexes that are better, larger, and more subject specific.

Standard Periodical Directory. Annual. New York, NY: Oxbridge Communications Inc. Lists 90,000 U.S. and Canadian periodicals arranged by subject matter into 230 classifications and indexed by title. This directory makes it difficult to claim your subject has "never been done!"

Statistical Abstract of the United States. Annual. Washington, DC: U.S. Dept. of Government, Bureau of the Census. This provides the statistical answers to Census questions of a political, social, and economic nature.

American Statistics Index. Washington DC: Congressional Information Service. This is a comprehensive index to 3000 statistical directories published by federal and state agencies, commercial publishers, and intergovernmental organizations.

Ulrich's International Periodical Directory. Annual. New Providence, NJ: R.R. Bowker. A subject-arranged list of more than 160,000 active periodicals, irregular serials, and annuals published throughout the world. A great help to comprehensive research of what's reaching the general public and the specialist reader.

Web Resources

Starting out:

www.zuzu.com

Major search engines
    www.altavista.com
    www.excite.com
    www.infoseek.com
    www.yahoo.com
    www.google.com

Minor search engines:
    www.about.com; www.askjeeves.com

Directories and databases:
    www.cyword.com

Newsgroups:
    www.dejanews.com; www.liszt.com
    www.reference.com

Finding experts:
    www.askanexpert.com; www.profnet.com

ON WRITING AND EDITING

Baker, Russel, ed. and Zinsser, William, ed. *Inventing the Truth: The Art and Craft of the Memoir.* New York: Houghton-Mifflin, 1998, revised edition. A must-read for anyone writing memoir. Includes lively dialogues from some of the great memoir writers of our times such as Frank McCourt, Annie Dillard, Toni Morrison, and Russel Baker.

Bates, Jefferson D. *Writing With Precision: How to Write So That You Cannot Possibly Be Misunderstood.* New York: Penguin USA, 2000. This is a super book to guide you through self-editing. Checklists, clear headings, and exercises allow you to pull out what you need. Sections have been added for the computer age, and include organizing, file management, and word processing.

Bennett, Hal Z. *How to Write With a Collaborator.* Cincinnati, OH: Writer's Digest Books, 1988. Out of print. Helpful guidelines to anyone who plans to team up with another writer, an expert, or a celebrity to coauthor books, articles, and short stories.

Cheney, Theodore A. Rees. *Getting the Words Right: How to Edit, Rewrite, & Revise*. Cincinnati, OH: Writer's Digest Books, 1990. If you want to delve into editing, this book will take you on an extensive journey into craft. Less of a shopping mall of easy-fix editing ideas, this book will give you the fundamental concepts—reduction, rearranging, and rewording—to make you an all-round better writer.

Cheney, Theodore A. Rees. *Writing Creative Nonfiction: How to Use Fiction Techniques to Make Your Nonfiction More Interesting, Dramatic, and Vivid*. Berkeley, CA: Ten Speed Press, 1991.

The Chicago Manual of Style. Chicago, IL: University of Chicago Press. Long considered the "last word" in editorial disputes, I couldn't live (i.e. edit) without it. *The Chicago Manual of Style* gives you the security of answering every conceivable question and trusting the source.

Cool, Lisa Collier. *How to Write Irresistible Query Letters*. Cincinnati, OH: Writer's Digest Books, 1990. Although primarily focused upon writing queries for magazine articles, this book lets you know how all queries are structured and what they are meant to accomplish.

Dumond, Val. *Grammar for Grownups: A Guide to Grammar and Usage for Everyone*. New York: HarperCollins, 1994. What I love about Val's book is the feeling of sitting down with her across the kitchen table and learning about grammar. She brings her own voice and personality into this normally dry subject matter, using colorful examples from adult experiences.

Gerard, Philip. *Creative Nonfiction: Researching and Crafting Stories of Real Life*. Cincinnati, OH: Story Press, 1996. Easy to read without loss of depth, this book will help you define what creative nonfiction is and isn't. It will help you create personal essays, autobiography, or memoir from evaluating and developing your idea to revising your finished work.

Henson, Kenneth T. *The Art of Writing for Publication.* Needham Heights, MA: Simon & Schuster, 1994. Out of print. Terrific book for everyone, but especially for writers steeped in academic or technical jargon. This book will lead you from dissertation writing to writing for journals to book publication with university presses and to professional writing of trade books for the public. Also includes grant-proposal writing.

Judd, Karen. *Copyediting, A Practical Guide,* second edition. Menlo Park, CA: Crisp Publications Inc., 1992. For authors, publishing personnel, writers, editors, journalists, teachers, desktop publishers, and computer software workers. Learn to recognize and use all those squiggly marks and produce clean, clear, copy.

Klauser, Henriette Anne. *Writing on Both Sides of the Brain: Breakthrough Techniques for People Who Write.* San Francisco, CA: Harper San Francisco, 1987. Inspirations and practical techniques to bulldoze through "writer's block," and to silence "The Critic" during the production of your proposal.

Markel, Michael H. *Technical Communication.* New York, NY: St. Martin's Press, 1997. Don't be put off by the word "technical" in the title. This is one of those bibles that will help any nonfiction writer organize research, select a method of organization, and outline.

The National Writers Association correspondence course in Freelance Writing. Suite 620, 1450 S. Havana, Aurora, CO 80012. I was an enrollee long ago. Their course is a great way to review the techniques of freelance writing or learn how to write in the special style required for publication. You will also enjoy the benefit of a published teacher responding personally to your letters and lessons.

Neuleib, Janice and Maurice Scharton. *Things Your Grammar Never Told You.* Needham Heights, MA: Allyn & Bacon, 1999. This is one of the many available, desktop grammar guides. Spiral bound and about 3½" X 6", it fits in my hand and seems easy to grab and find answers to common self-editing questions.

Perry, Susan K. *Writing in the Flow: Keys to Enhanced Creativity.* Cincinnati, OH: Writer's Digest Books, 1999. Originally based on the author's dissertation, this critically acclaimed book is well conceived and will help you understand and solve problems related to writing a long work. Although the seventy-six authors whose experiences are included in the book are poets or fiction writers, their insights into the process of writing itself will help the nonfiction writer as well.

Poynter, Dan, and Mindy Bingham. *Is There a Book Inside You? How to Successfully Author a Book Alone or Through a Collaborator,* fifth edition. Santa Barbara, CA: Para Publishing, 1998. A step-by-step formula for researching and writing a book, and how to find and work with a collaborator.

Provost, Gary. *Make Your Words Work,* iUniverse, a print-on-demand book, 2001. Formerly published by Writers Digest Books. Gary Provost's books are among the best for learning how to write popular nonfiction. His writing is proof of what he teaches; you're absorbed and entertained while learning. Provost's book is one to own and come back to again and again.

Provost, Gary. *100 Ways to Improve Your Writing.* New York, NY: Mentor Books, Reissue edition, 1985. You'll take away *one thousand* ways to improve your writing. A must for any writer who is having trouble translating expert or technical vocabulary into everyday communication.

Roberts, Ellen. *Nonfiction for Children: How to Write It, How to Sell It.* Cincinnati, OH: Writer's Digest Books, 1986. Although this book is out-of-print, there are so few how-to guides on writing nonfiction for children, it's worth chasing down a used copy (check amazon.com). This book stands out as the definitive work on the subject. It's thorough, well written, and offers as much to the writer of adult nonfiction as to the writer of children's nonfiction.

Tarshis, Barry. *How to be Your Own Best Editor: The Toolkit for Everyone Who Writes.* New York, NY: Three Rivers Press, 1998. The secret to a book on editing that you'll actually use is that it include not too much and not too little. This book meets those criteria, and has the kind of presentation that encourages yearly rereading, like *Elements of Style.* Not so much a desktop reference, this book, however, will help you learn matters of grammar and style permanently.

Writer's Digest correspondence course in nonfiction writing. 4700 Galbraith Rd., Cincinnati, OH 45236. Although I haven't sampled their nonfiction correspondence courses, I've heard positive testimonials from others who have. Correspondence courses offer a way to learn the techniques of writing for publication and have the benefit of a one-on-one relationship with an assigned teacher. *See also online correspondence courses under Web Resources.*

Zinsser, William. *On Writing Well: The Classic Guide to Writing Nonfiction,* 25th Anniversary issue. New York, NY: Harper Resource, 2001. When I first started my writing career, I read Zinsser's book and practically enshrined it. It's simple, elegant, and inspiring. It's one of those books you can read again and again. His book set a standard to which I still aspire.

Web Resources

OnWriting:
www.tipsforwriters.com
www.onlinelearning.net (UCLA extension)
www.zuzu.com

On Grammar:
> www.edunet.com/

On Editing:
> www.elizabethlyon.com
> www.4-edit.com

ON MARKET GUIDES FOR FINDING PUBLISHERS AND LITERARY AGENTS

Children's Writer's & Illustrator's Market. Annual. Cincinnati, OH: Writer's Digest Books. Comprehensive listings of children's book publishers and their specifications, including an age-level index. Also includes book and magazine markets for children writers and artists.

Herman, Jeff. *Writer's Guide to Book Editors, Publishers, and Literary Agents.* Annual. Rocklin, CA: Prima Publishing. Not just a directory, this book provides a brief history of 500 United States and Canadian publishers that include large, university, and religious/spiritual publishers. The guide is unique in listing current names of some 1000 editors at these houses, by specialty. Part II features answers by 200 agents about their education and personal preferences. The Guide includes statistics about rejection rates, numbers of new authors represented in the past year, and numbers of titles sold in the past year.

Guide to Literary Agents. Annual. Cincinnati, OH: Writer's Digest Books. Provides the listings, contact names, and specifications of some 500 agents, including indexes by subject and geographic location.

International Directory of Little Magazines and Small Presses. Annual, updated biannually. Len Fulton, editor. Paradise, CA: Dustbooks. Gives contact information and specifications for roughly 5000 book and magazine publishers, many of which are "tiny ventures" not listed elsewhere. Offers subject and regional indexes.

International Literary Market Place, updated annually. New Providence, RI: R.R. Bowker.

Literary Market Place. Annual. New York: R.R. Bowker. Long considered "the bible" of the publishing industry, this tome lists over 40,000 companies and individuals in the U.S. and Canadian publishing. It is divided into headings for book publishers, editorial services, literary agents, advertising, marketing and publicity (including book clubs), direct mail specialists, magazines that feature books, book manufacturing, book distributors, wholesalers, book producers, services and supplies, contests, and grants, book trade events, and much more. If you register online but do not subscribe, you can get contact information at the least (www.literarymarket-place.com).

Publishers, Distributors, and Wholesalers of the United States. Annual. New Providence, RI: R.R. Bowker. A directory of some 64,500 active U.S. publishers, distributors, associations, and wholesalers that list editorial and ordering addresses. Includes small and independent presses, producers of software, and audio cassettes by fields of activity.

Writers Northwest Handbook, seventh edition. Biennial. Portland, OR: Media Weavers, 2000. Essays and how-to articles by writers comprise about one third of this handbook, while the rest offers the listings and specifications of some 3000 book and magazine publishers, as well as other resources for writers in the Pacific Northwest.

Writer's Market. Annual. Cincinnati, OH: Writer's Digest Books. Lists more than 4000 places where freelance writers can sell articles, books, novels, stories, fillers, scripts, and more. You can get specifications and editors' names for about 1200 publishers (and about 80 agents).

Writer's Market: The Electronic Edition with CD-ROM. In addition to the same features as the paper version, this edition includes customized search capabilities, a submission tracker, and a writer's encyclopedia.

Web Resources

Overall Literary Resource:
www.zuzu.com (10,000 resources)

Book publishers:
www.bookwire.com/index/publishers/html
www.tipsforwriters

Literary agents:
www.bookwire.com/AAR/;www.literaryagent.com
www.literarymarketplace.com
www.writers.net/agents/htm/

ON PROMOTION

Best, Don and Peter Goodman. *The Author's Guide to Marketing Your Book: From Start to Success, for Writers and Publishers.* Berkeley, CA: Stone Bridge Press, 2000.

Celebrity Address Handbook and Autograph Guide 2000. Lee Ellis, editor. Spiral bound. Americana Group Publishing, 1999. Lists 5000 names and addresses of well-known celebrities in 30 career categories.

Celebrity Directory. Biennial. Ann Arbor, MI: Axiom Information Resources, 2001. Described as a directory of over 8000 celebrities from entertainment to business who may be contacted for testimonials for the book trade.

Encyclopedia of Associations. Annual. Detroit, MI: Gale Research Inc. Arranged by topic, this guide lists more than 20,000 national organizations of the U.S. From this guide and the *National Trade and Professional Associations* guide, you can find groups through which you may be able to promote your book. List these in "About the Market," and/or in "About

Promotion." After you've written your book, follow up and offer yourself as a workshop or conference speaker. A librarian can help you check the *Associations Reference File* on microform to actually see the full text of brochures and official literature offered by organizations listed in the *E.A.*

Gale Directory of Publications and Broadcast Media, 2000. Gale Group.

Kremer, John. *1001 Ways to Market Your Books—For Authors and Publishers,* sixth edition. Fairfield, IA: Open Horizons Publishing Co., 2002. This book could have been titled "Everything You Ever Needed to Know to Write a Great Promotions Section in Your Proposal." Includes planning and design, advertising, distribution, subsidiary rights, and spin-offs.

Levine, Michael. *The Address Book Direct Access to Over 4000 Celebrities, Corporate Execs, and Other VIPs.* New York: Perigee, 1999.

Spratt, Steven D. and Lee G. Spratt. *Networking at Writer's Conferences: From Contacts to Contracts.* New York, NY: John Wiley & Sons, 1995. This well-organized book will provide even the veteran conference goer with refinements on getting the most from a conference. Divided into "before," "during," and "after" the conference, read this guide and you'll be well on your way to becoming a book marketing expert.

Ortman, Mark. *A Simpler Guide to Marketing Your Book: What an Author and Publisher Can Do to Sell More Books.* Seattle, WA: Wise Owl Books, 1998. Simple and clear, this book covers the bases: marketing plans, distribution channels, pre- and post-publication publicity, media interviews, author tours, the Internet, and more.

Otte, Miriam. *Marketing with Speeches and Seminars: Your Key to More Clients and Referrals.* Seattle, WA: Zest Press, 1998. This guide zeros in on one, all-important set of skills for book sales—author presentations and speeches. You'll get just as many ideas from this book if you're a pro or a beginner with knocking knees.

National Trade and Professional Associations of the United States. Annual. Washington, DC: Columbia Books, Inc. Gives data on 7500 trade associations, professional societies, and labor unions with national memberships. Uses broad subject headings in its index.

Ross, Marilyn, and Tom Ross. *Jump Start Your Book Sales: A Money-Making Guide for Authors, Independent Publishers and Small Presses.* Buena Vista, CO: Communication Creativity, 1999. Authors detail winning strategies for promoting and selling books and generating author publicity. Follow a quarter of their ideas and you'll accomplish ten times more sales than if you hadn't.

Web Resources

On Conferences:
www.shawguides.com

On Web Site Development:
www.useit.com/papers/webwriting/writing/html;
www.scribe.com/resource/htm;
www.zuzu.com

Appendix 3

Publication Consent Agreement

    I hereby give _____ author of _____ (working title of what is henceforth referred to as the Property), the absolute right and permission to copyright and/or publish or to have copyrighted or have published information about me contained in the above mentioned Property. I understand that a pseudonym is being used in place of my real name and that other physical attributes have been fictionalized in order to protect my right to privacy.

    I also hereby waive any right to inspect and/or approve not only the final edited-for-publication versions of the book, but also any advertising copy that may be used in connection therewith.

    I also agree that _____ or the publisher shall have all the irrevocable and unconditional dramatic and subsidiary rights to the Property, and can cause an actor to depict actions in incidents related to, based upon, or adapted from me as depicted by the "character" based upon me in the above mentioned Property. Further, such adaptations may include fictional scenes, incidents or episodes based upon but not specifically included in the Property in preparation or production of a picture, and I waive all rights to the exploitation of such a picture in all media throughout the world, and in connection with customary advertising and publicity related there to.

    I represent that I will not assert or institute any claim or action against _____ or the publisher or other purchaser of rights based on the Property, on the grounds that their use of the above-described rights violates my right of privacy or any other right belonging to me. Nothing contained herein shall be construed as prejudicial to any rights to which I may otherwise be entitled as a member of the public.

None of the warranties or indemnities I make pursuant to this Release or elsewhere herein shall extend to (a) any changes or additions made in the Property, or (b) any elements of the Property which are undertaken to fictionalize for dramatic purposes. I agree to indemnify and hold harmless the author, publisher, or subsidiary rights' purchasers from and against any claims arising from such Changes.

Date _____

Signature _____

Phone _____ Address _____

Date _____

Witness _____

Appendix 4

Model Author/Agent Agreement

LITERARY AGENCY AGREEMENT

(provided by Anne Sheldon and Michael Vidor of The Hardy Agency)

This agreement is entered into on [date] by and between [agency name] a [state where agency is located] partnership [or sole proprietor business] hereinafter referred to as "Agent," and [author's name], hereinafter referred to as "Author."

This agreement is concerning the following manuscript: [title of book], hereinafter referred to as "the Work."

Author hereby appoints Agent as sole and exclusive agent of the Work, throughout the world pursuant to the following agreements and understanding:

1. SCOPE

Agent shall counsel and advise Author professionally and shall market all of the Author's literary rights in the Work, primary and subsidiary, including but not limited to print publishing, audio tape, video tape, motion picture, electronic, radio, and television rights in the Work.

2. SUB-AGENTS

Agent may, with prior notice to and approval by Author, appoint others to assist in fulfilling this agreement, including sub-agents.

3. AUTHOR'S APPROVAL

Agent agrees to submit to Author any offers received. No agreement shall bind Author without Author's consent and signature.

4. COLLECTIONS

a. Agent agrees to collect and receive for Author all monies due from marketing and selling Author's literary rights, to hold money safely in a separate bank account while it is in Agent's possession and control, and to remit to Author, less agency commission and any uncollected expenses, within five (5) business days after funds clear Agent's account.

b. Author is responsible for Author's own tax liabilities and Agent is not responsible for the collecting or payment of taxes due by Author.

c. In the event any monies due Agent are paid directly to Author, Author will remit the appropriate commission, as defined in paragraph 7, within five business days.

5. COMMISSIONS

Agent shall be entitled to retain as Agent's full agency commission for the full life of the copyright and any renewals:

a. Fifteen percent (15%) of all monies collected from the sale of the primary or

b. secondary rights in the Work for print publication within North America.

c. Twenty percent (20%) of all monies collected from the sale of the primary or

d. secondary rights in the Work for print publication outside of North America.

e. Twenty percent (20%) of all monies collected from the sale of motion picture, audio tape, videotape, electronic, radio, or television rights.

f. Whenever foreign taxes, fees, or commissions are deducted at the source of monies due, Agent's commission shall be based on the balance after said deductions.

6. EXPENSES

Author is responsible for out-of-pocket expenses relating to the marketing of the Work, limited to photocopying and postage for manuscript submission, and any bank charges for the collection and payment of the Author's royalties. Agent will not bill Author for other expenses unless previously approved by Author.

7. RECORDS

Agent shall maintain accurate books and records of Author's royalty account and shall submit complete and accurate statements to Author semiannually or when they are received from the publisher.

8. TERM

a. This agreement shall have an initial term of six (6) months, beginning upon the signing of this agreement. After the initial six-month period, this agreement may be terminated by either party upon thirty (30) days advance written notice.

b. If within three months after the date of termination, Author, or an agent representing Author, enters into a contract for the sale of literary rights with a buyer whom Agent had been negotiating prior to the termination, then that contract shall be deemed entered into during the term of this agreement.

c. Should the death of the Author occur during the term of this contract, the contract will remain in full force, and all of the Author's rights and monies due under this agreement shall transfer to the Author's heirs.

d. Should the death of the Agent occur during the term of this contract, the contract shall remain in full force and all monies due to Agent shall transfer to Agent's heirs or legal assignees.

e. Should Agent sell the business or make a change in ownership, Author shall have the right to cancel this contract upon written notice. Representation of any rights that remain unsold at that time will revert back to Author.

9. INDEMNITY

Author shall indemnify and hold Agent harmless against any suit, proceeding, action, claim, or liability of any nature that may arise from the creation, publishing, or marketing of the Work.

10. MAIL

Mail addressed to the Author may be opened and processed by Agent unless marked "Personal" or is otherwise apparently personal in nature, in which event, it shall be forwarded promptly to Author.

11. RIGHT TO CONTRACT

Both Agent and Author represent and warrant that they are free to enter into and fully perform this agreement and that they do not have nor shall have any contract or obligations which conflict with any of its provisions.

12. MODIFICATION OF WAIVER

This agreement represents the entire contract made by the parties. Its terms cannot be modified except by written document signed by the parties. A waiver of any form will not be construed as a continuing waiver of the other breaches of the same or other provision of the contract. If any part of this agreement is held to be illegal, void, or unenforceable, this shall not affect the validity of any other part of this contract.

13. INTERPRETATION

This Agreement shall be governed by and interpreted in all respects in accordance with the Law of the United States, State of [location of agent's business].

_____   _____
[signature of author] (Author)   Date

_____   _____
[signature of agent(s)]   (Agent)   Date

Author's address and Social Security number for payments under this agreement:

_____

(address)

_____

(city, state, zip)

_____

(social security number)

Index

About the Author

Elizabeth Lyon is an independent book editor through Editing International, LLC. Since 1998 she has worked with writers from the United States, Canada, and abroad, helping them with their proposals, queries, novels, and synopses. A popular speaker and workshop teacher, she gives presentations on proposals, novel craft, and all aspects of writing and marketing to organizations and conferences.

Born in Toledo, Ohio, she attended Arizona State University and Whittier College. She holds a masters degree in counseling. She lives in Eugene, Oregon, with her two children, Kris and Elaine. Elizabeth Lyon is also the author of *The Sell Your Novel Tool Kit: Everything You Need to Know About Queries, Synopses, Marketing & Breaking In*. Coming in 2003, her new series: *A Writer's Compass*. The author's web sites are: www.elizabethlyon.com and www.4-edit.com.

A WEALTH OF EXPERT ADVICE AT YOUR FINGERTIPS FROM ELIZABETH LYON

- ### *Manuscript Makeover*
Revision Techniques No Fiction Writer Can Afford to Ignore

- ### *Nonfiction Book Proposals Anybody Can Write*
How to Get a Contract and Advance *Before* Writing Your Book

- ### *The Sell Your Novel Tool Kit*
Everything You Need to Know About Queries, Synopses, Marketing, and Breaking In

- ### *A Writer's Guide to Fiction*

- ### *A Writer's Guide to Nonfiction*

"Whether you're learning the craft, revising your manuscript, or looking to position it for the best chance of getting published, read Elizabeth Lyon."

—Robert Dugoni, *New York Times* bestselling author of *The Jury Master*

Perigee Books penguin.com